Implementing the
Framework for Teaching in
Enhancing
Professional Practice

An ASCD Action Tool

CHARLOTTE DANIELSON

with Darlene Axtell

Paula Bevan

Bernadette Cleland

Candi McKay

Elaine Phillips

Karyn Wright

Implementing the Framework for Teaching in *Enhancing* Professional Practice

ASCD

Alexandria, Virginia USA

an ASCD
Action*TOOL*

1703 North Beauregard St. • Alexandria, VA 22311-1714 USA
Phone: 1-800-933-2723 or 1-703-578-9600 • Fax: 1-703-575-5400
Web site: www.ascd.org • E-mail: member@ascd.org
Author guidelines: www.ascd.org/write

Gene R. Carter, *Executive Director*; Nancy Modrak, *Publisher*; Ann Cunningham-Morris, *Content Development*; Mary Beth Nielsen, *Director, Editorial Services*; Alicia Goodman, *Project Manager*; Gary Bloom, *Director, Design and Production Services*; Georgia Park, *Senior Graphic Designer*; Mike Kalyan, *Production Manager*; Keith Demmons, *Desktop Publishing Specialist*; Kyle Steichen, *Production Specialist*

Printed in the United States of America. Cover art © 2009 by ASCD. ASCD publications present a variety of viewpoints. The views expressed or implied in this book should not be interpreted as official positions of ASCD.

All Web links in this book are correct as of the publication date below but may have become inactive or otherwise modified since that time. If you notice a deactivated or changed link, please e-mail books@ascd.org with the words "Link Update" in the subject line. In your message, please specify the Web link, the book title, and the page number on which the link appears.

PAPERBACK ISBN: 978-1-4166-0919-3   ASCD Product #109047   n12/09

Quantity discounts for the paperback edition only: 10–49 copies, 10%; 50+ copies, 15%; for 1,000 or more copies, call 1-800-933-2723, ext. 5634, or 1-703-575-5634.

Library of Congress Cataloging-in-Publication Data
Danielson, Charlotte.
  Implementing the framework for teaching in enhancing professional practice / Charlotte Danielson with Darlene Axtell ... [et al.].
    p. cm.
  Includes bibliographical references and index.
  ISBN 978-1-4166-0919-3 (pbk. : alk. paper) 1. Teaching. 2. Knowledge management 3. Instructional systems--Design. I. Axtell, Darlene. II. Title.
  LB1025.D1125 2010
  371.102--dc22
        2009030798

16 15 14 13 12   4 5 6 7 8 9 10

Implementing the Framework for Teaching in Enhancing Professional Practice

An ASCD Action Tool

DOMAIN 2: THE CLASSROOM ENVIRONMENT

DOMAIN 3: INSTRUCTION

DOMAIN 4: PROFESSIONAL RESPONSIBILITIES

Downloads

Electronic versions of some tools are available
for download at **www.ascd.org/downloads**.

Enter this unique key code
to unlock the files:
G428B-0298D-F791D

If you have difficulty accessing the files,
e-mail webhelp@ascd.org or call 1-800-933-ASCD for assistance.

Acknowledgments

The authors of this action tool acknowledge the gifts they have received from educators around the world who have inspired them with their use of the framework for teaching to enhance teaching and learning in their schools and classrooms. Working with the framework and exploring its application in many different settings has enriched all of us.

In particular, we want to recognize the outstanding educators who contributed ideas and materials to this action tool, from

- Bethel Public Schools in Bethel, Connecticut
- Clarkstown Central School District in New City, New York
- Forest Lake School District in Forest Lake, Minnesota

Introduction

An Action Tool for the Framework for Teaching

Since the framework for teaching was originally published in 1996 in the book *Enhancing Professional Practice: A Framework for Teaching*, educators in hundreds of schools around the world have adopted it either formally or informally. They use the framework in a number of settings for a wide range of purposes: professional preparation, recruitment and hiring, mentoring and induction, professional development, and performance appraisal.

All of these environments can offer the setting for important professional learning for teachers as they self-assess, reflect on practice, and engage in professional conversations. The framework provides the structure for such activities, offering a broad and comprehensive definition of practice within which to situate specific actions.

This action tool for the framework for teaching is designed to permit educators to focus on the different domains, components, and elements of the framework in analyzing and assessing their own practice and in devising techniques to strengthen that practice. The principal tools consist of structures for self-assessment and activities—for teachers to use themselves and for teachers to use with students—that address the different elements of the framework.

In addition, the description of each element elaborates on the practices that separate teaching at the distinguished level from that at the proficient level. Some educators, on first encountering the framework for teaching, do not immediately perceive the difference between the higher levels of performance; those are made clear in this book. The examples of teaching practices at the proficient and distinguished levels are written in general terms, and teachers must still translate those words to fit the specific conditions they face.

As educators know, there is only a single framework for teaching. There is not a separate framework for middle school science or high school English or elementary mathematics. Clearly teachers of high school students use different techniques than do teachers of primary students, but the underlying structure of what they do is the same. For example, all teachers need to engage students in learning and establish an environment of respect and rapport.

Introduction

Furthermore, the framework for teaching is not prescriptive; it does not endorse any particular teaching methodology. Instead, it provides a structure that educators can use as a guide against which to examine their own practice.

The unique contribution of this action tool lies in the fact that the strategies have been contributed from resources from around the United States. Thus teachers, as they consider how best to strengthen their teaching, are not limited to ideas from their own experience or even those of other teachers in their school. Teachers can adopt the strategies, approaches, and examples as they are presented or, more likely, adapt them for their classrooms.

FORMATS FOR USING THIS TOOL

The specific activities in this tool are only examples of the types of approaches teachers might use in their classrooms, and teachers should fully vet any strategy before implementing it. Indeed, it is unlikely that you will use any specific approach exactly as it is presented here. Rather, these examples are intended to stimulate discussion and the development of new practices.

Teachers may use this tool as they work on their own or with their colleagues in study groups or professional learning communities. Some of these applications are described below.

For Independent Work

The most powerful use of the framework—and the one that should accompany any other us—is self-assessment. Teachers are in a good position to assess their own practice. If they can be honest in their self-assessments, they can try new approaches as suggested in this tool and ascertain whether the approaches are suitable for their particular classroom and school.

Work by individual teachers is powerful because it is completely safe. Teachers working on their own do not have to be concerned that their colleagues will think less of them if they admit to wanting to work on a specific area of their practice. They don't need to worry that this effort will be perceived as a weakness or a deficiency. Moreover, teachers can freely explore new approaches to continuing challenges in their practice within the privacy of their own classrooms.

With Peers or Instructional Coaches

Sometimes individuals do not see their own practice accurately, and they need another set of eyes to interpret everyday events in the classroom. After identifying an area of need, either through self-assessment or with the assistance of a colleague, the teacher together with a colleague can identify practices from this tool that are promising for filling that need.

An Action Tool for the Framework for Teaching

Such an effort depends on a culture of professional inquiry and an environment in which it is safe for teachers to acknowledge that they want to explore an instructional area. This culture may be far from the reality in many schools, where teachers work as independent contractors sharing a building. Openness to others involves a deprivatization of practice, a norm that, in some schools, may need to be established.

In Professional Learning Communities

Teams of teachers working together in study groups or professional learning communities may also productively use this action tool. Groups typically meet regularly to examine some aspect of practice and to plan new approaches. This action tool is filled with specific suggestions for teachers to examine, possibly modify, and then implement in their own classrooms. A study group is a powerful mechanism to critically review new ideas.

However, a culture that supports this kind of work between teachers and individual colleagues must first be in place. Members of a professional learning community or an instructional team must have made a commitment to each other that instructional improvement is part of their definition of a profession, that it does not signal deficiency, and that no one person holds the monopoly on good ideas. Strengthening practice is a shared effort to which every individual contributes.

Most teachers will find the strategies and tools presented here as only a starting point for their planning, but the ideas will, no doubt, infuse the conversations that ensue with ideas they might not otherwise have considered.

Organization of This Action Tool

The action tool for the framework for teaching is organized by domain, with a chapter focused on each of the four domains: Planning and Preparation, The Classroom Environment, Instruction, and Professional Responsibilities. At the end of this introduction, you can use the self-assessment to evaluate your practice at the broadest level in the framework for teaching: that of the four domains. A summary of each domain with a rubric lets you determine where you should concentrate your professional development efforts.

Each of the following sections is organized according to the components and then specific elements of a domain. For each element, keywords in the descriptions of the higher levels of performance are italicized to clarify the distinctions between the proficient and distinguished levels. In addition, each element includes examples of activities common to teaching practice at the proficient and distinguished levels.

Each section adheres to a consistent format that encourages teachers to engage in the following activities:

- **Self-assessment**, in which you use component-level rubrics to assess your practice in each domain.
- **Element reflection**, in which you consider the elements of a component in the setting of your own classroom.
- **Planning**, in which you examine the tools and strategies presented and, possibly following conversation with colleagues, decide on a course of action.
- **Action**, in which you undertake a new practice and record the results of using the technique in the classroom with students.
- **Strategy reflection**, in which you consider what you have done, the results you achieved, and how you may want to modify the approach in the future.

The strategies are specific to the elements within each of the components of the framework for teaching. Some of them are more appropriate for elementary classrooms and others are more appropriate for middle and high school classes. Such differences constitute the

Introduction

content for much of the professional conversation that should accompany teachers' consideration of the approaches and help them determine which techniques can be useful in their unique setting.

ELECTRONIC TOOLS AND RESOURCES

The tools are available for download. To access these documents, visit www.ascd.org/downloads and enter the key code found on page ix. All files are saved in Adobe Portable Document Format (PDF). The PDF is compatible with both personal computers (PCs) and Macintosh computers. The main menu will let you navigate through the various sections, and you can print individual tools or sections in their entirety. If you are having difficulties downloading or viewing the files, contact webhelp@ascd.org for assistance, or call 1-800-933-ASCD.

Mininum System Requirements

Program: The most current version of the Adobe Reader software is available for free download at www.adobe.com.

PC: Intel Pentium Processor; Microsoft Windows XP Professional or Home Edition (Service Pack 1 or 2), Windows 2000 (Service Pack 2), Windows XP Tablet PC Edition, Windows Server 2003, or Windows NT (Service Pack 6 or 6a); 128 MB of RAM (256 MB recommended); up to 90 MB of available hard-disk space; Internet Explorer 5.5 (or higher), Netscape 7.1 (or higher), Firefox 1.0, or Mozilla 1.7.

Macintosh: PowerPC G3, G4, or G5 processor, Mac OS X v.10.2.8–10.3; 128 MB of RAM (256 MB recommended); up to 110 MB of available hard-disk space; Safari 1.2.2 browser supported for MAC OS X 10.3 or higher.

Getting Started

Select "Download files." Designate a location on your computer to save the zip file. Choose to open the PDF file with your existing version of Adobe Acrobat Reader, or install the newest version of Adobe Acrobat Reader from www.adobe.com. From the Main Menu, select a section by clicking on its title. To view a specific tool, open the Bookmarks tab in the left navigation pane and then click on the title of the tool.

Printing Tools

To print a single tool, select the tool by clicking on its title via the Bookmarks section and the printer icon, or select File then Print. In the Print Range section, select Current Page to print the page on the screen. To print several tools, enter the page range in the "Pages from" field. If you wish to print all of the tools in the section, select All in the Printer Range section and then click OK.

The Four Domains Self-Assessment

The first step in focusing your energy on new professional methods and techniques is to determine your needs. That requires honest self-assessment and planning. First, take a few moments to reflect on your practice and ask yourself, Where am I now?

Then review the performance descriptors for the components of each domain, underlining or highlighting keywords that best describe your teaching practice. Note that the words don't have to all be under one level. For example, you may highlight words in both the basic and proficient columns. Finally, mark the level that best matches your teaching performance for each domain.

As a result of this self-assessment, on which domain will you focus first?

□ 7

The Four Domains Self-Assessment

Domain 1: Planning and Preparation				
COMPONENT	UNSATISFACTORY	BASIC	PROFICIENT	DISTINGUISHED
1a: Demonstrating Knowledge of Content and Pedagogy	The teacher's plans and practice display little knowledge of the content, prerequisite relationships between different aspects of the content, or the instructional practices specific to that discipline. ☐	The teacher's plans and practice reflect some awareness of the important concepts in the discipline, prerequisite relationships between them, and the instructional practices specific to that discipline. ☐	The teacher's plans and practice reflect solid knowledge of the content, prerequisite relationships between important concepts, and the instructional practices specific to that discipline. ☐	The teacher's plans and practice reflect extensive knowledge of the content and the structure of the discipline. The teacher actively builds on knowledge of prerequisites and misconceptions when describing instruction or seeking causes for student misunderstanding. ☐
1b: Demonstrating Knowledge of Students	The teacher demonstrates little or no knowledge of students' backgrounds, cultures, skills, language proficiency, interests, and special needs, and does not seek such understanding. ☐	The teacher indicates the importance of understanding students' backgrounds, cultures, skills, language proficiency, interests, and special needs, and attains this knowledge for the class as a whole. ☐	The teacher actively seeks knowledge of students' backgrounds, cultures, skills, language proficiency, interests, and special needs, and attains this knowledge for groups of students. ☐	The teacher actively seeks knowledge of students' backgrounds, cultures, skills, language proficiency, interests, and special needs from a variety of sources, and attains this knowledge for individual students. ☐

Source: From *The Handbook for Enhancing Professional Practice: Using the Framework for Teaching in Your School* (pp. 129–135), by C. Danielson, 2008, Alexandria, VA: ASCD. © 2008 by ASCD. Reprinted with permission.

The Four Domains Self-Assessment

COMPONENT	UNSATISFACTORY	BASIC	PROFICIENT	DISTINGUISHED
1c: Setting Instructional Outcomes	Instructional outcomes are unsuitable for students, represent trivial or low-level learning, or are stated only as activities. They do not permit viable methods of assessment. ☐	Instructional outcomes are of moderate rigor and are suitable for some students, but consist of a combination of activities and goals, some of which permit viable methods of assessment. They reflect more than one type of learning, but the teacher makes no attempt at coordination or integration. ☐	Instructional outcomes are stated as goals reflecting high-level learning and curriculum standards. They are suitable for most students in the class, represent different types of learning, and can be assessed. The outcomes reflect opportunities for coordination. ☐	Instructional outcomes are stated as goals that can be assessed, reflecting rigorous learning and curriculum standards. They represent different types of content, offer opportunities for both coordination and integration, and take account of the needs of individual students. ☐
1d: Demonstrating Knowledge of Resources	The teacher demonstrates little or no familiarity with resources to enhance own knowledge, to use in teaching, or for students who need them. The teacher does not seek such knowledge. ☐	The teacher demonstrates some familiarity with resources available through the school or district to enhance own knowledge, to use in teaching, or for students who need them. The teacher does not seek to extend such knowledge. ☐	The teacher is fully aware of the resources available through the school or district to enhance own knowledge, to use in teaching, or for students who need them. ☐	The teacher seeks out resources in and beyond the school or district in professional organizations, on the Internet, and in the community to enhance own knowledge, to use in teaching, and for students who need them. ☐

Source: From *The Handbook for Enhancing Professional Practice: Using the Framework for Teaching in Your School* (pp. 129–135), by C. Danielson, 2008, Alexandria, VA: ASCD. © 2008 by ASCD. Reprinted with permission.

The Four Domains Self-Assessment

COMPONENT	UNSATISFACTORY	BASIC	PROFICIENT	DISTINGUISHED
1e: Designing Coherent Instruction	The series of learning experiences is poorly aligned with the instructional outcomes and does not represent a coherent structure. The experiences are suitable for only some students.	The series of learning experiences demonstrates partial alignment with instructional outcomes, and some of the experiences are likely to engage students in significant learning. The lesson or unit has a recognizable structure and reflects partial knowledge of students and resources.	The teacher coordinates knowledge of content, of students, and of resources to design a series of learning experiences aligned to instructional outcomes and suitable for groups of students. The lesson or unit has a clear structure and is likely to engage students in significant learning.	The teacher coordinates knowledge of content, of students, and of resources, to design a series of learning experiences aligned to instructional outcomes, differentiated where appropriate to make them suitable to all students and likely to engage them in significant learning. The lesson or unit structure is clear and allows for different pathways according to student needs.
	☐	☐	☐	☐

Source: From *The Handbook for Enhancing Professional Practice: Using the Framework for Teaching in Your School* (pp. 129–135), by C. Danielson, 2008, Alexandria, VA: ASCD. © 2008 by ASCD. Reprinted with permission.

The Four Domains Self-Assessment

COMPONENT	UNSATISFACTORY	BASIC	PROFICIENT	DISTINGUISHED
1f: Designing Student Assessments	The teacher's plan for assessing student learning contains no clear criteria or standards, is poorly aligned with the instructional outcomes, or is inappropriate for many students. The results of assessment have minimal impact on the design of future instruction. ☐	The teacher's plan for student assessment is partially aligned with the instructional outcomes, without clear criteria, and inappropriate for at least some students. The teacher intends to use assessment results to plan for future instruction for the class as a whole. ☐	The teacher's plan for student assessment is aligned with the instructional outcomes, uses clear criteria, and is appropriate to the needs of students. The teacher intends to use assessment results to plan for future instruction for groups of students. ☐	The teacher's plan for student assessment is fully aligned with the instructional outcomes, with clear criteria and standards that show evidence of student contribution to their development. Assessment methodologies may have been adapted for individuals, and the teacher intends to use assessment results to plan future instruction for individual students. ☐
Domain 2: The Classroom Environment				
COMPONENT	UNSATISFACTORY	BASIC	PROFICIENT	DISTINGUISHED
2a: Creating an Environment of Respect and Rapport	Classroom interactions, both between the teacher and students and among students, are negative, inappropriate, or insensitive to students' cultural backgrounds and are characterized by sarcasm, put-downs, or conflict. ☐	Classroom interactions, both between the teacher and students and among students, are generally appropriate and free from conflict, but may be characterized by occasional displays of insensitivity or lack of responsiveness to cultural or developmental differences among students. ☐	Classroom interactions between the teacher and students and among students are polite and respectful, reflecting general warmth and caring, and are appropriate to the cultural and developmental differences among groups of students. ☐	Classroom interactions between the teacher and individual students are highly respectful, reflecting genuine warmth and caring and sensitivity to students' cultures and levels of development. Students themselves ensure high levels of civility among members of the class. ☐

Source: From *The Handbook for Enhancing Professional Practice: Using the Framework for Teaching in Your School* (pp. 129–135), by C. Danielson, 2008, Alexandria, VA: ASCD. © 2008 by ASCD. Reprinted with permission.

The Four Domains Self-Assessment

COMPONENT	UNSATISFACTORY	BASIC	PROFICIENT	DISTINGUISHED
2b: Establishing a Culture for Learning	The classroom environment conveys a negative culture for learning, characterized by low teacher commitment to the subject, low expectations for student achievement, and little or no student pride in work. ☐	The teacher's attempt to create a culture for learning is partially successful, with little teacher commitment to the subject, modest expectations for student achievement, and little student pride in work. Both the teacher and students appear to be only "going through the motions." ☐	The classroom culture is characterized by high expectations for most students and genuine commitment to the subject by both teacher and students, with students demonstrating pride in their work. ☐	High levels of student energy and teacher passion for the subject create a culture for learning in which everyone shares a belief in the importance of the subject and all students hold themselves to high standards of performance—for example, by initiating improvements to their work. ☐
2c: Managing Classroom Procedures	Much instructional time is lost because of inefficient classroom routines and procedures for transitions, handling of supplies, and performance of noninstructional duties. ☐	Some instructional time is lost because classroom routines and procedures for transitions, handling of supplies, and performance of noninstructional duties are only partially effective. ☐	Little instructional time is lost because of classroom routines and procedures for transitions, handling of supplies, and performance of noninstructional duties, which occur smoothly. ☐	Students contribute to the seamless operation of classroom routines and procedures for transitions, handling of supplies, and performance of noninstructional duties. ☐

Source: From *The Handbook for Enhancing Professional Practice: Using the Framework for Teaching in Your School* (pp. 129–135), by C. Danielson, 2008, Alexandria, VA: ASCD. © 2008 by ASCD. Reprinted with permission.

The Four Domains Self-Assessment

COMPONENT	UNSATISFACTORY	BASIC	PROFICIENT	DISTINGUISHED
2d: Managing Student Behavior	There is no evidence that standards of conduct have been established and little or no teacher monitoring of student behavior. Response to student misbehavior is repressive or disrespectful of student dignity. ☐	It appears that the teacher has made an effort to establish standards of conduct for students. The teacher tries, with uneven results, to monitor student behavior and respond to student misbehavior. ☐	Standards of conduct appear to be clear to students, and the teacher monitors student behavior against those standards. The teacher's response to student misbehavior is appropriate and respects the students' dignity. ☐	Standards of conduct are clear, with evidence of student participation in setting them. The teacher's monitoring of student behavior is subtle and preventive, and the teacher's response to student misbehavior is sensitive to individual student needs. Students take an active role in monitoring the standards of behavior. ☐
2e: Organizing Physical Space	The physical environment is unsafe, or some students don't have access to learning. Alignment between the physical arrangement and the lesson activities is poor. ☐	The classroom is safe, and essential learning is accessible to most students; the teacher's use of physical resources, including computer technology, is moderately effective. The teacher may attempt to modify the physical arrangement to suit learning activities, with partial success. ☐	The classroom is safe, and learning is accessible to all students; the teacher ensures that the physical arrangement is appropriate to the learning activities. The teacher makes effective use of physical resources, including computer technology. ☐	The classroom is safe, and the physical environment ensures the learning of all students, including those with special needs. Students contribute to the use or adaptation of the physical environment to advance learning. Technology is used skillfully, as appropriate to the lesson. ☐

Source: From *The Handbook for Enhancing Professional Practice: Using the Framework for Teaching in Your School* (pp. 129–135), by C. Danielson, 2008, Alexandria, VA: ASCD. © 2008 by ASCD. Reprinted with permission.

The Four Domains Self-Assessment

Domain 3: Instruction				
COMPONENT	UNSATISFACTORY	BASIC	PROFICIENT	DISTINGUISHED
3a: Communicating with Students	Expectations for learning, directions and procedures, and explanations of content are unclear or confusing to students. The teacher's use of language contains errors or is inappropriate for students' cultures or levels of development. ☐	Expectations for learning, directions and procedures, and explanations of content are clarified after initial confusion; the teacher's use of language is correct but may not be completely appropriate for students' cultures or levels of development. ☐	Expectations for learning, directions and procedures, and explanations of content are clear to students. Communications are appropriate for students' cultures and levels of development. ☐	Expectations for learning, directions and procedures, and explanations of content are clear to students. The teacher's oral and written communication is clear and expressive, appropriate for students' cultures and levels of development, and anticipates possible student misconceptions. ☐
3b: Using Questioning and Discussion Techniques	The teacher's questions are low-level or inappropriate, eliciting limited student participation and recitation rather than discussion. ☐	Some of the teacher's questions elicit a thoughtful response, but most are low-level, posed in rapid succession. The teacher's attempts to engage all students in the discussion are only partially successful. ☐	Most of the teacher's questions elicit a thoughtful response, and the teacher allows sufficient time for students to answer. All students participate in the discussion, with the teacher stepping aside when appropriate. ☐	Questions reflect high expectations and are culturally and developmentally appropriate. Students formulate many of the high-level questions and ensure that all voices are heard. ☐

Source: From *The Handbook for Enhancing Professional Practice: Using the Framework for Teaching in Your School* (pp. 129–135), by C. Danielson, 2008, Alexandria, VA: ASCD. © 2008 by ASCD. Reprinted with permission.

The Four Domains Self-Assessment

COMPONENT	UNSATISFACTORY	BASIC	PROFICIENT	DISTINGUISHED
3c: Engaging Students in Learning	Activities and assignments, materials, and groupings of students are inappropriate for the instructional outcomes or students' cultures or levels of understanding, resulting in little intellectual engagement. The lesson has no structure or is poorly paced. ☐	Activities and assignments, materials, and groupings of students are partially appropriate to the instructional outcomes or students' cultures or levels of understanding, resulting in moderate intellectual engagement. The lesson has a recognizable structure, but that structure is not fully maintained. ☐	Activities and assignments, materials, and groupings of students are fully appropriate for the instructional outcomes and students' cultures and levels of understanding. All students are engaged in work of a high level of rigor. The lesson's structure is coherent, with appropriate pace. ☐	Students, throughout the lesson, are highly intellectually engaged in significant learning, and make material contributions to the activities, student groupings, and materials. The lesson is adapted as necessary to the needs of individuals, and the structure and pacing allow for student reflection and closure. ☐
3d: Using Assessment in Instruction	Assessment is not used in instruction, either through monitoring of progress by the teacher or students, or through feedback to students. Students are unaware of the assessment criteria used to evaluate their work. ☐	Assessment is occasionally used in instruction, through some monitoring of progress of learning by the teacher and/or students. Feedback to students is uneven, and students are aware of only some of the assessment criteria used to evaluate their work. ☐	Assessment is regularly used in instruction, through self-assessment by students, monitoring of progress of learning by the teacher and/or students, and high-quality feedback to students. Students are fully aware of the assessment criteria used to evaluate their work. ☐	Assessment is used in a sophisticated manner in instruction, through student involvement in establishing the assessment criteria, self-assessment by students, monitoring of progress by both students and teacher, and high-quality feedback to students from a variety of sources. ☐

Source: From *The Handbook for Enhancing Professional Practice: Using the Framework for Teaching in Your School* (pp. 129–135), by C. Danielson, 2008, Alexandria, VA: ASCD. © 2008 by ASCD. Reprinted with permission.

Introduction

The Four Domains Self-Assessment

COMPONENT	UNSATISFACTORY	BASIC	PROFICIENT	DISTINGUISHED
3e: **Demonstrating Flexibility and Responsive-ness**	The teacher adheres to the instruction plan, even when a change would improve the lesson or address students' lack of interest. The teacher brushes aside student questions; when students experience difficulty, the teacher blames the students or their home environment. ☐	The teacher attempts to modify the lesson when needed and to respond to student questions, with moderate success. The teacher accepts responsibility for student success, but has only a limited repertoire of strategies to draw on. ☐	The teacher promotes the successful learning of all students, making adjustments as needed to instruction plans and accommodating student questions, needs, and interests. ☐	The teacher seizes an opportunity to enhance learning, building on a spontaneous event or student interests. The teacher ensures the success of all students, using an extensive repertoire of instructional strategies. ☐
Domain 4: Professional Responsibilities				
COMPONENT	UNSATISFACTORY	BASIC	PROFICIENT	DISTINGUISHED
4a: **Reflecting on Teaching**	The teacher does not accurately assess the effectiveness of the lesson and has no ideas about how the lesson could be improved. ☐	The teacher provides a partially accurate and objective description of the lesson but does not cite specific evidence. The teacher makes only general suggestions as to how the lesson might be improved. ☐	The teacher provides an accurate and objective description of the lesson, citing specific evidence. The teacher makes some specific suggestions as to how the lesson might be improved. ☐	The teacher's reflection on the lesson is thoughtful and accurate, citing specific evidence. The teacher draws on an extensive repertoire to suggest alternative strategies and predicts the likely success of each. ☐

Source: From *The Handbook for Enhancing Professional Practice: Using the Framework for Teaching in Your School* (pp. 129–135), by C. Danielson, 2008, Alexandria, VA: ASCD. © 2008 by ASCD. Reprinted with permission.

The Four Domains Self-Assessment

COMPONENT	UNSATISFACTORY	BASIC	PROFICIENT	DISTINGUISHED
4b: Maintaining Accurate Records	The teacher's systems for maintaining both instructional and noninstructional records are either nonexistent or in disarray, resulting in errors and confusion. ☐	The teacher's systems for maintaining both instructional and noninstructional records are rudimentary and only partially effective. ☐	The teacher's systems for maintaining both instructional and noninstructional records are accurate, efficient, and effective. ☐	The teacher's systems for maintaining both instructional and noninstructional records are accurate, efficient, and effective, and students contribute to its maintenance. ☐
4c: Communicating with Families	The teacher's communication with families about the instructional program or about individual students is sporadic or culturally inappropriate. The teacher makes no attempt to engage families in the instructional program. ☐	The teacher adheres to school procedures for communicating with families and makes modest attempts to engage families in the instructional program. But communications are not always appropriate to the cultures of those families. ☐	The teacher communicates frequently with families and successfully engages them in the instructional program. Information to families about individual students is conveyed in a culturally appropriate manner. ☐	The teacher's communication with families is frequent and sensitive to cultural traditions; students participate in the communication. The teacher successfully engages families in the instructional program, as appropriate. ☐
4d: Participating in a Professional Community	The teacher avoids participating in a professional community or in school and district events and projects; relationships with colleagues are negative or self-serving. ☐	The teacher becomes involved in the professional community and in school and district events and projects when specifically asked; relationships with colleagues are cordial. ☐	The teacher participates actively in the professional community and in school and district events and projects, and maintains positive and productive relationships with colleagues. ☐	The teacher makes a substantial contribution to the professional community and to school and district events and projects, and assumes a leadership role among the faculty. ☐

Source: From *The Handbook for Enhancing Professional Practice: Using the Framework for Teaching in Your School* (pp. 129–135), by C. Danielson, 2008, Alexandria, VA: ASCD. © 2008 by ASCD. Reprinted with permission.

ASCD   ☐ 17

The Four Domains Self-Assessment

COMPONENT	UNSATISFACTORY	BASIC	PROFICIENT	DISTINGUISHED
4e: **Growing and Developing Professionally**	The teacher does not participate in professional development activities and makes no effort to share knowledge with colleagues. The teacher is resistant to feedback from supervisors or colleagues. ☐	The teacher participates in professional development activities that are convenient or are required, and makes limited contributions to the profession. The teacher accepts, with some reluctance, feedback from supervisors and colleagues. ☐	The teacher seeks out opportunities for professional development based on an individual assessment of need and actively shares expertise with others. The teacher welcomes feedback from supervisors and colleagues. ☐	The teacher actively pursues professional development opportunities and initiates activities to contribute to the profession. In addition, the teacher seeks feedback from supervisors and colleagues. ☐
4f: **Showing Professional-ism**	The teacher has little sense of ethics and professionalism and contributes to practices that are self-serving or harmful to students. The teacher fails to comply with school and district regulations and time lines. ☐	The teacher is honest and well intentioned in serving students and contributing to decisions in the school, but the teacher's attempts to serve students are limited. The teacher complies minimally with school and district regulations, doing just enough to get by. ☐	The teacher displays a high level of ethics and professionalism in dealings with both students and colleagues and complies fully and voluntarily with school and district regulations. ☐	The teacher is proactive and assumes a leadership role in making sure that school practices and procedures ensure that all students, particularly those traditionally underserved, are honored in the school. The teacher displays the highest standards of ethical conduct and takes a leadership role in seeing that colleagues comply with school and district regulations. ☐

Source: From *The Handbook for Enhancing Professional Practice: Using the Framework for Teaching in Your School* (pp. 129–135), by C. Danielson, 2008, Alexandria, VA: ASCD. © 2008 by ASCD. Reprinted with permission.

Domain 1

Planning and Preparation

Planning and Preparation

The components in Domain 1 describe how a teacher organizes the content students are supposed to learn—how the teacher designs instruction. This domain covers all aspects of instructional planning, beginning with a deep understanding of content and pedagogy and an understanding and appreciation of students and what they bring to educational encounters. Beyond simply understanding the content, teachers are responsible for engaging students in learning it.

Instructional design transforms content into sequences of activities and exercises that make it accessible to students. All elements of instructional design—learning activities, materials, and strategies—must be appropriate to both the content and the students and align with larger instructional goals. In addition, the content and process of assessment techniques must reflect the instructional outcomes, and they should document student progress during and at the end of the lesson. In designing assessment strategies, teachers must consider how to use assessments formatively so that they provide diagnostic opportunities. If students can demonstrate their level of understanding during an instructional sequence, teachers can make instructional adjustments.

Based on the results of the self-assessment you took in the introduction (see page 7), turn to the page of the component on which you will focus first. Each of the following sections explores the elements of these components in detail and includes tools that you can use in your professional practice.

Component 1a

Demonstrating Knowledge of Content and Pedagogy

OVERVIEW

To guide student learning, teachers must have a command of the subjects they teach. They must know which concepts and skills are central to a discipline and which are peripheral. They must know how the discipline has evolved into its 21st century form and incorporate such issues as global awareness and cultural diversity, as appropriate.

Accomplished teachers understand the internal relationships within the disciplines they teach, knowing which concepts and skills are prerequisite to the understanding of others. Teachers occasionally withhold information from students to encourage them to think on their own, but what information they do convey is accurate and reflects deep understanding. Teachers are also aware of typical student misconceptions in the discipline and work to dispel them. But knowledge of the content is not sufficient. In advancing student understanding, teachers are familiar with the particular pedagogical approaches best suited to each discipline.

SELF-ASSESSMENT

Assess your practice in Component 1a against the levels of performance below, then check the box that best matches the level of your own teaching for each element.

Component 1a: Demonstrating Knowledge of Content and Pedagogy				
	Level of Performance			
ELEMENT	UNSATISFACTORY	BASIC	PROFICIENT	DISTINGUISHED
Knowledge of content and the structure of the discipline	In planning and practice, teacher makes content errors or does not correct errors made by students. ☐	Teacher is familiar with the important concepts in the discipline but may display lack of awareness of how these concepts relate to one another. ☐	Teacher displays solid knowledge of the important concepts in the discipline and how these relate to one another. ☐	Teacher displays extensive knowledge of the important concepts in the discipline and how these relate both to one another and to other disciplines. ☐

Component 1a

ELEMENT	Level of Performance			
	UNSATISFACTORY	BASIC	PROFICIENT	DISTINGUISHED
Knowledge of prerequisite relationships	Teacher's plans and practice display little understanding of prerequisite relationships important to student learning of the content. ☐	Teacher's plans and practice indicate some awareness of prerequisite relationships, although such knowledge may be inaccurate or incomplete. ☐	Teacher's plans and practice reflect accurate understanding of prerequisite relationships among topics and concepts. ☐	Teacher's plans and practices reflect understanding of prerequisite relationships among topics and concepts and a link to necessary cognitive structures by students to ensure understanding. ☐
Knowledge of content-related pedagogy	Teacher displays little or no understanding of the range of pedagogical approaches suitable to student learning of the content. ☐	Teacher's plans and practice reflect a limited range of pedagogical approaches or some approaches that are not suitable to the discipline or to the students. ☐	Teacher's plans and practice reflect familiarity with a wide range of effective pedagogical approaches in the discipline. ☐	Teacher's plans and practice reflect familiarity with a wide range of effective pedagogical approaches in the discipline, anticipating student misconceptions. ☐

Source: From *Enhancing Professional Practice: A Framework for Teaching, 2nd Edition* (p. 47), by C. Danielson, 2007, Alexandria, VA: ASCD. © 2007 by ASCD. Reprinted with permission.

As a result of this self-assessment, on which element will you focus first? Turn to the pages following to explore the elements of the component in detail. After you've reviewed the tools, you can use the Action Planning and Reflection form to document the results of implementing the strategies in your classroom.

Domain 1

Element

Knowledge of Content and the Structure of the Discipline

Description

Teachers are familiar with the major concepts and skills of the subjects they teach and with the principal strands within each discipline and how they relate to each another. Furthermore, they recognize the connections between the subjects they teach and other disciplines.

A Closer Look

To help you recognize the subtle differences between the higher levels of performance for this element, note the keywords emphasized in the descriptions below and review the activities common to those levels.

PROFICIENT

The teacher displays *solid knowledge* of the important concepts in the discipline and how these relate *to one another.*

At the proficient level of performance, teaching practices may include the following types of activities:

- Teacher consistently provides a clear explanation of the content verbally to students.
- Teacher answers students' questions accurately.
- Teacher provides feedback to students that furthers their learning.
- Teacher relates concepts within the discipline to one another.
- Teacher is able to identify the important concepts of the discipline.
- Teacher coaches or mentors other teachers on the content.
- Teacher's plans reflect an understanding of which concepts are central to the discipline and which are peripheral.

DISTINGUISHED

The teacher displays *extensive knowledge* of the important concepts in the discipline and how these relate to *both one another and to other disciplines.*

At the distinguished level of performance, teaching practices may include the following types of activities:

Knowledge of Content and the Structure of the Discipline

- Teacher consistently provides multiple, clear explanations of the content both verbally and in writing to students.
- Teacher answers questions accurately with multiple explanations.
- Teacher provides extensive feedback to students that furthers their learning.
- Teacher relates concepts to others within the discipline and to concepts in other disciplines.
- Teacher is able to identify the important concepts of the discipline and relate those concepts across disciplines.
- Teacher coaches, mentors, and provides professional development on the content.
- Teacher's plans reflect an understanding of the complexities of the discipline.

The tools that follow will help you explore how to put the activities of these high levels of performance into practice in your classroom.

Knowledge of Content and the Structure of the Discipline

Element Reflection

✔ **Teacher tool**   __ **Student tool**

1. Describe a few interesting questions related to the content you teach for which there are no single or simple answers.

2. How has professional understanding of the subject or subjects you teach evolved over the last 20 years?

Domain 1

Knowledge of Content and the Structure of the Discipline

Thinking Through What I Want Students to Learn

✔ **Teacher tool**   __ **Student tool**

Think through the important concepts of the discipline and how you can relate them to other disciplines to deepen student understanding of the content.

1. What concepts do I want students to learn from this lesson?

2. How might I include other disciplines to deepen the understanding?

Domain 1

Element

Knowledge of Prerequisite Relationships

Description

Through knowing the prerequisite relationships within a discipline, teachers can readily determine the basis of a student's misunderstanding of the content. By knowing that students must understand Point A before they can master Point B, the experienced teacher will check the student's command of Point A if the student fails to understand Point B.

A Closer Look

To help you recognize the subtle differences between the higher levels of performance for this element, note the keywords emphasized in the descriptions and review the activities common to those levels.

PROFICIENT

The teacher's plans and practice reflect *accurate understanding* of prerequisite relationships among topics and concepts.

At the proficient level of performance, teaching practices may include the following types of activities:

- Teacher plans instruction that scaffolds skills and concepts to build student understanding.
- Teacher relates the skills and concepts of the discipline to other skills and concepts within the discipline.
- Teacher plans learning experiences that build on the students' prior understanding of the skills and concepts.
- Teacher designs questions that build on students' background in the content area.

DISTINGUISHED

The teacher's plans and practice reflect understanding of prerequisite relationships among topics and concepts and the necessity of students *linking cognitive structures* to ensure understanding.

At the distinguished level of performance, teaching practices may include the following types of activities:

Knowledge of Prerequisite Relationships

- Teacher accurately assesses student understanding of the content and designs instruction that scaffolds skills and concepts for individual students.
- Teacher relates skills and concepts of the discipline to skills and concepts of other disciplines to help students make connections.
- Teacher plans learning experiences that build on individual students' prior understanding of the skills and concepts.
- Teacher designs questions that uncover student misconceptions to address gaps in student understanding.

The tools that follow will help you explore how to put the activities of these high levels of performance into practice in your classroom.

Domain 1

Knowledge of Prerequisite Relationships

Element Reflection

✔ **Teacher tool**   __ **Student tool**

1. Describe a situation in your teaching when a student's lack of understanding of a prerequisite concept seriously hindered further learning.

2. What can you do to ensure that students have the prerequisite understanding necessary to be successful?

Domain 1

Prerequisite Relationships Template

✔ **Teacher tool**   __ **Student tool**

Identify the prerequisites for understanding and knowledge of important concepts, and monitor whether your students have met the prerequisites.

Grade Level: _____   Content Area: _____

Knowledge: _____

Prerequisite to understanding the identified knowledge:

Student Demonstration of Prerequisite Knowledge					
Student	**Concept:**	**Concept:**	**Concept:**	**Concept:**	**Concept:**

Prerequisite Relationships Example

Grade Level: <u>4</u>   Content Area: <u>Math</u>

Knowledge: Ordering decimals

| 0.3 | 0.13 | 0.25 | 0.53 | 0.4 |

Which of the following number sets correctly arranges the above numbers from least to greatest value?

A. 0.13   0.25   0.53   0.3   0.4

B. 0.13   0.25   0.3   0.4   0.53

C. 0.53   0.3   0.4   0.25   0.13

Prerequisite to understanding the identified knowledge:

- Writing Decimal Numbers
  - Tenths
  - Thousandths
- Ordering Whole Numbers
  - 3 Digits
  - 4 Digits

- Whole Number Place Value (Millions)
- Reading Whole Numbers (Millions)
- Writing Whole Numbers
  - Thousands
  - Ten Thousands
  - Millions

Student Demonstration of Prerequisite Knowledge						
Student	Writing Whole Numbers	Reading Whole Numbers	Whole Number Place Value	Ordering Whole Numbers	Writing Decimals	Ordering Decimals
Andrews, G.	X	X	X	X		
Baez, V.	X	X	X	X	X	X
Bennett, R.	X	X	X		X	X
Diaz, P.	X	X	X	X		
Delia, E.	X	X	X	X		
Monroe, T.	X	X	X	X	X	X

Domain 1

Element

Knowledge of Content-Related Pedagogy

Description

Every discipline has its content-specific pedagogy. Experienced teachers know that the particular techniques used in teaching literacy are specific to that discipline and are fundamentally different from those used in science or history. As they gain experience, teachers acquire the strategies designed for the subjects they teach.

A Closer Look

To help you recognize the subtle differences between the higher levels of performance for this element, note the keywords emphasized in the descriptions and review the activities common to those levels.

PROFICIENT

The teacher's plans and practice reflect a familiarity with a *wide range* of *effective* pedagogical approaches in the discipline.

At the proficient level of performance, teaching practices may include the following types of activities:

- Teacher selects appropriate strategies to engage students in the content.
- Teacher is able to plan alternative strategies within a lesson to meet the learning needs of most students.
- Teacher selects strategies that best align with the concepts being taught.
- Teacher is open to trying new strategies to help students understand the content.

DISTINGUISHED

The teacher's plans and practice reflect familiarity with a wide range of effective pedagogical approaches in the discipline and *anticipate student misconceptions*.

At the distinguished level of performance, teaching practices may include the following types of activities:

Knowledge of Content-Related Pedagogy

- Teacher selects appropriate strategies to engage all students in the content, including those with special needs.
- Teacher is able to plan multiple strategies within a lesson to meet the learning needs of all students.
- Teacher selects multiple strategies that clearly align with the concepts being taught.
- Teacher incorporates new strategies in planning documents to help students understand the content.
- Teacher anticipates student misconceptions and addresses them in planning the lesson.

The tools that follow will help you explore how to put the activities of these high levels of performance into practice in your classroom.

Domain 1

Knowledge of Content-Related Pedagogy

 # Element Reflection

✔ **Teacher tool**   __ **Student tool**

1. Describe a pedagogical approach that is unique to the subjects you teach.

2. What are some typical student misconceptions in the subjects you teach?

Domain 1

Knowledge of Content-Related Pedagogy

Effective Pedagogical Approach Template

✔ Teacher tool   __ **Student tool**

Contrast the way the same skill might be presented in two different disciplines, carefully considering how the learning is scaffolded to cognitively engage students. Grade-level or interdisciplinary teams may find it helpful to complete this tool together.

Skill: _____   Discipline: _____

Pedagogical Approach:

[ ]

Skill: _____   Discipline: _____

Pedagogical Approach:

[ ]

Domain 1

Example Effective Pedagogical Approach

Skill: <u>Distinguishing fact from opinion</u>   Discipline: <u>Social studies</u>

Pedagogical Approach:

The students select a current magazine article of their choice. Using a graphic organizer, they will identify the facts and opinions presented in the article.

Topic of Article: The U.S. Economy	
Facts in the Article	Opinions in the Article
• U.S. deficit is $1.2 trillion. • Roosevelt's Emergency Relief Appropriation Act of 1935 was $4.9 billion. • Johnson's Economic Opportunity Act of 1964 was $948 million.	• Washington can't prove that it spends money wisely. • Politicians are going to include pet projects in the stimulus plan. • Politicians love to cut ribbons.

How do you know the things you listed are facts?
The author of the article cited sources for the facts listed.

Skill: <u>Distinguishing fact from opinion (to make valid observations)</u>   Discipline: <u>Science</u>

Pedagogical Approach:

Students will answer the following question and discuss the reasons why each answer is or is not
correct.

Question: Which of the following is NOT a scientific observation?

A. The tree is 15 meters tall.

B. The solution smells bad.

C. The water tasted sweet.

D. The first sound was higher pitched than the second sound.

Students will next conduct an experiment and record their observations using factual/valid language.

Knowledge of Content-Related Pedagogy

Misconceptions Template

✔ Teacher tool   __ Student tool

By identifying student misconceptions before a unit or lesson, you can improve instruction. Identify the main concepts in a unit of study you will teach and some probable student misconceptions. Then plan how you will incorporate clarifying activities into your instruction.

Concept	Possible Student Misconception	Clarifying Activity

Knowledge of Content-Related Pedagogy

Example Math Misconceptions

Concept	Possible Student Misconception	Clarifying Activity
In a fraction, the denominator divides the numerator.	A bigger denominator denotes a larger number. For example, 1/8 is bigger than 1/4 because 8 is bigger than 4.	To help reinforce understanding of fractions, have students cut pre-divided circles into eighths and quarters and then compare the sizes of the slices.
To order decimals, first line up the decimal points.	The more digits a number has, the bigger the number is. For example, 3.24 is bigger than 4.6 because it has more digits. For the first few years of learning, students had only come across whole numbers, where the "digits rule" did work.	First line up the decimal points. Then, beginning at the left, find the first place where the digits are different. Compare the value of the different digits; the higher digit is the bigger number. 54.677 54.567 .6 is greater than .5 so 54.677 > 54.567
Regular shapes are the same regardless of their orientation.	A square isn't the same as a regular diamond.	Invite students to look at the basic properties of shapes by occasionally drawing shapes in a different orientation: upside down, facing a different direction, or just tilted over.
The multiplication "shortcuts" of whole numbers don't always apply to decimals.	To multiply by 10, just add a 0. For decimals, student thinks 54.3 x 10 = 54.30.	Have students place the decimal point in the product by counting the number of places to the right of the decimal point in each factor. This total tells how many places there will be to the right of the decimal point in the product. 54.3 x 10 = 543.0

Source: Teachernet. *Math misconceptions.* Retrieved May 29, 2009, from http://www.teachernet.gov.uk/teachers/issue42/primary/features/Mathsmisconceptions/

Domain 1

Component 1a

Domain 1

 ## Action Planning and Reflection

✔ **Teacher tool**   __ **Student tool**

Look over the tools for this component and choose a strategy or strategies that you are committed to trying in your classroom. Then return to this page and record what happened. If there was a change, what evidence indicates the extent to which this strategy was successful? Finally, think about what you might do differently to continue to bring about further growth in this component.

What will I try?	How did it go?	What will I do differently next time?

Component 1b

Demonstrating Knowledge
of Students

OVERVIEW

Educators don't teach content in the abstract; they teach it to students. To ensure student learning, therefore, teachers must not only know their content and its related pedagogy but also the students to whom they wish to teach that content.

Students have lives beyond school that include athletic and musical pursuits, activities in their neighborhoods, and family and cultural traditions. Teachers, when planning lessons and identifying resources that will ensure student understanding, must also consider whether students' first language is English and whether they have other special needs.

In ensuring student learning, teachers must appreciate what recent research in cognitive psychology has confirmed: namely that students learn through active intellectual engagement with content. Although there are patterns in the cognitive, social, and emotional developmental stages that are typical of different age-groups, students learn in their individual ways and may have gaps or misconceptions that teachers need to uncover to plan appropriate learning activities.

SELF-ASSESSMENT

Assess your practice in Component 1b against the levels of performance below, then check the box that best matches the level of your own teaching for each element.

Component 1b

Domain 1

Component 1b: Demonstrating Knowledge of Students				
	Level of Performance			
ELEMENT	UNSATISFACTORY	BASIC	PROFICIENT	DISTINGUISHED
Knowledge of child and adolescent development	Teacher displays little or no knowledge of the developmental characteristics of the age-group. ☐	Teacher displays partial knowledge of the developmental characteristics of the age-group. ☐	Teacher displays accurate understanding of the typical developmental characteristics of the age-group, as well as exceptions to the general patterns. ☐	In addition to accurate knowledge of the typical developmental characteristics of the age-group and exceptions to the general patterns, teacher displays knowledge of the extent to which individual students follow the general patterns. ☐
Knowledge of the learning process	Teacher sees no value in understanding how students learn and does not seek such information. ☐	Teacher recognizes the value of knowing how students learn, but this knowledge is limited or outdated. ☐	Teacher's knowledge of how students learn is accurate and current. Teacher applies this knowledge to the class as a whole and to groups of students. ☐	Teacher displays extensive and subtle understanding of how students learn and applies this knowledge to individual students. ☐
Knowledge of students' skills, knowledge, and language proficiency	Teacher displays little or no knowledge of students' skills, knowledge, and language proficiency and does not indicate that such knowledge is valuable. ☐	Teacher recognizes the value of understanding students' skills, knowledge, and language proficiency but displays this knowledge only for the class as a whole. ☐	Teacher recognizes the value of understanding students' skills, knowledge, and language proficiency and displays this knowledge for groups of students. ☐	Teacher displays understanding of individual students' skills, knowledge, and language proficiency and has a strategy for maintaining such information. ☐

Component 1b

ELEMENT	Level of Performance			
	UNSATISFACTORY	BASIC	PROFICIENT	DISTINGUISHED
Knowledge of students' interests and cultural heritage	Teacher displays little or no knowledge of students' interests or cultural heritage and does not indicate that such knowledge is valuable. ☐	Teacher recognizes the value of understanding students' interests and cultural heritage but displays this knowledge only for the class as a whole. ☐	Teacher recognizes the value of understanding students' interests and cultural heritage and displays this knowledge for groups of students. ☐	Teacher recognizes the value of understanding students' interests and cultural heritage and displays this knowledge for individual students. ☐
Knowledge of students' special needs	Teacher displays little or no understanding of students' special learning or medical needs or why such knowledge is important. ☐	Teacher displays awareness of the importance of knowing students' special learning or medical needs, but such knowledge may be incomplete or inaccurate. ☐	Teacher is aware of students' special learning and medical needs. ☐	Teacher possesses information about each student's learning and medical needs, collecting such information from a variety of sources. ☐

Source: From *Enhancing Professional Practice: A Framework for Teaching, 2nd Edition* (p. 50), by C. Danielson, 2007, Alexandria, VA: ASCD. © 2007 by ASCD. Reprinted with permission.

Domain 1

As a result of this self-assessment, on which element will you focus first? Turn to the pages following to explore the elements of the component in detail. After you've reviewed the tools, you can use the Action Planning and Reflection form to document the results of implementing the strategies in your classroom.

Element

Knowledge of Child and Adolescent Development

Description

Developmental research has revealed important and universal patterns in child development. The patterns in cognition, in particular, have important implications for how teachers should introduce concepts to students and how students demonstrate understanding.

A Closer Look

To help you recognize the subtle differences between the higher levels of performance for this element, note the keywords emphasized in the descriptions and review the activities common to those levels.

PROFICIENT

The teacher displays *accurate* understanding of the *typical* developmental characteristics of the age-group, as well as *exceptions* to the general patterns.

At the proficient level of performance, teaching practices may include the following types of activities:

- Teacher develops lessons that are developmentally appropriate for the age level.
- Teacher assesses student learning through developmentally appropriate methods.
- Teacher plans learning activities and experiences that reflect an understanding of the needs of the age-group.
- Teacher gathers information through informal observations during instructional activities and during less structured times, such as lunch, recess, assemblies, and homeroom.
- Teacher describes, orally or in writing, how the exceptions to the general development of the age-group are relevant to a lesson or unit.

DISTINGUISHED

In addition to accurate knowledge of the typical developmental characteristics of the age-group and exceptions to the general patterns, the teacher displays knowledge of the *extent to which individual students follow the general patterns.*

44 □

Knowledge of Child and Adolescent Development

At the distinguished level of performance, teaching practices may include the following types of activities:

- Teacher consistently develops lessons that are intellectually, emotionally, and socially appropriate for the age level and modifies these lessons for students who do not follow the general pattern of development.
- Teacher assesses student learning through developmentally appropriate methods and differentiates for those learners who may have different needs.
- Teacher paces lessons to maximize learning for the age-group and adjusts for those students who need an accelerated or slower pace.
- Teacher plans learning activities and experiences that reflect an understanding of the needs of each individual student in the age-group.
- Teacher identifies which students reflect exceptions and makes referrals to programs such as gifted or special education as appropriate.
- Teacher is aware of students whose social or intellectual development is asynchronous and adapts instruction accordingly.

The tools that follow will help you explore how to put the activities of these high levels of performance into practice in your classroom.

Domain 1

Knowledge of Child and Adolescent Development

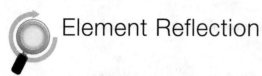 Element Reflection

✔ **Teacher tool** ___ **Student tool**

1. Describe some typical developmental patterns for students of the age you teach.

2. How could you ascertain the extent to which your students follow the typical developmental patterns?

Domain 1

Knowledge of Child and Adolescent Development

Taking a Look at Developmental Differences

✔ Teacher tool   **___ Student tool**

To learn about the developmental differences among elementary students, ask the following questions of five children of different ages—5, 8, and 10, for example.

- Why is it hotter in the summer than in the winter?
- What is the difference between a pizza that is cut into eight pieces and one cut into four pieces?
- Why are clouds sometimes white and sometimes dark?
- Why do we only see part of the moon at certain times?
- Where does sand come from?

1. What are the main differences in the students' responses?

2. How does this information support your own understanding of developmental differences?

3. How might this information inform the way you plan instruction for your own students?

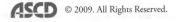

Birth Date Chart

✔ Teacher tool   __ **Student tool**

Knowing your students' dates of birth can help you understand individual developmental characteristics and provide a picture of your class's developmental characteristics.

Student	Date of Birth	Age at Start of School Year

1. How will knowing your students' ages inform your planning?

2. What social, emotional, and cognitive differences might you expect between older students and younger students?

Domain 1

Element

Knowledge of the Learning Process

Description

Students—as well as adults—learn through active intellectual engagement in important content. In some situations physical activity may contribute to learning, but intellectual activity is what is important. In other words, while school may sometimes be hands-on, it should always be minds-on.

A Closer Look

To help you recognize the subtle differences between the higher levels of performance for this element, note the keywords emphasized in the descriptions and review the activities common to those levels.

PROFICIENT

The teacher's knowledge of how students learn is *accurate* and *current*, and the teacher applies this knowledge to *the class as a whole* and to *groups of students*.

At the proficient level of performance, teaching practices may include the following types of activities:

- Lesson plans include some activities in which students are engaged in inquiry.
- Teacher plans to make thinking skills explicit in instruction, labeling and identifying such cognitive processes as comparing, analyzing, applying, translating, predicting, and evaluating.
- Lesson plans make use of mental models, thinking maps, and visual tools for problem solving and decision making appropriate for the developmental stage of students.
- Teacher understands the current research on the brain and its connection to student learning.
- Teacher understands how the students' preexisting knowledge relates to how they develop new understandings.
- Teacher understands that learning is a reciprocal process, in which individuals influence group thinking and vice versa, and designs activities accordingly.

Domain 1

DISTINGUISHED

The teacher displays *extensive* and *subtle* understanding of how students learn and applies this knowledge to *individual students*.

At the distinguished level of performance, teaching practices may include the following types of activities:

- Lesson plans make extensive use of activities in which students engage in inquiry to construct their understanding of concepts.
- Teacher develops a comprehensive learning profile for each student that includes not only learning style preference but also intelligence preferences, culture-influenced preferences, and gender-based preferences.
- Teacher understands the current research on the brain and its connection to student learning and regularly uses that information to design lessons.
- Teacher regularly uses students' prior knowledge in planning lessons that further their understandings.
- Teacher differentiates instruction to meet the learning needs of individual students.
- Students are self-aware of the ways they learn best and can make classroom choices based on their preferences.
- Teacher provides opportunities for student metacognition in the lesson design.

The tools that follow will help you explore how to put the activities of these high levels of performance into practice in your classroom.

Knowledge of the Learning Process

Element Reflection

✔ **Teacher tool**   __ **Student tool**

1. Why is it important to understand the basic principles of human learning when planning instruction?

2. Describe several implications that the research on learning has for your own planning.

The Learning Process

✔ **Teacher tool**   __ **Student tool**

Complete the following activity in groups of two or more.

1. Take a few minutes to think about something you are good at, such as math, golf, writing, or skiing.

I am good at:

2. How did you learn it? Write down some of the things you did to become so skilled in that area.

I became good at this by:

3. Share your learning experience with your colleague or a group of colleagues. What attributes of how you developed skill in your chosen area did you have in common?

Common attributes:

4. Usually people discover that they learn best by doing. Active learning, where the learner is cognitively engaged, results in deeper understanding and confidence in the area of study. Did you and your colleague find this to be true?

5. How will you modify the learning activities for your students based on your learning process discoveries?

6. How can you ensure that your students are "doing" in order to learn?

Element

Knowledge of Students' Skills, Knowledge, and Language Proficiency

Description

For their work to be as productive as possible, teachers need to target instructional activities to their students' current levels of knowledge and skill. This entails having systems in place to acquire such information and to keep it current.

A Closer Look

To help you recognize the subtle differences between the higher levels of performance for this element, note the keywords emphasized in the descriptions and review the activities common to those levels.

PROFICIENT

The teacher *recognizes* the value of understanding students' skills, knowledge, and language proficiency and displays this knowledge for *groups of students*.

At the proficient level of performance, teaching practices may include the following types of activities:

- Teacher studies standardized and state test results, diagnostic test results, and report cards from the prior and current year and draws conclusions for groups of students for instructional planning.
- Teacher uses ongoing assessment strategies, including pre-tests, to ascertain the skill levels of students.
- Teacher uses accurate skill-level assessments to flexibly group and regroup students in learning activities.
- Teacher has a formal method for recording ongoing skill and language proficiency assessments.
- Teacher gathers information through observations of students in instructional and noninstructional activities.
- Teacher includes in a parent survey questions about students' language proficiency and provides a translation of the survey when needed.

Domain 1

DISTINGUISHED

The teacher displays understanding of *individual students'* skills, knowledge, and language proficiency and has a *strategy for maintaining such information.*

At the distinguished level of performance, teaching practices may include the following types of activities:

- Teacher studies standardized and state test results, diagnostic test results, and report cards from the prior and current year and draws conclusions for individual students for instructional planning.
- Teacher uses ongoing assessment strategies to ascertain the skill levels of the students and uses that information to tailor instruction for individual students.
- Teacher has a formal method, which incorporates multiple data sources, for recording ongoing skill and language proficiency assessments.
- Teacher's strategy for maintaining individual student information is easily accessible by other professionals and by parents and students as appropriate.
- Students maintain and update a profile of their own knowledge and skills, using technology as appropriate.
- Teacher conferences with each student prior to end of each marking period, inviting student reflection on progress and the next steps for growth.
- Teacher keeps anecdotal, running records on individual students beyond those for whom it is required by an individual education program (IEP) or other policy.

The tools that follow will help you explore how to put the activities of these high levels of performance into practice in your classroom.

Knowledge of Students' Skills, Knowledge, and Language Proficiency

Element Reflection

✔ **Teacher tool**   __ **Student tool**

1. What techniques do you use to ascertain your students' levels of knowledge, skill, and language proficiency?

2. Describe the implications of the range of student knowledge and skill for your instructional planning. In other words, how do you regularly differentiate for groups and individuals?

Domain 1

Tracking Student Progress

✔ **Teacher tool**   __ **Student tool**

As students master the expected skills and knowledge, record the date that they achieve proficiency. Providing dates helps you assess whether students are progressing at the appropriate rate. It also helps you plan how to accommodate for those students who have well-developed skills and those who need more support. You should closely monitor students for whom language proficiency is a challenge to ensure that they are learning at the same rate as other students.

Skill Set: _____   Grade: _____

Student	Skill:	Skill:	Skill:	Skill:	Skill:

Notes:

Element

Knowledge of Students' Interests and Cultural Heritage

Description

Students engage in many activities and family events outside of school. These experiences both reflect their individual passions and contribute to their approach to learning new material. Furthermore, students' cultural heritage enriches classroom life and may influence students' interactions with teachers and other students.

A Closer Look

To help you recognize the subtle differences between the higher levels of performance for this element, note the keywords emphasized in the descriptions and review the activities common to those levels.

PROFICIENT

The teacher *recognizes the value* of understanding students' interests and cultural heritage and displays this knowledge for *groups of students*.

At the proficient level of performance, teaching practices may include the following types of activities:

- Teacher has students complete an interest survey and uses this information when designing learning experiences for groups of students.
- Teacher solicits information from parents or guardians about their student and takes that information into account when designing learning experiences for groups of students.
- Teacher designs lessons that allow for some choice.
- Teacher seeks out information about the cultural heritage of students and uses that information when designing learning activities.
- Teacher examines resources and materials for cultural sensitivity.
- Teacher holds individual interviews with each student during the first week of the course or term or upon enrollment.
- Teacher writes a letter to students to welcome them on the first day of class, and students respond in a letter to tell the teacher about their interests.

Domain 1

- Students maintain interactive journals with the teacher.
- Teacher plans homework assignments or projects that offer opportunities for students to explore their families' cultural heritage and share it with the class.

DISTINGUISHED

The teacher recognizes the value of understanding students' interests and cultural heritage and displays this knowledge for *individual students*.

At the distinguished level of performance, teaching practices may include the following types of activities:

- Teacher has students complete an interest survey and uses this information to design individual learning experiences.
- Teacher solicits information from parents or guardians about their student and takes this into account when designing learning experiences for individual students.
- Teacher regularly designs lessons that allow for individual choice.
- Teacher experiences cultural traditions and practices firsthand, such as by attending an event at the local cultural center, and uses this experiential learning when designing lessons.
- Teacher examines resources and materials for cultural sensitivity and adjusts materials, resources, and the lesson design as appropriate.
- Teacher's lesson plan reflects student-initiated ideas for incorporating culturally relevant activities and assignments.
- Teacher understands cultural expectations while being sensitive to the individual variations within the cultural group.
- Teacher attends cultural events in the community to enhance understanding of and appreciation for the culture.

The tools that follow will help you explore how to put the activities of these high levels of performance into practice in your classroom.

Knowledge of Students' Interests and Cultural Heritage

Element Reflection

✔ **Teacher tool**   __ **Student tool**

1. How do you learn about your students' interests and cultural backgrounds?

2. Describe the implications of the range of student backgrounds for your planning.

Domain 1

Letter to Send Home to Students Before School Starts

__ **Teacher tool**   ✔ **Student tool**

Dear [student name],

Hello, my name is Mr./Ms. _____. I'd like to welcome you to our

_____ classroom.

[You might want to include a paragraph here about yourself and your interests.]

I am looking forward to working together in the coming school year. I'm interested in knowing more about you and your interests. Please fill out the following information and return this sheet to me by mail, by e-mail, or by dropping it off at the school office. Feel free to add anything not included that would help me learn more about you.

Thank you.

My name is _____

I like to be called _____

My favorite activities are _____

_____

My favorite subject in school is _____

I participate in the following cocurricular activities:

Knowledge of Students' Interests and Cultural Heritage

Designing Student Interest Inventories

__ **Teacher tool**   ✔ **Student tool**

Teachers needs to know students' attitudes about the subject area they are teaching as well as what interests students outside of school, including the activities they participate in, the music they listen to, and the movies they watch. An interest inventory, usually given the first day of class and throughout the year to any new students, paves the way to get to know your students.

If a student has academic difficulty or behavioral issues in the class, the teacher can refer back to the interest inventory for insight about potential sources of the problem and open up a conversation. For example, if a student does not turn in homework assignments, the interest inventory may reveal that the student works late hours or participates in a sport. The interest inventory also gives teachers ideas about rewards that may work with a particular set of students.

There is no minimum or maximum number of questions for the inventory, but make sure that questions are about

- **Your subject area and school in general.** Do students like your subject area? What is the hardest aspect about your subject area? Elementary school teachers may want to ask which subjects their students like the most, feel most confident in, and so forth.
- **Interests in sports or other extracurricular activities, music, and movies.**
- **Work schedules and home life**, such as how many people live in your student's house.

If you work with elementary or kindergarten students, parents may be able to better articulate the strengths and interests of their children. Before the school year starts, you can send a letter and survey to students' homes to introduce yourself and solicit information from parents. You can also modify the letter to send to the homes of students who enroll throughout the year.

You can customize the following samples of inventories to suit your needs, or create your own.

Domain 1

Domain 1

STUDENT INTEREST INVENTORY: HIGH SCHOOL ENGLISH

Your full name: _____

The name you prefer, if different from above: _____

Your birthday (month, day, year): _____

Name of parents/guardians: _____

Names and ages of your brothers and sisters: _____

In what grade did you first enter _____ Public Schools? _____

1. As you think about your English classes throughout middle school, what was your most valuable learning experience?

2. What did your teacher do that helped make it such a valuable learning experience?

3. Here are some areas of study in English classes. Place a plus beside those that you enjoy the most and a check by those that you would like to practice more.

☐ Reading literature   ☐ Writing essays/expository writing

☐ Presenting speeches   ☐ Writing a research paper

☐ Writing fiction/creative writing   ☐ Reading/acting in dramas

4. What do you most enjoy doing in your out-of-school time?

5. What school activities (sports, government, band, etc.) are you taking part in this semester?

6. What job, if any, do you hold? If you do have a job, approximately how many hours a week do you work?

7. What will make this English class a success for you?

STUDENT INTEREST INVENTORY: KINDERGARTEN AND ELEMENTARY LEVEL

Dear families,

In anticipation of the new school year, we would like to welcome you to our classroom. We are looking forward to getting to know your child and working with you to make this a wonderful year.

Our classroom is sensitive to the strengths and needs of each child. Because you are the person who knows your child the best, we would like to invite you to share your thoughts about your child. Anything you can think of will be helpful. This reflection will help us better match our teaching styles and the curriculum to your child and her individual needs.

Thank you!

Student's Name: _____

Date of Birth: _____

1. What do you enjoy most about your child?

2. When your child is upset, what are some strategies that you find helpful?

3. When your child has conflicts with other children, what are some ways he works them out?

4. Has your child experienced any traumatic events in her lifetime?

5. Did your child attend preschool?

6. What are your child's key personality characteristics?

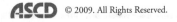

Domain 1

7. By what means do you prefer me to communicate with you?

☐ E-mail: _____

☐ Telephone: _____

☐ Written notes

☐ Other: _____

8. What is the first language spoken in your home?

9. Are there important holidays or celebrations that you observe?

10. What do I need to know about your child to teach him best?

Academically:

Emotionally:

Socially:

Culturally:

Other:

Element

Knowledge of Students' Special Needs

Description

Many classrooms include students with special needs, sometimes—although not always—accompanied by an instructional aide. Special needs students, while enriching the classroom environment, increase the complexity of instructional planning.

A Closer Look

To help you recognize the subtle differences between the higher levels of performance for this element, note the keywords emphasized in the descriptions and review the activities common to those levels.

PROFICIENT

The teacher is *aware* of students' special learning and medical needs.

At the proficient level of performance, teaching practices may include the following types of activities:

- Teacher meets with other school personnel, such as the school nurse, guidance counselor, or special educator, to understand the needs of students.
- Teacher maintains records that pertain to the medical or learning needs of students.
- Teacher has a system for relating pertinent medical or learning needs to substitutes or other adults who interact with the class.
- Teacher is mindful of designing lessons that accommodate the medical or learning needs of students.
- Teacher proactively seeks and uses reports from physicians, counselors, instructional consultants, or parents to build relationships with individual students.

Domain 1

DISTINGUISHED

The teacher possesses information about each student's learning and medical needs, *collecting such information* from a variety of sources.

At the distinguished level of performance, teaching practices may include the following types of activities:

- Teacher meets regularly with other school personnel, such as the school nurse, guidance counselor, or special educator, to understand the current needs of each individual student.
- Teacher maintains regularly updated records that pertain to the medical or learning needs of each student.
- Teacher has a system for relating pertinent medical or learning needs to substitutes or other adults who interact with the students and for following up afterward.
- Teacher carefully designs lessons that accommodate the medical or learning needs of students, are inclusive, and do not appear to be unlike the lessons of students who do not have medical or special learning needs.
- Teacher proactively organizes ongoing information exchange with other classroom teachers of special needs children they have in common.

The tools that follow will help you explore how to put the activities of these high levels of performance into practice in your classroom.

Knowledge of Students' Special Needs

Element Reflection

✔ **Teacher tool**   __ **Student tool**

1. How do you learn about your students' special needs?

2. Describe the challenges presented by students' special needs in your lesson planning.

Domain 1

Domain 1

Modifications and Accommodations Template

✔ Teacher tool　　　　　　　__ **Student tool**

A student's individual education program (IEP) can be a bulky document to keep at hand, but there is important information in it that all teachers must use to plan lessons to make sure that they are meeting the student's needs. Use this template to extract the modifications or accommodations from the IEP that you need to have in place on a daily basis. Keep this template inside a plan book as a reminder when planning lessons.

Student:	**Student:**	**Student:**	**Student:**
Modifications/ Accommodations	Modifications/ Accommodations	Modifications/ Accommodations	Modifications/ Accommodations

Component 1b

Action Planning and Reflection

✔ Teacher tool   **__ Student tool**

Look over the tools for this component and choose a strategy or strategies that you are committed to trying in your classroom. Then return to this page and record what happened. If there was a change, what evidence indicates the extent to which this strategy was successful? Finally, think about what you might do differently to continue to bring about further growth in this component.

What will I try?	How did it go?	What will I do differently next time?

Domain 1

Component 1c

Setting Instructional Outcomes

OVERVIEW

Establishing instructional outcomes entails identifying exactly what students will be expected to learn. Instructional outcomes do not describe what students will *do* but what they will *learn.* The instructional outcomes must reflect important learning and must lend themselves to various forms of assessment so that all students are able to demonstrate their understanding of the content. Insofar as the outcomes influence instructional activities, the resources teachers use, and the methods of assessment teachers employ, they hold a central place in Domain 1.

Teachers must be able to determine the sequence in which they should teach skills and concepts so that students can build their understanding from one concept to the next. Additionally, teachers must select outcomes that allow students to transfer their understanding among disciplines and that are appropriate for all students in the class, no matter their learning needs. Instructional outcomes must be presented to students in language that is clear to them and conveys exactly what learning is expected from them.

Outcomes for a lesson should be specific and doable in the time provided, and activities become the means by which the students demonstrate their learning of the intended outcomes. When outlining your instructional outcomes, be sure that they represent what you want students to learn and aren't activities masquerading as outcomes. For example, consider the following:

Activity: Students will work in small groups using the number line and will work individually on worksheet page 23.
Outcome: At the end of math class today, you will be adding two-digit numbers accurately.

This outcome allows the teacher to assess how well students can add two-digit numbers and to determine which students may need more individual instruction and which students are ready to move on.

Activity: Read question #3 on page 47. Work with a partner to answer the question.
Outcome: Today you will use your problem-solving skills to resolve the following dilemma...

The outcome is not about the answer to the dilemma, but rather the thinking students engage in to come to a resolution. The outcome allows the teacher to uncover how students are thinking about a situation and provides an opportunity to probe for deeper thinking.

Activity: Students will begin working on their research paper.

Outcome: Students will develop a thesis statement to begin the research project.

The lesson outcome is not the research project, but rather a specific step in the process of the research project. The teacher is able to assess how well students understand the concept of thesis statements as well as guide the scope of the project.

SELF-ASSESSMENT

Assess your practice in Component 1c against the levels of performance below, then check the box that best matches the level of your own teaching for each element.

Component 1c: Setting Instructional Outcomes				
	Level of Performance			
ELEMENT	UNSATISFACTORY	BASIC	PROFICIENT	DISTINGUISHED
Value, sequence, and alignment	Outcomes represent low expectations for students and lack of rigor. They do not reflect important learning in the discipline or a connection to a sequence of learning. ☐	Outcomes represent moderately high expectations and rigor. Some reflect important learning in the discipline and at least some connection to a sequence of learning. ☐	Most outcomes represent high expectations and rigor and important learning in the discipline. They are connected to a sequence of learning. ☐	All outcomes represent high expectations and rigor and important learning in the discipline. They are connected to a sequence of learning both in the discipline and in related disciplines. ☐
Clarity	Outcomes are either not clear or are stated as activities, not as student learning. Outcomes do not permit viable methods of assessment. ☐	Outcomes are only moderately clear or consist of a combination of outcomes and activities. Some outcomes do not permit viable methods of assessment. ☐	All the instructional outcomes are clear, written in the form of student learning. Most suggest viable methods of assessment. ☐	All the outcomes are clear, written in the form of student learning, and permit viable methods of assessment. ☐

Source: From *Enhancing Professional Practice: A Framework for Teaching, 2nd Edition* (p. 54), by C. Danielson, 2007, Alexandria, VA: ASCD. © 2007 by ASCD. Reprinted with permission.

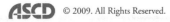

Domain 1

Component 1c

Domain 1

ELEMENT	Level of Performance			
	UNSATISFACTORY	BASIC	PROFICIENT	DISTINGUISHED
Balance	Outcomes reflect only one type of learning and only one discipline or strand. ☐	Outcomes reflect several types of learning, but teacher has made no attempt at coordination or integration. ☐	Outcomes reflect several different types of learning and opportunities for coordination. ☐	Where appropriate, outcomes reflect several different types of learning and opportunities for both coordination and integration. ☐
Suitability for diverse learners	Outcomes are not suitable for the class or are not based on any assessment of student needs. ☐	Most of the outcomes are suitable for most of the students in the class based on global assessments of student learning. ☐	Most of the outcomes are suitable for all students in the class and are based on evidence of student proficiency. However, the needs of some individual students may not be accommodated. ☐	Outcomes are based on a comprehensive assessment of student learning and take into account the varying needs of individual students or groups. ☐

Source: From *Enhancing Professional Practice: A Framework for Teaching, 2nd Edition* (p. 54), by C. Danielson, 2007, Alexandria, VA: ASCD. © 2007 by ASCD. Reprinted with permission.

As a result of this self-assessment, on which element will you focus first? Turn to the pages following to explore the elements of the component in detail. After you've reviewed the tools, you can use the Action Planning and Reflection form to document the results of implementing the strategies in your classroom.

Element

Value, Sequence, and Alignment

Description

When establishing instructional outcomes, teachers should make sure that they represent important learning and are organized in a sequence that respects the structure of the discipline.

A Closer Look

To help you recognize the subtle differences between the higher levels of performance for this element, note the keywords emphasized in the descriptions and review the activities common to those levels.

PROFICIENT

Most outcomes represent high expectations and rigor and important learning in the discipline. They are connected to a *sequence of learning*.

At the proficient level of performance, teaching practices may include the following types of activities:

- Teacher uses national, state, or local standards to align outcomes and shows in writing or orally the connection of individual lesson outcomes to standards.
- Outcomes represent the big ideas of the discipline but are tailored for the lesson and unit.
- Outcomes are scaffolded, build on prior learning, and establish a foundation for future learning.
- Teacher's plan references previous lessons and units to sequence outcomes in the discipline.

DISTINGUISHED

All outcomes represent high expectations and rigor and important learning in the discipline. They are connected to a sequence of learning *both in the discipline and in related disciplines.*

At the distinguished level of performance, teaching practices may include the following types of activities:

Value, Sequence, and Alignment

Domain 1

- Teacher regularly develops outcomes based on national, state, or local standards.
- Outcomes represent the big ideas of the discipline and connect to the big ideas of other disciplines.
- Outcomes are scaffolded, build on prior learning, and establish a foundation for future learning in related disciplines.
- Outcomes represent deep understanding of the content that can be transferred to other content areas.
- Teacher's plan shows use of curricular frameworks, blueprints, or other references to ensure accurate sequencing of outcomes in the discipline.

The tools that follow will help you explore how to put the activities of these high levels of performance into practice in your classroom.

Value, Sequence, and Alignment

Element Reflection

✔ Teacher tool   **___ Student tool**

1. Describe how your instructional outcomes represent important, rather than trivial, learning.

2. How do your instructional outcomes relate to your state's or district's curriculum standards? How do they help students acquire the knowledge and skill they need?

Domain 1

Analyzing Your Instructional Outcomes

✔ Teacher tool   **__ Student tool**

Instructional outcomes represent what you want students to *learn*, not what they are going to do. Examine the value of your instructional outcomes by asking yourself the following questions.

1. Is this important learning?

2. Does the outcome represent high expectations for all students?

3. Is the outcome rigorous? If not, how might I rewrite it to be more rigorous?

4. Does the outcome reflect the curriculum standards or the state framework?

5. Does this outcome naturally follow what students have previously learned?

6. Does this outcome connect to what students are learning in other disciplines?

Element

Clarity

> ## Description
>
> The outcome is not that the students will "complete page 38 and answer the questions" but what they will learn as a consequence of answering the questions on page 38. Confusion on this point leads to muddled instructional planning throughout Domain 1.

A Closer Look

To help you recognize the subtle differences between the higher levels of performance for this element, note the keywords emphasized in the descriptions and review the activities common to those levels.

PROFICIENT

All the instructional outcomes are *clear* and *written in the form of student learning. Most* suggest viable methods of assessment.

At the proficient level of performance, teaching practices may include the following types of activities:

- Teacher describes the instructional outcomes in terms of what students will *learn* rather than what students will *do.*
- Outcomes are specific and doable in the time allotted.
- Outcomes are written with consideration of how students will demonstrate their achievement of the outcomes.
- Teacher plans how to show students the connection between the current outcome and previous outcomes.
- Teacher solicits feedback from colleagues on the clarity of outcomes and makes revisions accordingly.

DISTINGUISHED

All the outcomes are clear, written in the form of student learning, and permit viable methods of assessment.

At the distinguished level of performance, teaching practices may include the following types of activities:

- Teacher describes the instructional outcomes in terms of what students will *learn* rather than what students will *do*. Outcomes are written in terms that students can understand.
- Outcomes are specific, doable, and allow for informal assessment within the time allotted.
- Teacher and students work together to determine how students will demonstrate understanding of the outcome.
- Teacher and students make connections between the current outcome and previous outcomes.
- Teacher audits outcomes from previous units, terms, or years to check for clarity and revises outcomes as necessary.
- Teacher audits outcomes from previous units, terms, or years to check alignment with assessment measures and revises outcomes or assessments as necessary.

The tools that follow will help you explore how to put the activities of these high levels of performance into practice in your classroom.

Clarity

Element Reflection

✔ **Teacher tool**   __ **Student tool**

1. How can you ensure that your instructional outcomes represent student learning rather than activities?

2. To what extent are your instructional outcomes expressed in a manner that permits you to assess them?

Domain 1

Domain 1

Outcome or Activity?

✔ **Teacher tool**   ___ **Student tool**

Outcomes should be

- clearly stated
- appropriately focused, neither to broad nor too specific
- measurable
- focused on student learning needs
- aligned with state or local standards or curriculum frameworks

Work with a small group to evaluate the following statements and determine if they are outcomes or activities. Rewrite the activities to make them outcomes.

1. Students will analyze cultural interactions among diverse groups.
☐ Outcome.

☐ Activity. Rewrite:

2. Students will write a journal entry from the perspective of a pioneer settling in the West.
☐ Outcome.

☐ Activity. Rewrite:

3. Students will use models and formulas to find surface area and volumes.
☐ Outcome.

☐ Activity. Rewrite:

Clarity

4. Students will understand essential concepts about diet and nutrition.

☐ Outcome.

☐ Activity. Rewrite:

5. Students will examine different diet plans for their nutritional value.

☐ Outcome.

☐ Activity. Rewrite:

6. Students will read chapter 10 in the math textbook and do the odd-numbered problems on page 235.

☐ Outcome.

☐ Activity. Rewrite:

Domain 1

Element

Balance

Description

Instructional outcomes represent factual knowledge and procedural skills as well as thinking and reasoning, conceptual understanding, and skills in collaboration—in addition to aesthetic appreciation of, for example, literature. Outcomes should reflect a balance among these types of learning.

A Closer Look

To help you recognize the subtle differences between the higher levels of performance for this element, note the keywords emphasized in the descriptions and review the activities common to those levels.

PROFICIENT

Outcomes reflect *several different types of learning* and *opportunities for coordination*.

At the proficient level of performance, teaching practices may include the following types of activities:

- Teacher develops outcomes related to social skills, thinking skills, task management, and knowledge-related outcomes.
- Outcomes coordinate with learning among several disciplines.
- Teacher plans lessons that require factual and higher-order thinking skills.
- Process and content align with the outcome.
- Teacher develops a matrix or spreadsheet to track different types of instructional outcomes—factual, conceptual, reasoning, social, management, and communication—to assess the balance of outcomes over time.
- Most outcomes push students to take appropriate educational risks.

DISTINGUISHED

Where appropriate, outcomes reflect several different types of learning and opportunities for *both coordination and integration.*

At the distinguished level of performance, teaching practices may include the following types of activities:

Balance

- Instructional outcomes represent the different types of learning and also permit students to integrate their learning across several disciplines.
- Students demonstrate that they've achieved outcomes through processes, such as writing or presentation, that integrate with other disciplines.
- Teacher presents lessons that require higher-order thinking; students are responsible for searching out the necessary factual information.
- Processes and content directly align with the outcome and to other disciplines.
- Teacher develops a matrix or spreadsheet to track different types of instructional outcomes to assess the balance of outcomes for each student over time.
- Outcomes are differentiated to encourage individual students to take appropriate educational risks.

The tools that follow will help you explore how to put the activities of these high levels of performance into practice in your classroom.

Domain 1

Balance

Element Reflection

✔ **Teacher tool**   __ **Student tool**

1. To what extent can you incorporate instructional outcomes for thinking skills, writing, and collaboration along with factual and procedural knowledge in your lessons?

2. Describe how you are able to coordinate or integrate the instructional outcomes in one discipline with those in another.

Balancing Instructional Outcomes

✔ **Teacher tool**   __ **Student tool**

High-quality instructional outcomes reflect a balance of the different types of skills students need to succeed. Review the instructional outcomes for one of your units and mark which category or categories of skills they fall into. When you've filled out the chart, note which skills you don't address and consider how you can modify your lesson plans to include them.

Overall Unit Outcome:

Instructional Outcomes	Factual Knowledge	Procedural Knowledge	Conceptual Understanding	Communication Skills	Reasoning Skills	Collaboration Skills	Dispositions

Domain 1

Balancing Instructional Outcomes Example: U.S. History

Overall Unit Outcome: Students will understand the causes of the American Revolution, the ideas and interests involved in shaping the revolutionary movement, and reasons for the American victory.

Instructional Outcomes	Factual Knowledge	Procedural Knowledge	Conceptual Understanding	Communication Skills	Reasoning Skills	Collaboration Skills	Dispositions
Know the events of the pre-Revolutionary War period	X						
Understand the critical differences between a monarchy and a republic			X				
Formulate questions to be investigated					X		
Determine evidence needed to answer important questions; locate that evidence					X		
Demonstrate appropriate and imaginative use of electronic technology in conducting investigations and making a presentation		X			X		
Analyze data regarding the pre-Revolutionary War period					X		
Understand the perspectives of different groups involved in the effort for independence							X
Work cooperatively with others						X	
Illustrate results through visual representation				X	X		
Make a presentation to classmates summarizing findings				X			
Write a well-organized essay with findings				X			

Element

Suitability for Diverse Learners

Description

Because every classroom includes students with a range of backgrounds and levels of proficiency, teachers may have to adapt their overall instructional outcomes to different students.

A Closer Look

To help you recognize the subtle differences between the higher levels of performance for this element, note the keywords emphasized in the descriptions and review the activities common to those levels.

PROFICIENT

Most of the outcomes are *suitable* for all students in the class and are based on evidence of student proficiency. However, the needs of some individual students *may not* be accommodated.

At the proficient level of performance, teaching practices may include the following types of activities:

- Teacher considers students' cultures, special needs, and skill levels when planning instructional outcomes for groups of students.
- Teacher plans instructional strategies that allow most students to achieve the outcomes.
- Teacher plans for choice by groups of students to work toward achieving outcomes.

DISTINGUISHED

Outcomes are based on a *comprehensive* assessment of student learning and take into account the varying needs of *individual students or groups*.

At the distinguished level of performance, teaching practices may include the following types of activities:

- Teacher considers students' cultures, special needs, and skill levels when planning instructional outcomes for students, individualizing where necessary.
- Teacher differentiates the learning experiences so that each student can work toward achieving the outcomes.

- Teacher differentiates the assessment of students' achievement of the outcomes.
- Teacher plans learning experiences around the outcomes that are culturally sensitive, as well as sensitive to the special needs and skill levels of each student.

The tools that follow will help you explore how to put the activities of these high levels of performance into practice in your classroom.

ASCD © 2009. All Rights Reserved.

Domain 1

Suitability for Diverse Learners

Element Reflection

✔ **Teacher tool**   __ **Student tool**

1. What strategies do you use to determine the diverse learning needs of your students?

2. Describe how the range of students in your class affects your choice of instructional outcomes.

Domain 1

89

Outcome Suitability Template

✔ **Teacher tool**   __ **Student tool**

Instructional outcomes reflect an expectation for all students. Some students will achieve the outcome sooner than others, and some students will need to have instruction presented differently before they can demonstrate their understanding. Think about the different groups and individuals in your classroom and what you need to do to make sure that they attain the desired outcome.

Outcome:		
Groups	**Groups (Proficient)**	**Individuals (Distinguished)**
Advanced Learners	Names:	Names:
Struggling Learners	Names:	Names:
ELLs	Names:	Names:
Other	Names:	Names:

Domain 1

Component 1c

Action Planning and Reflection

✔ **Teacher tool**   __ **Student tool**

Look over the tools for this component and choose a strategy or strategies that you are committed to trying in your classroom. Then return to this page and record what happened. If there was a change, what evidence indicates the extent to which this strategy was successful? Finally, think about what you might do differently to continue to bring about further growth in this component.

What will I try?	How did it go?	What will I do differently next time?

Domain 1

91

Component 1d

Demonstrating Knowledge of Resources

OVERVIEW

Student learning is enhanced by a teacher's skillful use of resources. Some of the resources are provided by the school as official materials, and others are secured by teachers through their own initiative. Resources fall into several different categories:

- Those used in the classroom by students.
- Those available beyond the classroom walls to enhance student learning.
- Those for teachers to further their own professional knowledge and skill.
- Those that can provide noninstructional assistance to students.

In selecting resources, teachers recognize the importance of discretion, choosing those that align directly with the instructional outcomes and will be most useful to students. Accomplished teachers also ensure that materials and resources are appropriately challenging for every student. Texts, for example, are available at various reading levels to make sure that all students can access the content and successfully demonstrate understanding of the instructional outcomes. Furthermore, expert teachers look beyond the school for resources to bring their subjects to life and to assist students who need help in their academic or nonacademic lives.

SELF-ASSESSMENT

Assess your practice in Component 1d against the levels of performance below, then check the box that best matches the level of your own teaching for each element.

Component 1d

Component 1d: Demonstrating Knowledge of Resources				
	Level of Performance			
ELEMENT	UNSATISFACTORY	BASIC	PROFICIENT	DISTINGUISHED
Resources for classroom use	Teacher is unaware of resources for classroom use available through the school or district.	Teacher displays awareness of resources available for classroom use through the school or district but no knowledge of resources available more broadly.	Teacher displays awareness of resources available for classroom use through the school or district and some familiarity with resources external to the school and on the Internet.	Teacher's knowledge of resources for classroom use is extensive, including those available through the school or district, in the community, through professional organizations and universities, and on the Internet.
	☐	☐	☐	☐
Resources to extend content knowledge and pedagogy	Teacher is unaware of resources to enhance content and pedagogical knowledge available through the school or district.	Teacher displays awareness of resources to enhance content and pedagogical knowledge available through the school or district but no knowledge of resources available more broadly.	Teacher displays awareness of resources to enhance content and pedagogical knowledge available through the school or district and some familiarity with resources external to the school and on the Internet.	Teacher's knowledge of resources to enhance content and pedagogical knowledge is extensive, including those available through the school or district, in the community, through professional organizations and universities, and on the Internet.
	☐	☐	☐	☐

Source: From *Enhancing Professional Practice: A Framework for Teaching, 2nd Edition* (p. 56), by C. Danielson, 2007, Alexandria, VA: ASCD. © 2007 by ASCD. Reprinted with permission.

Domain 1

Component 1d

ELEMENT	Level of Performance			
	UNSATISFACTORY	BASIC	PROFICIENT	DISTINGUISHED
Resources for students	Teacher is unaware of resources for students available through the school or district.	Teacher displays awareness of resources for students available through the school or district but no knowledge of resources available more broadly.	Teacher displays awareness of resources for students available through the school or district and some familiarity with resources external to the school and on the Internet.	Teacher's knowledge of resources for students is extensive, including those available through the school or district, in the community, and on the Internet.
	☐	☐	☐	☐

Source: From *Enhancing Professional Practice: A Framework for Teaching, 2nd Edition* (p. 56), by C. Danielson, 2007, Alexandria, VA: ASCD. © 2007 by ASCD. Reprinted with permission.

As a result of this self-assessment, on which element will you focus first? Turn to the pages following to explore the elements of the component in detail. After you've reviewed the tools, you can use the Action Planning and Reflection form to document the results of implementing the strategies in your classroom.

Domain 1

Element

Resources for Classroom Use

Description

To enhance the learning experiences of their students, teachers must be keenly aware of both the resources provided officially through the school and those available to teachers from a wide variety of sources that align with the teacher's instructional outcomes.

A Closer Look

To help you recognize the subtle differences between the higher levels of performance for this element, note the keywords emphasized in the descriptions and review the activities common to those levels.

PROFICIENT

The teacher displays *awareness* of resources available for classroom use through the school or district and *some familiarity* with resources outside the school and on the Internet.

At the proficient level of performance, teaching practices may include the following types of activities:

- Teacher selects several resources for students to use.
- Teacher selects resources that contain the same content but are written at varying reading levels.
- Teacher extends the lesson with resources outside of the classroom, such as guest speakers and field experiences.
- Teacher prepares students to use the Internet appropriately and provides students with access to the Internet as a tool for extending their learning.
- Teacher appropriately incorporates Internet resources, such as a virtual tour of the Smithsonian, with classroom instruction.
- Teacher often uses resources from professional organizations to support student learning.
- Teacher incorporates the media center, computer lab, and other school resources in lesson activities and assignments.
- Teacher uses multidisciplinary resources.
- Teacher uses artifacts available at the district or school level, such as media kits, science kits, physical models, and CDs, for hands-on or other applications in the classroom.

Domain 1

- Teacher incorporates community resources such as Junior Achievement projects; business mentors; fire, bike, and vehicle safety drills; science trunks; history primary sources; and art museum works-on-loan to enrich and complement lesson objectives.
- Teacher creates an annotated list of guest speakers and field trips and shares it with colleagues.

DISTINGUISHED

The teacher's knowledge of resources for classroom use is *extensive* and includes resources available through the school or district, in the community, through professional organizations and universities, and on the Internet.

At the distinguished level of performance, teaching practices may include the following types of activities:

- Teacher offers students a variety of resources from which to choose.
- Teacher offers students resources that contain the same content written at reading levels that match the students' levels.
- Teacher extends the lesson with resources outside of the classroom, such as guest speakers, field experiences, and so forth, and connects the resources to other disciplines.
- Teacher gives students access to researched sites on the Internet.
- Teacher explores the resources that are singular and unique to the topics or concepts under study that are available at the local public library, local businesses, and local colleges.
- Teacher provides resources that match students' skill levels.
- Teacher regularly researches resources on the Internet, checking them for validity and appropriateness, and keeps updated electronic files of resources that include but are not limited to Web sites.
- Teacher regularly uses resources from professional organizations to support student learning.
- Teacher has an ongoing relationship with colleges and universities that support student learning.
- Teacher compiles a list of resources that publish student work and recommends work for publication.
- Teacher develops a parent partner list, eliciting ideas from parents, and provides opportunities for parents themselves to share careers, hobbies, service, or civic activities to enrich classroom instruction.

Domain 1

- Teacher keeps a log of contacts with external resources that includes evaluative comments about the experience and recommendations for improvement.

The tools that follow will help you explore how to put the activities of these high levels of performance into practice in your classroom.

Domain 1

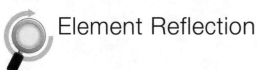

Element Reflection

✔ **Teacher tool**   ___ **Student tool**

1. How do you become aware of the range of resources available for classroom use?

2. To what extent is the Internet a useful resource to you in your teaching? How do you evaluate the quality of material you find there?

Planning Log of Visiting Classroom Experts and Guests

✔ **Teacher tool**   __ **Student tool**

Teacher: _____ School Year: _____

Date/ Time	Name of Experts or Guests	Sponsoring Organization	Purpose of Visit	Related Learner Outcome	Evaluative Comments	Invite Again?
						Yes No
						Yes No
						Yes No
						Yes No
						Yes No

Domain 1

Local Experts Checklist

✔ Teacher tool   __ **Student tool**

Once you've located a community expert to support your curriculum, you want to ensure that you both understand and agree on expectations for the visit to your classroom, including the length of the visit, the materials needed, and how students will be involved in the learning experience. Use the checklist to guide your planning.

☐ Send a letter of welcome.

☐ Confirm date, time, and location.

☐ Enclose a map to your site, noting the visitor parking area and preferred entry door.

☐ Inform of school visitor protocol.

    ☐ Sign in and out at main office.

    ☐ Wear a name badge at all times.

    ☐ Identify who will meet and escort to your classroom.

☐ Provide a fact sheet or otherwise share pertinent information about your school.

☐ Share class norms for behavior and any other relevant information about the class.

☐ Follow your district and school policies pertaining to community visitors.

☐ Request that the local expert complete an evaluation.

☐ Send a handwritten thank-you note from your students or yourself.

Domain 1

Local Expert Feedback Questionnaire

✔ Teacher tool   __ **Student tool**

Using local experts as learning resources can be especially effective if you have goals and feedback mechanisms. Feedback can help you refine the planning process and improve the experience of the students and the expert. After the visitation, ask the expert to complete the questionnaire.

Teacher's Name: Class Grade:

Expert's Name: Date:

Subject of Presentation:

1. I understood the purpose of my visit and how my presentation fit with the curriculum.

Needs Improvement		Satisfactory		Outstanding
1	2	3	4	5

2. I received adequate information to prepare me for visiting the school.

Needs Improvement		Satisfactory		Outstanding
1	2	3	4	5

3. Students were prepared with the background necessary for this presentation.

Needs Improvement		Satisfactory		Outstanding
1	2	3	4	5

4. Students expressed interest in this topic by being attentive and respectful.

Needs Improvement		Satisfactory		Outstanding
1	2	3	4	5

5. Students showed thinking skills through their questioning and participation.

Needs Improvement		Satisfactory		Outstanding
1	2	3	4	5

Comments:

Domain 1

Element

Resources to Extend Content Knowledge and Pedagogy

Description

In improving their own professional knowledge and skill, experienced teachers seek out resources both within the school and beyond for information and insight. Some of these are formal professional organizations while others are more informal networks.

A Closer Look

To help you recognize the subtle differences between the higher levels of performance for this element, note the keywords emphasized in the descriptions and review the activities common to those levels.

PROFICIENT

The teacher displays *awareness* of resources to enhance content and pedagogical knowledge available through the school or district and has *some familiarity* with resources outside the school and on the Internet.

At the proficient level of performance, teaching practices may include the following types of activities:

- Teacher uses multiple avenues, including the Internet, to deepen content knowledge.
- Teacher explores district offerings that enhance content knowledge or pedagogical knowledge.
- Teacher works with colleagues through both structured means—such as a lesson study, professional learning communities, critical friends groups, and groups that look at student work—and more informal means, such as team meetings, to expand content knowledge or pedagogical skill.
- Teacher explores connections with professional organizations to enhance knowledge of the content.
- Teacher explores options offered by universities to deepen professional content knowledge as well as student content knowledge.

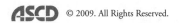

DISTINGUISHED

The teacher's knowledge of resources to enhance content and pedagogical knowledge is *extensive*, including resources available through the school or district, in the community, through professional organizations and universities, and on the Internet.

At the distinguished level of performance, teaching practices may include the following types of activities:

- Teacher researches Internet information about the content and checks the information for bias, validity, and authenticity.
- Teacher advocates for school and district support to enhance knowledge or pedagogical skill.
- Teacher regularly seeks out colleagues with whom to share and expand content knowledge or pedagogical skill.
- Teacher has an ongoing connection to professional organizations that enhance knowledge of the content and pedagogy.
- Teacher has an ongoing relationship with colleges and universities to enhance professional content knowledge as well as student content knowledge.
- Teacher investigates opportunities for participating in internships, shadowing, mentoring, and apprenticeships in business, industry, health, law, and other areas to stay current in a discipline, its knowledge base and skills, and related careers.
- Teacher seeks student critique of specific instructional material.
- Teacher invites students, as appropriate, for membership on the textbook selection committee at the department, school, or district level.

The tools that follow will help you explore how to put the activities of these high levels of performance into practice in your classroom.

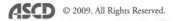

Domain 1

Resources to Extend Content Knowledge and Pedagogy

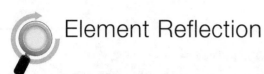

Element Reflection

✔ **Teacher tool**   __ **Student tool**

1. What school and district resources are available to help you stay abreast of the subject you teach?

2. Describe the advances in pedagogy in your field, the resources you have found to assist you, and how you have incorporated these advances into your practice.

Resources to Extend Content Knowledge and Pedagogy

Resource Log for Teachers

✔ **Teacher tool**   __ **Student tool**

Use the planning template to support and document your ongoing professional learning.

Resource	Activity	Lessons Learned/ Use in Teaching
Peers Observations, professional conversations, book study groups, sharing lesson activities		
Mentor/Coach Observations, coplanning, sharing lesson ideas, sharing instructional strategies		
Field Experts Observations, professional conversations, visiting sites		
Courses/Workshops College or other courses, school or district workshops		
Texts Professional texts, journals, articles		
Online Learning/Web Sites Content-specific sites, research information		

Domain 1

Element

Resources for Students

Domain 1

Description

Resources that help ensure students' success in school aren't always academic. Some of the resources may relate to nonacademic matters. These resources may include such things as Big Brother or Big Sister programs, mentoring and tutoring programs, community physical and mental health resources, and the like.

A Closer Look

To help you recognize the subtle differences between the higher levels of performance for this element, note the keywords emphasized in the descriptions and review the activities common to those levels.

PROFICIENT

The teacher displays *awareness* of resources for students available through the school or district and *some familiarity* with resources outside the school and on the Internet.

At the proficient level of performance, teaching practices may include the following types of activities:

- Teacher creates lists of community resources and Web sites and makes them available to students in multiple formats, including electronically on the school or classroom Web site.
- Teacher suggests resources that are available to students outside of school, such as the local public libraries and museums.
- Teacher provides resources that match various levels of students' skills.
- Teacher encourages students to use resources to expand learning beyond the school term or year, including resources for summer or vacation time.
- Teacher compiles a list of school and district resources, including social, health, and cultural as well as academic, for students and shares it with the team or school.
- Teacher makes direct contact with a resource contact or liaison to determine the availability and procedures for accessing the resource (e.g., social service agency).

DISTINGUISHED

The teacher's knowledge of resources for students is *extensive*, including knowledge of resources available through the school or district, in the community, and on the Internet.

At the distinguished level of performance, teaching practices may include the following types of activities:

- Teacher provides an extensive, annotated, and current selection of resources for student use and encourages students to add to the classroom collection of resources.
- Teacher requires students to use outside resources to expand independent student learning.
- Teacher, independently or in collaboration with others, organizes a resource fair to familiarize parents and students with resources available in the community.
- Teacher fosters student involvement in contests, enrichment activities, and competitions that nurture student talents and special needs.
- Teacher keeps logs of students' contact and involvement with external resources that includes evaluative comments about the experiences.
- Teacher develops personal relationships with a resource contact or liaison so that immediate access is available for students when needed.
- Teacher assumes leadership in familiarizing colleagues with their responsibilities in recognizing signals of students who need assistance and the resources available to help them.

The tools that follow will help you explore how to put the activities of these high levels of performance into practice in your classroom.

Domain 1

Resources for Students

Element Reflection

✔ **Teacher tool**   ___ **Student tool**

1. How do you become aware of resources in the school or community for needy students?

2. Describe how you help your students maintain their dignity when you offer them assistance for personal items, such as winter coats.

Domain 1

Resources for Students

✔ **Teacher tool**   __ **Student tool**

Use this template to plan for the resources you will make available to students to support their learning.

Unit of Study:
Unit Standards/Goals:

Resource	Lesson	Activity
Classroom Materials and Resources Teacher-made as well as other classroom materials, such as texts, maps, or manipulatives		
School Materials and Resources Library resources as well as school personnel, such as ESOL teacher, guidance counselor, or school psychologist		
Electronic Resources Web sites, Smart Boards, clickers, etc.		
Community Resources Local experts, local libraries, local sites such as a river or a business, local food shelf, local counseling center, boys and girls club, etc.		
Other Resources Peers, parents, counselors, big brother/big sister, etc.		

Domain 1

☐ 109

Questions for Examining Web Sites

✔ **Teacher tool**   ✔ **Student tool**

Teachers and students should be able to determine the validity of the information on the Internet. When examining Web sites for unbiased information, ask the following questions.

1. What is the date of the information?

2. Who created the information? (one person, an organization, etc.)

3. What is the author's purpose for presenting the information?

4. Does the author have a bias toward a particular viewpoint?

5. Is the information presented as fact or opinion?

6. Does the author offer contact information?

7. Does the author provide a variety of authentic sources?

8. Can you locate other Web sites that contain similar information?

Domain 1

Log of Student Contacts with External Resources

✔ **Teacher tool**   __ **Student tool**

Use this type of log to monitor service learning projects, mentor programs, senior project exhibitions, or other external student projects that contribute to your overall learning program.

Teacher: _____   School Year: _____

Domain 1

Date Range	Student	Contact Name and Organization	Reason for Project/Referral	Outcome and Comments

Component 1d

Action Planning and Reflection

✔ Teacher tool   **__ Student tool**

Look over the tools for this component and choose a strategy or strategies that you are committed to trying in your classroom. Then return to this page and record what happened. If there was a change, what evidence indicates the extent to which this strategy was successful? Finally, think about what you might do differently to continue to bring about further growth in this component.

What will I try?	How did it go?	What will I do differently next time?

Domain 1

Component 1e

Designing Coherent Instruction

OVERVIEW

Designing coherent instruction is the heart of planning and requires educators to have a clear understanding of the content; the curriculum; and the state, district, and school expectations for student learning. It also requires teachers to understand the characteristics of the students they teach and the active nature of student learning.

Educators must determine how best to sequence instruction to advance student learning through the required content. Thoughtfully constructed lessons contain cognitively engaging learning activities, incorporate appropriate resources and materials, and involve intentional student groupings. Proficient practice in this component recognizes that a well-designed instruction plan addresses the learning needs of various groups of students; one size does not fit all. At the distinguished level, the teacher plans instruction that takes into account the specific learning needs of each student and solicits ideas from students on how best to structure the learning.

This component involves planning that teachers will implement in Component 3c: Engaging Students in Learning (see page 304).

SELF-ASSESSMENT

Assess your practice in Component 1e against the levels of performance below, then check the box that best matches the level of your own teaching for each element.

Domain 1

	Level of Performance			
Component 1e: Designing Coherent Instruction				
ELEMENT	UNSATISFACTORY	BASIC	PROFICIENT	DISTINGUISHED
Learning activities	Learning activities are not suitable to students or to instructional outcomes and are not designed to engage students in active intellectual activity.	Only some of the learning activities are suitable to students or to the instructional outcomes. Some represent a moderate cognitive challenge, but with no differentiation for different students.	All of the learning activities are suitable to students or to the instructional outcomes, and most represent significant cognitive challenge, with some differentiation for different groups of students.	Learning activities are highly suitable to diverse learners and support the instructional outcomes. They are all designed to engage students in high-level cognitive activity and are differentiated, as appropriate, for individual learners.
Instructional materials and resources	Materials and resources are not suitable for students and do not support the instructional outcomes or engage students in meaningful learning.	Some of the materials and resources are suitable to students, support the instructional outcomes, and engage students in meaningful learning.	All of the materials and resources are suitable to students, support the instructional outcomes, and are designed to engage students in meaningful learning.	All of the materials and resources are suitable to students, support the instructional outcomes, and are designed to engage students in meaningful learning. There is evidence of appropriate use of technology and of student participation in selecting or adapting materials.

Component 1e

	Level of Performance			
ELEMENT	UNSATISFACTORY	BASIC	PROFICIENT	DISTINGUISHED
Instructional groups	Instructional groups do not support the instructional outcomes and offer no variety.	Instructional groups partially support the instructional outcomes, with an effort at providing some variety.	Instructional groups are varied as appropriate to the students and the different instructional outcomes.	Instructional groups are varied as appropriate to the students and the different instructional outcomes. There is evidence of student choice in selecting the different patterns of instructional groups.
	☐	☐	☐	☐
Lesson and unit structure	The lesson or unit has no clearly defined structure, or the structure is chaotic. Activities do not follow an organized progression, and time allocations are unrealistic.	The lesson or unit has a recognizable structure, although the structure is not uniformly maintained throughout. Progression of activities is uneven, with most time allocations reasonable.	The lesson or unit has a clearly defined structure around which activities are organized. Progression of activities is even, with reasonable time allocations.	The lesson's or unit's structure is clear and allows for different pathways according to diverse student needs. The progression of activities is highly coherent.
	☐	☐	☐	☐

Source: From *Enhancing Professional Practice: A Framework for Teaching, 2nd Edition* (pp. 60–61), by C. Danielson, 2007, Alexandria, VA: ASCD. © 2007 by ASCD. Reprinted with permission.

As a result of this self-assessment, on which element will you focus first? Turn to the pages following to explore the elements of the component in detail. After you've reviewed the tools, you can use the Action Planning and Reflection form to document the results of implementing the strategies in your classroom.

Domain 1

Element

Learning Activities

Description

It is through the design of learning activities that teachers make their content real to students. Viable learning activities are ones that engage students in thinking and reasoning, permitting them to acquire deep understanding of complex concepts, and involving, where possible, opportunities for student choice and collaboration.

A Closer Look

To help you recognize the subtle differences between the higher levels of performance for this element, note the keywords emphasized in the descriptions and review the activities common to those levels.

PROFICIENT

All of the learning activities are *suitable* to students or to the instructional outcomes and *most* represent *significant* cognitive challenge, with *some differentiation* for different groups of students.

At the proficient level of performance, teaching practices may include the following types of activities:

- Teacher ensures that units and lessons support instructional outcomes, reflecting important concepts of the content.
- Teacher designs an instructional map that builds on prior knowledge of groups of students and moves learning forward.
- Activities present students with opportunities for high-level thinking.
- Activities permit student choice and offer opportunities for students to work with their classmates.
- Learning experiences all align to the desired instructional outcomes.

DISTINGUISHED

Learning activities are *highly suitable* to diverse learners and support the instructional outcomes. They are *all* designed to engage students in high-level cognitive activity and are *differentiated for individual learners*, as appropriate.

Learning Activities

At the distinguished level of performance, teaching practices may include the following types of activities:

- Teacher tightly aligns units and lessons to instructional outcomes, reflecting important concepts of the content.
- Teacher designs an instructional map that builds on the prior knowledge of individual students to move all learners forward.
- Activities present students with increasingly complex opportunities for high-level thinking and are suitable for the range of student in the class.
- Activities permit student choice and provide opportunities for students to work with others, building on individual student strengths.
- Learning experiences directly align with the desired instructional outcomes and connect to other disciplines.

The tools that follow will help you explore how to put the activities of these high levels of performance into practice in your classroom.

Domain 1

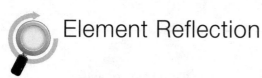

Element Reflection

✔ **Teacher tool**   __ **Student tool**

1. Describe the principal characteristics of engaging learning activities.

2. To what extent are the learning tasks you have planned likely to engage students in high-level cognitive activity?

Learning Activities

Lesson Planning Template

☑ **Teacher tool**   __ **Student tool**

Unit: Lesson: Date:	
Curriculum Standard(s) Identify the curriculum standards to be taught and how they connect to other standards within or outside of the discipline.	
Instructional Outcomes Identify the important concepts and skills that students will be expected to learn.	
Activities Include the warm-up or opening to lesson, activities to engage students in the intended instructional outcomes, and closure activities.	
Adjustments/Modifications Include any adjustments to the activities to accommodate student learning needs.	
Groups How will students be grouped for each activity in the lesson?	
Resources Identify resources and materials needed for the lesson.	
Assessments Identify the formative or summative assessments you will use to determine student progress toward achieving the instructional outcomes of the lesson.	

Domain 1

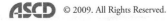

Curriculum Map: Secondary English Language Arts

✔ **Teacher tool**   __ **Student tool**

You can use this curriculum map template to provide a visual framework of the structure of the course. It can also help you organize the various learning experiences into a coherent schema that progresses student learning.

	Themes and Essential Questions	Standards-Based Essential Skills or Concepts to be Targeted/ Instructional Strategies	Formative or Summative Assessments (writing assignments, projects, performances)	Multigenre Thematic Texts (novels, drama, short fiction, poetry, nonfiction)
1st Quarter				
2nd Quarter				
3rd Quarter				
4th Quarter				

Domain 1

Learning Activities

Guidelines for Planning an Activity or Assignment

☑ **Teacher tool**   ___ **Student tool**

As you develop an activity or assignment, plan how you will engage students in important learning.

1. Concept students will learn or explore:

2. Description of how the activity or assignment fits within the prior and future learning of students in the class:

3. Description of opportunities for high-level thinking:

4. Description of differentiation of activity or assignment:

5. Description of opportunities for student choice:

6. Description of opportunities for students to work with others:

Domain 1

Assignments with a Twist

✔ Teacher tool   **__ Student tool**

To engage students in deeper exploration of the topics involved, try to give your assignments a twist. Review the example assignments and then design your own assignments with a twist.

Discipline	Topic	Traditional Assignment	Assignment with a Twist
U.S. History	Civil War	Write a 5-page report on the Second Battle of Bull Run.	Imagine that you were a Confederate (or Union) soldier in the Second Battle of Bull Run; write a letter home.
Mathematics	Area and Perimeter	Find the areas and perimeters of figures with the following dimensions...	Given 64 feet of fencing, what is the largest area you could enclose for a dog run?

Domain 1

Element

Instructional Materials
and Resources

Domain 1

Description

Teachers procure resources from a variety of sources that best align with their instructional outcomes and can engage students in learning. These resources can come from either inside or outside the school and may be suggested by the students themselves.

A Closer Look

To help you recognize the subtle differences between the higher levels of performance for this element, note the keywords emphasized in the descriptions and review the activities common to those levels.

PROFICIENT

All of the materials and resources are *suitable* to students, *support the instructional outcomes*, and are *designed to engage* students in meaningful learning.

At the proficient level of performance, teaching practices may include the following types of activities:

- Teacher finds a collection of materials and resources that support the intended learning.
- The learning resources are varied.
- The materials and resources appropriately challenge the students.
- The materials and resources engage students in their learning.
- Teacher revises commercially developed materials and resources to ensure that they are suitable.

DISTINGUISHED

All of the materials and resources are suitable to students, support the instructional outcomes, and are designed to engage students in meaningful learning. There is evidence of *appropriate use of technology* and of *student participation* in selecting or adapting materials.

At the distinguished level of performance, teaching practices may include the following types of activities:

Domain 1

- Teacher identifies a collection of materials and resources that tightly align with the intended learning.
- The resources are varied and include technological resources and suggestions from students.
- The materials and resources are differentiated and are appropriately challenging to every student.
- The resources and materials engage all students in their learning.
- Teacher revises commercially developed materials and resources to ensure that they are suitable, making revisions as needed.
- Teacher solicits students' critiques of piloted instructional materials and uses the comments in making a final decision.

The tools that follow will help you explore how to put the activities of these high levels of performance into practice in your classroom.

Instructional Materials and Resources

Element Reflection

✔ **Teacher tool**   __ **Student tool**

1. Describe the difficulties you encounter, if any, in locating appropriate materials for your classes.

2. What is the appropriate role of physical materials in your lessons? What about drawings and diagrams? How do you use all of them effectively?

Domain 1

Examining Materials and Resources
That Support Coherent Instruction

✔ Teacher tool   **__ Student tool**

Often textbooks alone do not provide the extent of engagement with a topic that students need to experience meaningful learning. Consider the degree to which the materials and resources enrich student learning. If the approved text or resource does not fulfill student needs, use this template to examine how you could use supplemental resources.

Approved Text/Resource: _____

1. Is it suitable for all students (advanced, struggling, ELL)?

Supplemental resource:

2. Does it align with state standards or frameworks?

Supplemental resource:

3. How does the resource support the instructional outcomes?

Supplemental resource:

4. How does the resource engage students cognitively?

Supplemental resource:

5. How does the resource integrate the use of technology?

Supplemental resource:

Element

Instructional Groups

Description

Teachers' grouping of students influences student learning, and teachers need to carefully consider whether groups should be homogeneous or heterogeneous, permanent or temporary. Regardless of the grouping system, instructional groups should enhance student learning.

A Closer Look

To help you recognize the subtle differences between the higher levels of performance for this element, note the keywords emphasized in the descriptions and review the activities common to those levels.

PROFICIENT

Instructional groups are *varied* as appropriate to the students and the different instructional outcomes.

At the proficient level of performance, teaching practices may include the following types of activities:

- Teacher considers the intended learning of the lesson when determining groups.
- Teacher considers the different learning needs of the students when determining groups.
- Teacher considers the number of students per group that will maximize learning.
- Teacher's plan shows provisions for sharing the expected roles and responsibilities of group members.
- Teacher can demonstrate through a matrix or chart use of a variety of grouping strategies.

DISTINGUISHED

Instructional groups are varied as appropriate to the students and the different instructional outcomes. There is evidence of *student choice* in selecting the different patterns of instructional groups.

At the distinguished level of performance, teaching practices may include the following types of activities:

- Teacher incorporates the intended learning of the lesson into the development of groups.
- Teacher considers the learning needs of each student when grouping.
- Teacher incorporates the suggestions offered by students for the development of groups, including numbers of members, roles and responsibilities, and group decision-making processes.
- Students reflect on the effectiveness of their participation in groups to enhance their learning.
- Students contribute to the teacher's awareness of the effectiveness of different grouping strategies.

The tools that follow will help you explore how to put the activities of these high levels of performance into practice in your classroom.

Element Reflection

✔ **Teacher tool**   __ **Student tool**

1. What factors do you consider when determining how to group your students?

2. To what extent should you permit your students to select their own work groups?

Planning Guide for Forming Instructional Groups

✔ **Teacher tool**   __ **Student tool**

Every grouping configuration has benefits and drawbacks, and you should take these into consideration when planning instructional groups for any lesson or unit.

Type of Group	Advantages	Disadvantages
Friends	Students get along well	Too much socializing
Random	Student perceive as "fair"	Can be unbalanced
Student Choice	Student buy-in	May not select the best people to work with
Learning Styles	Styles complement each other	May have difficulty working to each other's strengths
Same Skill Level	Can work on the same skill together; easier for teacher	Lack of diversity
Mixed Skill Level	Students can help one another	Students may get frustrated if other students' skill level is significantly different from their own

Unit/Lesson:

Dates:

Grouping Plan:

Rationale for Grouping Plan:

Evaluation of Grouping Plan:

What will you do next time as a result of what worked or didn't work this time?

Element

Lesson and Unit Structure

Description

The sequence of learning activities in a unit or lesson should ensure that students are not rushed and that they have the opportunity for reflection and closure in their learning. The amount of time devoted to parts of the lesson should be proportionate to their value to the lesson.

A Closer Look

To help you recognize the subtle differences between the higher levels of performance for this element, note the keywords emphasized in the descriptions and review the activities common to those levels.

PROFICIENT

The lesson or unit has a *clearly defined structure* around which activities are organized. Progression of activities is *even*, with *reasonable time allocations*.

At the proficient level of performance, teaching practices may include the following types of activities:

- Teacher plans units and lessons that allow sufficient time for students to engage in meaningful learning that ensures that students achieve the identified outcomes.
- Teacher structures each activity to build on the previous activities.
- Teacher's plan is complete, from opening to closure.
- Daily lesson plans show alignment and coherence with the overall unit plan.

DISTINGUISHED

The lesson's or unit's structure is clear and allows for *different pathways* according to diverse student needs. The progression of activities is *highly coherent*.

At the distinguished level of performance, teaching practices may include the following types of activities:

- Teacher plans units and lessons that allow ample time for students to engage in meaningful learning that ensures that every student achieves the identified outcomes.
- Teacher structures each activity to expand the learning of the previous activities.

- Teacher structures the lesson and unit to allow students with different learning needs to meet the intended outcomes.
- Daily lesson plans align and cohere with the overall unit plan and half-term plan.

The tools that follow will help you explore how to put the activities of these high levels of performance into practice in your classroom.

Lesson and Unit Structure

Element Reflection

✔ Teacher tool   __ **Student tool**

1. How important is it, in the subjects you teach, to establish an arc of the lesson or unit with a clearly defined beginning, middle, and end?

2. In your unit and lesson planning, how can you ensure that students have the opportunity for both reflection and closure?

ASCD © 2009. All Rights Reserved.

Domain 1

Action Planning and Reflection

✔ **Teacher tool**   __ **Student tool**

Look over the tools for this component and choose a strategy or strategies that you are committed to trying in your classroom. Then return to this page and record what happened. If there was a change, what evidence indicates the extent to which this strategy was successful? Finally, think about what you might do differently to continue to bring about further growth in this component.

What will I try?	How did it go?	What will I do differently next time?

Domain 1

Designing Student Assessments

OVERVIEW

Good teaching requires both assessment *of* learning and assessment *for* learning. Assessments *of* learning ensure that teachers know that students have achieved the intended outcomes. Teachers must design these assessments so that they provide evidence of the full range of instructional outcomes. For instance, different methods are needed to assess reasoning skills than to assess factual knowledge. Furthermore, teachers may need to adapt such assessments to the particular needs of individual students. An ESL student, for example, may need an alternative method of assessment to demonstrate understanding.

Assessments *for* learning enable teachers to incorporate assessments directly into the instruction and to modify or adapt instruction as needed to ensure student understanding. Even though such assessments are used during instruction, teachers must design them during the planning process. Such formative assessment strategies are ongoing, and both teachers and students can use them to monitor progress toward instructional outcomes.

SELF-ASSESSMENT

Assess your practice in Component 1f against the levels of performance below, then check the box that best matches the level of your own teaching for each element.

Component 1f: Designing Student Assessments				
	Level of Performance			
ELEMENT	UNSATISFACTORY	BASIC	PROFICIENT	DISTINGUISHED
Congruence with instructional outcomes	Assessment procedures are not congruent with instructional outcomes.	Some of the instructional outcomes are assessed through the proposed approach, but many are not.	All the instructional outcomes are assessed through the approach to assessment; assessment methodologies may have been adapted for groups of students.	Proposed approach to assessment is fully aligned with the instructional outcomes in both content and process. Assessment methodologies have been adapted for individual students, as needed.
	☐	☐	☐	☐

Source: From *Enhancing Professional Practice: A Framework for Teaching, 2nd Edition* (p. 63), by C. Danielson, 2007, Alexandria, VA: ASCD. © 2007 by ASCD. Reprinted with permission.

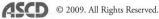

Component 1f

Domain 1

	Level of Performance			
ELEMENT	UNSATISFACTORY	BASIC	PROFICIENT	DISTINGUISHED
Criteria and standards	Proposed approach contains no criteria or standards. ☐	Assessment criteria and standards have been developed, but they are not clear. ☐	Assessment criteria and standards are clear. ☐	Assessment criteria and standards are clear; there is evidence that the students contributed to their development. ☐
Design of formative assessments	Teacher has no plan to incorporate formative assessment in the lesson or unit. ☐	Approach to the use of formative assessment is rudimentary, including only some of the instructional outcomes. ☐	Teacher has a well-developed strategy to using formative assessment and has designed particular approaches to be used. ☐	Approach to using formative assessment is well designed and includes student as well as teacher use of the assessment information. ☐
Use for planning	Teacher has no plans to use assessment results in designing future instruction. ☐	Teacher plans to use assessment results to plan for future instruction for the class as a whole. ☐	Teacher plans to use assessment results to plan for future instruction for groups of students. ☐	Teacher plans to use assessment results to plan future instruction for individual students. ☐

Source: From *Enhancing Professional Practice: A Framework for Teaching, 2nd Edition* (p. 63), by C. Danielson, 2007, Alexandria, VA: ASCD. © 2007 by ASCD. Reprinted with permission.

As a result of this self-assessment, on which element will you focus first? Turn to the pages following to explore the elements of the component in detail. After you've reviewed the tools, you can use the Action Planning and Reflection form to document the results of implementing the strategies in your classroom.

Element

Congruence with Instructional Outcomes

Description

Different types of instructional outcomes require different types of assessments. True/false or multiple-choice questions are suitable for factual knowledge, whereas longer, constructed-response questions are needed for conceptual understanding and reasoning skills. And for such outcomes as collaboration skills, only teacher observation will suffice.

A Closer Look

To help you recognize the subtle differences between the higher levels of performance for this element, note the keywords emphasized in the descriptions and review the activities common to those levels.

PROFICIENT

All the instructional outcomes are assessed through the approach to assessment. Assessment methodologies may have been *adapted for groups* of students.

At the proficient level of performance, teaching practices may include the following types of activities:

- Teacher's lesson plans show a connection of each instructional outcome to its corresponding assessment.
- Teacher designs or selects each assessment to match its corresponding type of instructional outcomes (e.g., a behavioral checklist self-assessment might be an assessment for a social skills outcome).
- Plans for students to demonstrate their understanding include performances, such as writing or presentation.
- Teacher's lesson plans show modifications or adaptations of an assessment for groups of students as needed.

DISTINGUISHED

The teacher's proposed approach to assessment *fully aligns* with the instructional outcomes in both content and process. Assessment methodologies have been *adapted for individual students* as needed.

At the distinguished level of performance, teaching practices may include the following types of activities:

- Teacher's lesson plans show modifications or adaptations of assessment for individual students.
- Teacher's unit plans show modification or adaptations of assessments of learning (summative assessments) for individual students.
- Teacher-designed assessments are authentic, with real-world applications.
- Teacher develops an alternative version of the same assessment as appropriate for diverse learners.

The tools that follow will help you explore how to put the activities of these high levels of performance into practice in your classroom.

Congruence with Instructional Outcomes

Element Reflection

✔ **Teacher tool**   __ **Student tool**

1. How can you ensure that your assessment methodologies are suitable for the range of instructional outcomes?

2. To what extent must you modify your approaches to assessment to accommodate individual students?

Domain 1

Domain 1

Choosing the Right Assessment

✔ **Teacher tool**   __ **Student tool**

Well-designed assessments tightly align with the instructional outcomes and are best tailored to suit the type of learning being asked of the student.

Fill in the Assessment Selection Chart with the knowledge and skills that compose the lesson's instructional outcomes. Then, based on the congruence matrix, check the boxes for the recommended types of assessments for each characteristic that applies to your outcome.

The assessments that you should include in your lesson will be those with multiple checks in the same column.

ASSESSMENT SELECTION CHART

Instructional Outcome(s)	Test		Product		Performance	
	Select	**Supply**	**Written**	**Physical**	**Structured**	**Spontaneous**
Knowledge						
Factual Knowledge						
Procedural Knowledge						
Conceptual Understanding						
Skills						
Thinking and Reasoning						
Communication Skills						
Social Skills						
Learning to Learn						
Aesthetics, Disposition, and Ethics						

Congruence with Instructional Outcomes

CONGRUENCE MATRIX

Assessment Methods Key

Test		Product		Performance	
Select	**Supply**	**Written**	**Physical**	**Structured**	**Spontaneous**
• True/false test • Multiple-choice test	• Short-answer questions • Essay test	• Essay • Term paper • Lab report	• Sculpture • Model	• Student reading • Speech or presentation • Musical performance • French or Spanish dialogue	• Group work

Type of Instructional Outcomes	Test		Product		Performance	
	Select	**Supply**	**Written**	**Physical**	**Structured**	**Spontaneous**
Knowledge						
Factual Knowledge	XX	XX	XX		X	
Procedural Knowledge	X	XX	X			
Conceptual Understanding	X	XX	XX	X	XX	X
Skills						
Thinking and Reasoning	X	XX	XX		XX	X
Communication Skills		XX	XX		XX	
Social Skills					X	XX
Learning to Learn		XX	XX	XX	XX	XX
Aesthetics, Disposition, and Ethics		XX	XX		XX	XX

Domain 1

Element

Criteria and Standards

Description

Students should never be assessed against criteria of which they are ignorant. Teachers should clearly write and convey the criteria, such as the essential elements of a satisfactory piece of student writing and the accompanying scoring guide or rubric, to students during instruction. If possible, students should themselves contribute to the articulation of assessment criteria.

A Closer Look

To help you recognize the subtle differences between the higher levels of performance for this element, note the keywords emphasized in the descriptions and review the activities common to those levels.

PROFICIENT

Assessment criteria and standards are *clear*.

At the proficient level of performance, teaching practices may include the following types of activities:

- Teacher can clearly articulate the assessment criteria for any desired instructional outcome.
- Teacher writes assessment criteria in student-friendly language to share with students.
- Teacher develops rubrics with clear criteria statements and descriptors of performance at several levels for most assessments.
- Teacher prepares and plans to explain to students the grading guidelines for major assessments.
- Teacher plans multiple assessments for students who may not meet standards on the first attempt.

DISTINGUISHED

Assessment criteria and standards are clear, and there is evidence that the *students contributed* to their development.

At the distinguished level of performance, teaching practices may include the following types of activities:

- Teacher's criteria for assessing student outcomes have been developed with student input.

Criteria and Standards

- Teacher plans to teach students about rubrics and checklists and then invites students to participate in the development of rubrics for specific assignments or activities.
- Teacher uses technology in developing rubrics.
- Teacher collects, selects, and shares with students examples of student work at each rubric level.
- Teacher lets students practice using the checklists and rubrics in scoring sample student work.

The tools that follow will help you explore how to put the activities of these high levels of performance into practice in your classroom.

Domain 1

Criteria and Standards

Element Reflection

✔ Teacher tool   ___ **Student tool**

1. What challenges do you encounter in formulating clear criteria and standards for your instructional outcomes?

2. What strategies do you use to elicit student participation in defining assessment criteria and standards?

Criteria and Standards

Checklist for Using Rubrics with Students

✔ **Teacher tool**   __ **Student tool**

Use the following checklist as a guide for introducing rubrics to students.

☐ Select from an established rubric bank or design a new rubric that could be incorporated into a lesson or assignment.

☐ Give each student a copy of the rubric.

☐ Invite students to study the rubric, and guide them in this effort to make sure that they understand the descriptors, the acceptable level of performance, and how you will use the rubric to score their work.

☐ As appropriate, share examples of student work (from previous classes perhaps) that demonstrate the different levels of performance, particularly at the proficient level.

☐ Give students the assignment and have them use the rubric as a guide to complete the task.

☐ Upon completion, have students self-assess their assignment using the rubric before handing it in. Provide adequate time for students to revise their work if needed before handing it in for scoring by the teacher.

☐ Use the same rubric to score the student's assignment.

Domain 1

Rubric Template

✔ **Teacher tool**   ✔ **Student tool**

Rubrics are meant to be instructive, formative assessments. The goal is to have students recognize what proficient work is and persevere until they meet that target. Performance levels don't translate neatly into grades because the work is criterion-referenced instead of norm-referenced.

Fill out the rubric template with the evaluation criteria and descriptions of the performance levels for each criterion. You can see an example of a completed rubric on the following page.

Rubric for _____

Criteria	1: Beginning	2: Developing	3: Proficient	4: Exemplary

Student Goals for Improvement:

Domain 1

EXAMPLE RUBRIC: RESEARCH AND INFORMATION GATHERING

Criteria	1: Beginning	2: Developing	3: Proficient	4: Exemplary
Search Strategies for Information Gathering	Uses basic search strategies with assistance. Sources or information gathered is not varied or specific to the task. Unable to identify primary resources.	Uses appropriate search strategies with assistance. Sources and information may not be specific to the task (may be too narrow or too broad) or lack variety. Has difficulty identifying primary resources.	Independently uses appropriate search strategies to find a variety of relevant sources and information specific to the task. Identifies primary and secondary sources.	Independently uses appropriate and advanced search strategies for a variety of relevant sources and information specific to the task. Identifies little-known or unique information resources or gathering techniques, including primary and secondary sources.
Assessment of Information	Makes little attempt to determine or totally misjudges credibility, relevance, or value of information specific to the task.	Has difficulty determining credibility, relevance, or value specific to the task. Uses a mix of relevant and irrelevant information.	Independently analyzes information to determine its credibility, relevance, and value specific to the task.	Independently analyzes information in detail, accurately, and insightfully to determine its credibility, relevance, and value specific to the task.
Interpretation and Synthesis of Information	Misinterprets the information specific to the task or fails to synthesize it.	Has difficulty interpreting the information specific to the task or synthesizes the information imprecisely or inaccurately.	Independently interprets information accurately. Concisely synthesizes information specific to the task.	Independently interprets information in accurate and highly insightful ways. Provides a highly creative and unique synthesis of the information specific to the task.
Citing of Information Gathered	Unable to create bibliographic records using MLA style. Does not understand the concept of plagiarism.	Creates, with assistance, bibliographic records using MLA style. Needs assistance recognizing information that requires quotes and documentation to avoid plagiarism.	Independently creates bibliographic records using MLA style. Cites all sources, using quotes and documentation to avoid plagiarism.	Independently creates bibliographic records using MLA style. Cites all sources, using quotes and documentation to avoid plagiarism.

Domain 1

Element

Design of Formative Assessments

Description

Formative assessment is a powerful instructional strategy, but one that requires considerable planning to use well. Experienced teachers develop questions prior to a lesson that they will be able to use both to ascertain the general level of student understanding and to diagnose particular student misconceptions.

A Closer Look

To help you recognize the subtle differences between the higher levels of performance for this element, note the keywords emphasized in the descriptions and review the activities common to those levels.

PROFICIENT

The teacher has a *well-developed* strategy for using formative assessment and has designed particular approaches.

At the proficient level of performance, teaching practices may include the following types of activities:

- Teacher develops checklists for each formative assessment and plans for students to use them.
- Teacher creates a matrix or spreadsheet to record by name each formative assessment and audits the matrix for variety, frequency, and quantity.
- Teacher reflects on the usefulness and effectiveness of formative assessments.
- Teacher continues to add to the repertoire of formative assessment approaches or strategies.
- Teacher shares with colleagues the rationale behind choosing a certain formative assessment to measure student progress on a specific skill, concept, or process.

DISTINGUISHED

The teacher's approach to using formative assessment is well designed, and *students as well as the teacher* use the assessment information.

Design of Formative Assessments

At the distinguished level of performance, teaching practices may include the following types of activities:

- For each formative assessment, teacher develops checklists designed to be used by both teacher and students, as well as parents and peers as appropriate.
- Teacher shares with students information gained from formative assessment and invites student reflection and next steps for the class as a whole.
- Teacher conferences with individual students to focus on what the student has learned from the assessment and possible next steps.
- Students are actively involved in collecting information from formative assessments.
- Students are invited to give input about the design of new formative assessments and modifications to existing ones.

The tools that follow will help you explore how to put the activities of these high levels of performance into practice in your classroom.

Domain 1

Design of Formative Assessments

Element Reflection

✔ **Teacher tool**   __ **Student tool**

1. What considerations do you bear in mind as you determine formative assessment strategies as part of the planning process?

2. How can you ensure that formative assessment strategies remain "formative" and are not incorporated into summative measures, such as grading?

Domain 1

Checking for Student Understanding

✔ **Teacher tool**   __ **Student tool**

Formative assessment requires teachers to determine, in advance, what successful and ongoing learning looks like and how to assess whether this is happening. If you establish that students are not learning, you can establish which elements of a lesson you need to reteach or which students are eligible for more advanced work. Below are examples of ways to check student understanding.

- **Questions Strips/Index Cards:** Distribute strips of paper or index cards at critical points in the lesson. Ask students to respond to a specific question or to paraphrase the main concept. You should be able to quickly read the responses and adjust the lesson if necessary.
- **Thumbs Up, Thumbs Down:** Students give a thumbs-up if they understand and a thumbs-down if they do not understand or are unsure. It is important that all students respond.
- **Traffic Light:** Students have red, yellow, and green disks on their desks. As they work on an assignment, they turn over the green disk if they are not having any difficulties, the yellow disk if they aren't sure about something, and the red disk if they are stuck and need assistance right away. You can work with the red-disk students and ask yellow-disk students to seek out a student who has a green disk displayed for assistance.
- **Whiteboards:** Students respond to a question or prompt on a whiteboard and then display the boards simultaneously for you to see and respond to. If whiteboards are not available, teachers can use transparent sleeves with a white sheet of paper inserted. Students can use overhead markers to write on the transparent sleeve and can remove the white paper to project their answer on an overhead projector.
- **Popcorn Questioning or Discussion:** Ask a question to a particular student. After that student answers, he selects a classmate to respond to or add to his answer. The second student responds and selects a third student to elaborate, and so forth.
- **Entrance or Warm-Up Slip:** Students respond to a question or prompt at the very beginning of class that references the previous day's learning or sets them up for the current day's learning. You can randomly select several students to share responses to assess readiness to move into the lesson.

- **Exit Ticket:** Prior to leaving class, students write one thing that they have learned and one question that they have about the lesson. You can adjust the next day's lesson based on students' exit ticket responses.

For each lesson you teach, keep track of the formative assessment techniques you used and whether they were successful or what modification you made based on students' responses.

Lesson:

Assessment	Used in This Lesson	Notes
Questions Strips/Index Cards		
Thumbs Up, Thumbs Down		
Traffic Light		
Whiteboards		
Popcorn Questioning or Discussion		
Entrance or Warm-Up Slip		
Exit Ticket		
Other:		

Domain 1

Element

Use for Planning

Description

The principal purpose of student assessment, both formal and informal, is to inform both student and teacher planning for future learning. Well-designed assessments enable such planning to be highly focused and specific to the needs of individuals and groups of students.

A Closer Look

To help you recognize the subtle differences between the higher levels of performance for this element, note the keywords emphasized in the descriptions and review the activities common to those levels.

PROFICIENT

The teacher uses assessment results to plan for future instruction for *groups of students.*

At the proficient level of performance, teaching practices may include the following types of activities:

- Teacher's plans show how the teacher uses information from state and district tests and assessments to instruct groups of students.
- Teacher communicates, orally or in writing, how grouping for future instruction is based on information from formative assessments.
- Teacher develops new assignments and activities in response to information from assessments.
- Teacher participates with colleagues in collecting samples of student work and analyzing it with a common protocol.
- Teacher uses the results of assessments to locate and select new or varied materials and resources, including technology resources.

DISTINGUISHED

The teacher uses assessment results to plan future instruction for *individual students.*

At the distinguished level of performance, teaching practices may include the following types of activities:

- Teacher's plans show how the teacher uses information from state and district tests to instruct individual students.
- Teacher communicates, orally or in writing, how information from formative assessments influences individualized instruction.
- Teacher takes the lead with colleagues in collecting samples of student work and analyzing it using a common protocol. As a result, the teacher modifies instruction for individual students.

The tools that follow will help you explore how to put the activities of these high levels of performance into practice in your classroom.

Domain 1

Use for Planning

Element Reflection

✔ **Teacher tool**   __ **Student tool**

1. To what degree is the assessment information you have sufficient to enable you to plan for groups of students and individuals? How could you supplement the information?

2. How does your students' language proficiency present challenges in your using assessment information for planning?

Domain 1

Use for Planning

Domain 1

Tracking Student Progress

✔ **Teacher tool**   __ **Student tool**

Students' responses to assessments can shed light on the success of a lesson and the progress of individual students. Fill in the students' names and the type and date of assessments to get a picture of what students understand.

Instructional Outcome:

Assessment										
Date										
Student	Not Yet	Got It	Not Yet	Got It	Not Yet	Got It	Not Yet	Got It	Not Yet	Got It

Evaluation:

Use for Planning

Example of Tracking Student Progress

Assessment	Index Cards		Exit Ticket		Essay		Popcorn Questions		Test	
Date	9/22/08		9/23/08		9/24/08		9/25/08		9/26/08	
Student	**Not Yet**	**Got It**	**Not Yet**	**Got It**	**Not Yet**	**Got It**	**Not Yet**	**Got It**	**Not Yet**	**Got It**
Adrian	X		X			X		X	X	
Bobby		X	X		X		X		X	
Dylan		X		X	X			X		X
Elisha	X		X			X		X		X
Michelle		X	X			X		X		X
Pedro		X	X		X			X		X
Sasha		X		X		X		X	X	
Terrence		X		X	X			X	X	

Evaluation:

- Bobby "got it" on the first day of instruction but did not demonstrate proficiency the rest of the week. What do I need to do to help Bobby reach proficiency?
- When I look at Elisha's progress, what does it tell me?
- How might I extend learning expectations for students who consistently demonstrate proficiency?

Component 1f

Action Planning and Reflection

✔ **Teacher tool**   __ **Student tool**

Look over the tools for this component and choose a strategy or strategies that you are committed to trying in your classroom. Then return to this page and record what happened. If there was a change, what evidence indicates the extent to which this strategy was successful? Finally, think about what you might do differently to continue to bring about further growth in this component.

What will I try?	How did it go?	What will I do differently next time?

Domain 1

Domain 2

The Classroom Environment

The Classroom Environment

Domain 2 focuses on classroom exchanges between the students and the teacher. Teachers who excel in this area have the ability to create classrooms in which students feel safe and comfortable. An atmosphere of warmth and caring coexists with professionalism: the teacher and students work together to effectively and efficiently deal with classroom management, behavior, and procedures.

Teachers who operate at the proficient and distinguished levels in Domain 2 show genuine concern for their students' needs and abilities both within and outside of the classroom. Their students consider these teachers to be adults who believe in their learning potential, care about them personally, and are reliable sources of support for their learning.

Based on the results of the self-assessment you took in the introduction (see page 7), turn to the page of the component on which you will focus first. Each of the following sections explores the elements of these components in detail and includes tools that you can use in your professional practice.

Domain 2

Component 2a

Creating an Environment
of Respect and Rapport

OVERVIEW

Respect and rapport both between the students and the teacher and among the students is a cornerstone of maintaining a learning environment in which students feel safe and valued. When adults recall their school experiences, the relationships are what dominate their recollections. A learning environment of respect and rapport looks different in various classrooms depending on a number of contextual factors, such as the age or culture of the students.

Respect and rapport are observable through teachers' verbal and nonverbal behavior. Nods, smiles, and hand gestures as well as the spoken word are all part of how teachers establish and maintain relationships with students. In classrooms where teachers demonstrate this component at a high level, all students feel valued and know that they will be treated with dignity by the teacher as well by other students. As is often said, "People will forget what you said. People will forget what you did. But they will never forget how you made them feel."

SELF-ASSESSMENT

Assess your practice in Component 2a against the levels of performance below, then check the box that best matches the level of your own teaching for each element.

Domain 2

Component 2a

Component 2a: Creating an Environment of Respect and Rapport				
	Level of Performance			
ELEMENT	UNSATISFACTORY	BASIC	PROFICIENT	DISTINGUISHED
Teacher interaction with students	Teacher interaction with at least some students is negative, demeaning, sarcastic, or inappropriate to the age or culture of the students. Students exhibit disrespect for the teacher. ☐	Teacher-student interactions are generally appropriate but may reflect occasional inconsistencies, favoritism, or disregard for students' cultures. Students exhibit only minimal respect for the teacher. ☐	Teacher-student interactions are friendly and demonstrate general caring and respect. Such interactions are appropriate to the age and cultures of the students. Students exhibit respect for the teacher. ☐	Teacher interactions with students reflect genuine respect and caring for individuals as well as groups of students. Students appear to trust the teacher with sensitive information. ☐
Student interactions with other students	Student interactions are characterized by conflict, sarcasm, or put-downs. ☐	Students do not demonstrate disrespect for one another. ☐	Student interactions are generally polite and respectful. ☐	Students demonstrate genuine caring for one another and monitor one another's treatment of peers, correcting classmates respectfully when needed. ☐

Source: From *Enhancing Professional Practice: A Framework for Teaching, 2nd Edition* (p. 66), by C. Danielson, 2007, Alexandria, VA: ASCD. © 2007 by ASCD. Reprinted with permission.

As a result of this self-assessment, on which element will you focus first? Turn to the pages following to explore the elements of the component in detail. After you've reviewed the tools, you can use the Action Planning and Reflection form to document the results of implementing the strategies in your classroom.

Domain 2

Element

Teacher Interaction with Students

Description

A teacher's interactions with students set the tone for the classroom. Without a positive tone, very little learning is possible.

A Closer Look

To help you recognize the subtle differences between the higher levels of performance for this element, note the keywords emphasized in the descriptions and review the activities common to those levels.

PROFICIENT

Teacher-student interactions are *friendly* and demonstrate general *caring and respect*. Such interactions are appropriate to the age and cultures of the students. Students exhibit respect for the teacher.

At the proficient level of performance, teaching practices may include the following types of activities:

- Teacher calls the students by name.
- Teacher greets students as they walk in the door.
- Teacher uses "we" statements to make students feel part of the group.
- Teacher listens to students with care.
- Teacher uses oral, written, and nonverbal language to convey caring for students.
- Polite language is used in interactions between the students and teacher.
- Teacher reaches out to families to learn about students.
- Teacher makes an effort to learn about how students feel about the class.

DISTINGUISHED

The teacher's interactions with students reflect genuine caring and respect for *individual students* as well as groups of students. Students exhibit respect for the teacher *as an individual*, beyond that for the role.

Teacher Interaction with Students

At the distinguished level of performance, teaching practices may include the following types of activities:

- Teacher sets aside time outside the classroom to help students.
- Teacher shares, in an appropriate manner, personal stories and situations that apply to the classroom setting.
- Students point out, as appropriate, if another student treats the teacher with disrespect.
- Teacher intentionally plans for and seeks out ways to build respect and rapport with students.

The tools that follow will help you explore how to put the activities of these high levels of performance into practice in your classroom.

Domain 2

165

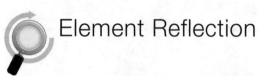

Element Reflection

✔ **Teacher tool**   __ **Student tool**

1. To what extent are your interactions with students a function of their cultural backgrounds? Gender? Cognitive abilities? What difference, if any, do these factors make?

2. What is the range of classroom situations in which you can show respect for your students?

Domain 2

Teacher Interaction with Students

KWL Chart About Students

✔ **Teacher tool**   __ **Student tool**

To guide you in building relationships with students, complete this KWL chart for the students in your classes. Review and update the chart at least once each semester.

Student	What I know about this student	What do I want to know about this student?	How will I learn more about this student?

Domain 2

☐ 167

Exit Ticket

__ **Teacher tool**   ✔ **Student tool**

Distribute this questionnaire to students at any time during the year to get feedback on their learning experience in your classroom. You can ensure that students answer honestly by giving them anonymity. Have a box by the door where students can drop completed sheets.

1. One thing I'd like to change about this class:

2. It would be easier for me to learn if:

3. I wish:

4. I feel:

5. I'd like to know more about:

6. One thing that would help me is:

7. The best thing about this class is:

8. The worst thing about this class is:

Domain 2

Element

Student Interactions with Other Students

Description

As important as the teacher's treatment of students is, students' treatment by their classmates is arguably even more important to students. Poor treatment can result in bullying, which can poison the environment of an entire school. On the other hand, positive interactions among students are mutually supportive, creating an emotionally healthy school environment. It's the teacher's responsibility to both model and teach students how to interact with one another respectfully.

A Closer Look

To help you recognize the subtle differences between the higher levels of performance for this element, note the keywords emphasized in the descriptions and review the activities common to those levels.

PROFICIENT

Student interactions are *generally polite* and *respectful*.

At the proficient level of performance, teaching practices may include the following types of activities:

- Students know each other's names and use them in their conversations.
- Students use polite language when they work together.
- Students work well together in a variety of group settings.
- Students listen carefully to one another during a class discussion.

DISTINGUISHED

Students demonstrate *genuine caring* for one another as individuals and as students. Students *monitor one another's treatment* of peers, correcting classmates respectfully when needed.

At the distinguished level of performance, teaching practices may include the following types of activities:

- Students correct each other, in an appropriate manner, when they see evidence of lack of respect for other students.
- Students display a sense of esprit de corps and are committed to the success of their peers.
- Students support each other's learning and offer each other assistance.
- Students ensure that their classmates listen respectfully to one another's views.

The tools that follow will help you explore how to put the activities of these high levels of performance into practice in your classroom.

Student Interactions with Other Students

Element Reflection

✔ **Teacher tool**   __ **Student tool**

1. How have you taught your students how to demonstrate respect for one another?

2. What strategies can you use with your students so that they will monitor one another's interactions?

Domain 2

Find a Person Who...

__ **Teacher tool**   ✔ **Student tool**

Give students an opportunity to get to know each other by having them find classmates who fit the descriptions in each of the squares. You might follow this up by collecting the sheets and making notes of information about each student. Modify this chart to fit the subject area or grade level of your students.

Variation: This can also be a bingo game. After the students have filled them out, collect the sheets and hand out new ones. Then call out a category and have students write in the name of a classmate who fits the category. Students who get a row or column filled in call out "bingo."

Likes math	Plays football	Likes drawing	Went to this school last year
Just moved here	Writes poetry	Has a sister	Has been out of the United States
Is an only child	Has a pet	Has a brother	Has really short hair
Has the same eye color as you	Went to a different school last year	Rides a bike to school	Has really long hair
Has read a book you have read	Was born in another state	Lives more than a mile from school	Is good on the computer
Speaks a language other than English	Wears the same size shoe as you	Gets an allowance	Has never attended a different school

Student Interactions with Other Students

What Is Respect?

__ **Teacher tool**   ✔ **Student tool (grades 5–12)**

Have students work individually to fill in circle #1 with the initials of three to five people they respect. These can be people they know, celebrities, or historical figures. Give them about three minutes. Then have students write down five characteristics of these people in circle #2.

Put students in cooperative groups, and have them share their characteristics. Ask them to reach a consensus on three words that best summarize their collective thinking about respect. As a class, generate a master list of words based on the report from each group. Start with one group and ask them to share one word, move on to the next group, and continue until you've recorded all the words they wrote.

Discuss the meaning of these words as a group, asking students what they do or say in the classroom that conveys these characteristics.

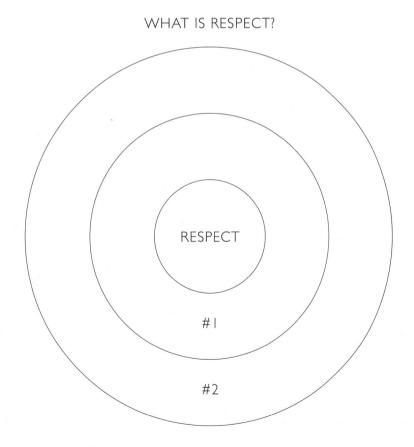

WHAT IS RESPECT?

RESPECT

#1

#2

Domain 2

Action Planning and Reflection

✔ **Teacher tool**   __ **Student tool**

Look over the tools for this component and choose a strategy or strategies that you are committed to trying in your classroom. Then return to this page and record what happened. If there was a change, what evidence indicates the extent to which this strategy was successful? Finally, think about what you might do differently to continue to bring about further growth in this component.

What will I try?	How did it go?	What will I do differently next time?

Domain 2

Component 2b

Establishing a Culture for Learning

OVERVIEW

A culture for learning refers to the atmosphere and energy level in a classroom where students are engaged in important work. The teacher conveys enthusiasm for the subject, letting students know that they are pursuing this knowledge because it's important, interesting, and fun—as opposed to learning something because it will be on the state test or is in the textbook. The teacher also communicates to students that although the content is challenging, it is within the reach of any student committed to working hard. In such classrooms, students respond by taking pride in their work and experience the feeling of satisfaction that comes from having achieved major goals.

SELF-ASSESSMENT

Assess your practice in Component 2b against the levels of performance below, then check the box that best matches the level of your own teaching for each element.

Component 2b: Establishing a Culture for Learning				
	Level of Performance			
ELEMENT	UNSATISFACTORY	BASIC	PROFICIENT	DISTINGUISHED
Importance of the content	Teacher or students convey a negative attitude toward the content, suggesting that it is not important or has been mandated by others.	Teacher communicates importance of the work but with little conviction and only minimal apparent buy-in by the students.	Teacher conveys genuine enthusiasm for the content, and students demonstrate consistent commitment to its value.	Students demonstrate through their active participation, curiosity, and taking initiative that they value the importance of the content.
	☐	☐	☐	☐

Source: From *Enhancing Professional Practice: A Framework for Teaching, 2nd Edition* (p. 69), by C. Danielson, 2007, Alexandria, VA: ASCD. © 2007 by ASCD. Reprinted with permission.

Domain 2

Component 2b

ELEMENT	Level of Performance			
	UNSATISFACTORY	BASIC	PROFICIENT	DISTINGUISHED
Expectations for learning and achievement	Instructional outcomes, activities and assignments, and classroom interactions convey low expectations for at least some students.	Instructional outcomes, activities and assignments, and classroom interactions convey only modest expectations for student learning and achievement.	Instructional outcomes, activities and assignments, and classroom interactions convey high expectations for most students.	Instructional outcomes, activities and assignments, and classroom interactions convey high expectations for all students. Students appear to have internalized these expectations.
	☐	☐	☐	☐
Student pride in work	Students demonstrate little or no pride in their work. They seem to be motivated by the desire to complete a task rather than to do high-quality work.	Students minimally accept the responsibility to do good work but invest little of their energy into its quality.	Students accept the teacher's insistence on work of high quality and demonstrate pride in that work.	Students demonstrate attention to detail and take obvious pride in their work, initiating improvements in it by, for example, revising drafts on their own or helping peers.
	☐	☐	☐	☐

Source: From *Enhancing Professional Practice: A Framework for Teaching, 2nd Edition* (p. 69), by C. Danielson, 2007, Alexandria, VA: ASCD. © 2007 by ASCD. Reprinted with permission.

Domain 2

As a result of this self-assessment, on which element will you focus first? Turn to the pages following to explore the elements of the component in detail. After you've reviewed the tools, you can use the Action Planning and Reflection form to document the results of implementing the strategies in your classroom.

Element

Importance of the Content

Description

In a classroom with a strong culture of learning, teachers convey the importance of what the students are learning.

A Closer Look

To help you recognize the subtle differences between the higher levels of performance for this element, note the keywords emphasized in the descriptions and review the activities common to those levels.

PROFICIENT

The teacher conveys *genuine enthusiasm* for the content, and students demonstrate *consistent commitment* to its value.

At the proficient level of performance, teaching practices may include the following types of activities:

- Teacher shares with students personal learning experiences, such as a new technique or strategy he is trying, a book he has read, or a peer observation with a colleague.
- Teacher shares the learning goal for the lesson and explains the lesson's importance and purpose.
- Teacher reinforces the importance of work with charts and posters that convey high expectations.
- Teacher's voice inflection and body language convey enthusiasm for the learning.
- Teacher provides opportunities for students to choose their own projects and methods for demonstrating their learning.

DISTINGUISHED

Students demonstrate through their *active participation*, *curiosity*, and *taking initiative* that they value the importance of the content.

At the distinguished level of performance, teaching practices may include the following types of activities:

- Students conduct research related to the current topic and share their results with each other.
- Students develop questions related to the current topic and ask these questions of each other as they share their findings.
- Students articulate the learning goal and can explain to each other why it is important.
- Students' voice inflection and body language convey enthusiasm for the learning.
- Students post relevant, high-quality work on a designated bulletin board.
- Students make posters or signs that convey positive learning expectations.
- Students take advantage of opportunities to choose their own projects and show individualism and creativity in their methods of demonstrating their learning.

The tools that follow will help you explore how to put the activities of these high levels of performance into practice in your classroom.

Domain 2

Importance of the Content

Element Reflection

✔ **Teacher tool**   __ **Student tool**

1. How do you convey the sense to your students that the work they are doing in your classroom is important? That it is fun?

2. What strategies do you use to reinforce and cultivate student curiosity?

Domain 2

179

Student Portfolio Selection Reflection

__ **Teacher tool**   ✔ **Student tool**

Distribute this template to students as they determine the work they will include in a required portfolio.

Work Selected	Why I Chose This Piece	What It Tells Me About My Learning

Domain 2

Element

Expectations for Learning and Achievement

Description

In classrooms with robust cultures for learning, all students receive the message that, although the work is challenging, they are capable of achieving the goals if they are prepared to work hard.

A Closer Look

To help you recognize the subtle differences between the higher levels of performance for this element, note the keywords emphasized in the descriptions and review the activities common to those levels.

PROFICIENT

Instructional outcomes, activities and assignments, and classroom interactions convey high expectations for *most students*.

At the proficient level of performance, teaching practices may include the following types of activities:

- Teacher develops and shares high-quality instructional outcomes and expectations with most students.
- Teacher develops a mission statement that points out the purpose of the work in the class.
- Teacher sets high standards for most students regarding completion of assignments.
- Teacher discusses the importance and significance of the content and shares personal experiences related to the topic.
- Teacher models high expectations through language when conversing with most students.
- Teacher attributes student success to hard work and effort rather than the task being easy or luck.

Domain 2

DISTINGUISHED

Instructional outcomes, activities and assignments, and classroom interactions convey high expectations for *all students*. Students appear to have *internalized these expectations*.

At the distinguished level of performance, teaching practices may include the following types of activities:

- Teacher develops and shares high-quality instructional outcomes and expectations with all students.
- Students help develop a mission statement that addresses the purpose and importance of the work in the class.
- Teacher holds all students to high standards for completion of assignments.
- Teacher models high expectations for all students when conversing with the class.
- Students determine the relevance of assignments to real-life examples. For example, in a lesson on the environment, students establish a recycling program for the classroom or the school and collect materials that can be recycled.
- Students attribute their success to hard work and effort rather than the task being easy or luck.

The tools that follow will help you explore how to put the activities of these high levels of performance into practice in your classroom.

Domain 2

Expectations for Learning and Achievement

 # Element Reflection

✔ Teacher tool   __ **Student tool**

1. Describe a situation in which you have conveyed a belief that a student was highly capable, even when the student did not seem to initially believe it.

2. How do you recognize high levels of student achievement in your class? To what extent do all students receive such recognition?

Domain 2

Expectations for Learning and Achievement

Creating a Class Mission Statement

__ **Teacher tool**   ✔ **Student tool**

Ask students to answer the following prompts on sticky notes, writing down as many answers for each prompt as they can. Then gather the notes and put them on a large version of the chart, arranging the answers into groups of similar ideas. Work as a class to write a mission statement based on the common themes.

Why are we here?	What do we have to do in order to successfully work together?	How will we make it happen?

Domain 2

Example Classroom Mission Statement

The mission of our class is to work together so that we are all top-quality learners and outstanding readers, writers, thinkers, and problem solvers.

As a class we will:

- Help each other understand the class.
- Create a positive, comfortable learning environment.
- Help each other work toward personal achievement of the goals.
- Work toward having the necessary skills to perform well on the chapter tests.
- Prepare for and get a 3 or better on the semester exam.

Domain 2

Element

Student Pride in Work

Description

When students are convinced of their capabilities, they are willing to devote energy to the task at hand, and they take pride in their accomplishments. They may undertake revisions on their own or show a visitor a recent paper or project they have produced.

A Closer Look

To help you recognize the subtle differences between the higher levels of performance for this element, note the keywords emphasized in the descriptions and review the activities common to those levels.

PROFICIENT

Students *accept the teacher's insistence* on work of high quality and demonstrate pride in that work.

At the proficient level of performance, teaching practices may include the following types of activities:

- Teacher consistently reinforces students' development of conceptual understanding. For example, students must retake some assessments until they demonstrate a level of proficiency.
- Students must turn in all work. Even if work is not completed within the given time frame, it must be completed.
- Students are engaged in their work and give their best effort at all times.
- Teacher creates and maintains an environment where students feel free to take risks and ask questions.

DISTINGUISHED

Students demonstrate *attention to detail* and take obvious pride in their work, *initiating improvements* in it by, for example, revising drafts on their own or helping peers.

At the distinguished level of performance, teaching practices may include the following types of activities:

- Students encourage each other to take risks and continually ask questions.

Domain 2

Student Pride in Work

- Students provide each other with assistance in understanding a concept.
- Students peer-edit writing, providing constructive feedback.
- Students encourage each other to continually deepen their understandings.
- Students reflect on their own work and consider how they might improve it.
- Students use blogs or wikis to keep a digital notebook of their work, editing and refining it throughout the year.[1]

The tools that follow will help you explore how to put the activities of these high levels of performance into practice in your classroom.

[1] Calvert, J. (2009). *Blogs in the classroom.* Retrieved June 11, 2009, from http://calvert.wiki.ccsd.edu/page/diff/Blogs+in+the+Classroom/69204799

Domain 2

Student Pride in Work

Element Reflection

✔ **Teacher tool**   __ **Student tool**

1. What evidence do you have that your students take pride in their work? How have you encouraged this attitude?

2. What strategies can you use to encourage students to take pride in their work and to acknowledge the good work of their classmates?

Domain 2

Student Pride in Work

Assignment Revision Checklist

__ **Teacher tool**   ✔ **Student tool**

☐ Review the work you are about to turn in.

☐ Review the standards for this assignment.

☐ Determine how you could improve your work based on the standards.

☐ Choose the improvements you will make and revise as necessary.

Domain 2

Peer Review Worksheet

__ **Teacher tool**   ✔ **Student tool**

Have students answer these questions as part of their peer review to help them provide constructive comments.

1. What were the standards for this assignment?

2. What areas of your peer's work meet or exceed the standards?

3. What areas of your peer's work do not meet the standards?

4. Make 1–2 suggestions to your peer for improving this work:

Domain 2

Student Pride in Work

I Blew It Card

___ **Teacher tool**   ✔ **Student tool**

To encourage students to try something new, hand out this coupon at the beginning of a unit. Alternatively, you could give each student a certain number for the term or year. Explain that you learn by taking risks, even if the risk was not successful.

I Blew It

I tried something new and innovative and it didn't work as well as I wanted.
This COUPON entitles me to be
free of criticism for my efforts and to try again.

I Blew It

I tried something new and innovative and it didn't work as well as I wanted.
This COUPON entitles me to be
free of criticism for my efforts and to try again.

I Blew It

I tried something new and innovative and it didn't work as well as I wanted.
This COUPON entitles me to be
free of criticism for my efforts and to try again.

Source: Patterson, J. L. (1993). *Leadership for tomorrow's schools.* Alexandria, VA: ASCD. Reprinted with permission.

Domain 2

Student Pride in Work

Take a Chance

___ **Teacher tool** **Student tool**

Distribute "Take a Chance Pads" to all students each semester. By periodically collecting the pads, you can determine what students are struggling with.

TAKE A CHANCE PAD

Use this pad to write down answers or solve problems, even when you are not sure of the answers. All tries are risk- and criticism-free.

Component 2b

Action Planning and Reflection

✔ **Teacher tool**   __ **Student tool**

Look over the tools for this component and choose a strategy or strategies that you are committed to trying in your classroom. Then return to this page and record what happened. If there was a change, what evidence indicates the extent to which this strategy was successful? Finally, think about what you might do differently to continue to bring about further growth in this component.

What will I try?	How did it go?	What will I do differently next time?

Domain 2

Component 2c

Managing Classroom Procedures

OVERVIEW

Simply put, successful teaching is not possible in a chaotic environment. To ensure learning, students must be engaged in meaningful activities, which requires that they be able to find their materials and know how to work with their classmates and that noninstructional routines don't consume undue amounts of time.

Good classroom management is not a substitute for high-quality instruction, but it is a prerequisite to it. In well-managed classrooms, transitions are seamless, with students assuming considerable responsibility for smooth operation. In addition, teachers have established routines that enable very little instructional time to be lost between activities or on noninstructional matters, such as taking attendance or establishing the lunch count. Such classrooms appear to be running themselves, and an untrained observer might conclude that the teacher is not doing very much. However, teachers are the ones who have to establish successful routines and teach them to students.

SELF-ASSESSMENT

Assess your practice in Component 2c against the levels of performance below, then check the box that best matches the level of your own teaching for each element.

Component 2c: Managing Classroom Procedures				
	Level of Performance			
ELEMENT	UNSATISFACTORY	BASIC	PROFICIENT	DISTINGUISHED
Management of instructional groups	Students not working with the teacher are not productively engaged in learning.	Students in only some groups are productively engaged in learning while unsupervised by the teacher.	Small-group work is well organized, and most students are productively engaged in learning while unsupervised by the teacher.	Small-group work is well organized, and students are productively engaged at all times, with students assuming responsibility for productivity.
	☐	☐	☐	☐

Component 2c

ELEMENT	Level of Performance			
	UNSATISFACTORY	BASIC	PROFICIENT	DISTINGUISHED
Management of transitions	Transitions are chaotic, with much time lost between activities or lesson segments. ☐	Only some transitions are efficient, resulting in some loss of instructional time. ☐	Transitions occur smoothly, with little loss of instructional time. ☐	Transitions are seamless, with students assuming responsibility in ensuring their efficient operation. ☐
Management of materials and supplies	Materials and supplies are handled inefficiently, resulting in significant loss of instructional time. ☐	Routines for handling materials and supplies function moderately well, but with some loss of instructional time. ☐	Routines for handling materials and supplies occur smoothly, with little loss of instructional time. ☐	Routines for handling materials and supplies are seamless, with students assuming some responsibility for smooth operation. ☐
Performance of noninstructional duties	Considerable instructional time is lost in performing noninstructional duties. ☐	Systems for performing noninstructional duties are only fairly efficient, resulting in some loss of instructional time. ☐	Efficient systems for performing noninstructional duties are in place, resulting in minimal loss of instructional time. ☐	Systems for performing noninstructional duties are well established, with students assuming considerable responsibility for efficient operation. ☐
Supervision of volunteers and paraprofessionals	Volunteers and paraprofessionals have no clearly defined duties and are idle most of the time. ☐	Volunteers and paraprofessionals are productively engaged during portions of class time but require frequent supervision. ☐	Volunteers and paraprofessionals are productively and independently engaged during the entire class. ☐	Volunteers and paraprofessionals make a substantive contribution to the classroom environment. ☐

Domain 2

Source: From *Enhancing Professional Practice: A Framework for Teaching, 2nd Edition* (p. 72), by C. Danielson, 2007, Alexandria, VA: ASCD. © 2007 by ASCD. Reprinted with permission.

As a result of this self-assessment, on which element will you focus first? Turn to the pages following to explore the elements of the component in detail. After you've reviewed the tools, you can use the Action Planning and Reflection form to document the results of implementing the strategies in your classroom.

Domain 2

Element

Management of Instructional Groups

Description

Much work in classrooms takes place in small groups, which enable students to work with their classmates, discuss possible approaches to a problem, and benefit from one another's thinking. But students cannot be expected to automatically know how to work productively in small groups. These skills, like others, must be taught.

A Closer Look

To help you recognize the subtle differences between the higher levels of performance for this element, note the keywords emphasized in the descriptions and review the activities common to those levels.

PROFICIENT

Small-group work is *well organized*, and *most students* are productively engaged in learning while *unsupervised* by the teacher.

At the proficient level of performance, teaching practices may include the following types of activities:

- Teacher has established procedures for group work, such as listening and sharing responsibilities.
- Teacher assigns students roles for work within the group.
- Teacher instructs on social skills that will promote expected group behavior.
- Teacher ensures that students understand what they are supposed to accomplish in the group and how they are supposed to do it.
- Teacher establishes instructional groups based on the instructional goal.
- Teacher provides students with feedback on how they have worked as a group.

Domain 2

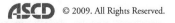

DISTINGUISHED

Small-group work is well organized, and students are productively engaged *at all times*, with *students assuming responsibility* for productivity.

At the distinguished level of performance, teaching practices may include the following types of activities:

- Expectations for group work have been developed with student input and are posted.
- Students assign their own roles in the group and can easily assume other roles.
- Students remind each other of their roles within the group.
- Students are able to explain to each other what the group is supposed to accomplish.
- Students self-assess how well their group worked together on that day.

The tools that follow will help you explore how to put the activities of these high levels of performance into practice in your classroom.

Domain 2

Management of Instructional Groups

Element Reflection

✔ **Teacher tool**   __ **Student tool**

1. What strategies can you use to teach students how to work productively in small groups, even when you are otherwise occupied?

2. How can you engage students in monitoring their own small-group work?

Domain 2

Management of Instructional Groups

Rubric for Working as a Group

__ **Teacher tool**   ✔ **Student tool**

Distribute this rubric to students to self-evaluate how they work together. Collect it from each group member at the conclusion of group assignments to use in your evaluation.

Criteria	We need to work on this	We're doing better but still need to remember this	We're doing a great job in this area
We followed through with our roles	☐ We didn't talk about or assume roles as directed.	☐ Sometimes our group members assumed and carried through with their assigned roles.	☐ Group members followed through with their assigned roles, or we politely reminded each other of the assigned roles.
We listened with respect to the ideas of others	☐ Group members interrupted each other and did not listen when others spoke.	☐ Group members were quiet when someone else was speaking but were pretty much just waiting for their turn to talk.	☐ Group members listened with respect to the ideas of others and reflected on those ideas, linking them to their own ideas when appropriate.
We met our learning goal	☐ None or only a few of the group members met the learning goal.	☐ Some of the group members met the learning goal.	☐ We worked together to make sure all of the group members met the learning goal.
We used our time wisely	☐ We didn't focus on the task and wasted time during group time.	☐ We had some trouble focusing, but most of us worked productively during group time.	☐ We focused on our task and all worked productively during group time.
We used appropriate voice levels	☐ Our voices were loud and disturbed the learning of other groups.	☐ At times our voices were loud enough to disturb the learning of other groups.	☐ We kept our voices at a level that was loud enough to be heard by each other but did not disturb the learning of the other groups.

Domain 2

Element

Management of Transitions

Description

Coherent lessons have clear beginnings and endings, with a discernible structure between the different parts. Little time is lost as students move from one activity to another. They know the drill and execute it seamlessly.

A Closer Look

To help you recognize the subtle differences between the higher levels of performance for this element, note the keywords emphasized in the descriptions and review the activities common to those levels.

PROFICIENT

Transitions occur *smoothly*, with *little loss* of instructional time.

At the proficient level of performance, teaching practices may include the following types of activities:

- Teacher brainstorms a list of transitions that occur throughout the day.
- Teacher establishes the procedures for each transition and teaches those procedures to students.
- Teacher models transition procedures for students.
- Teacher uses time as a motivational factor for students to move into groups. Timing devices might include a teacher countdown, a timer that rings after a given time, or a timing device projected on a screen.
- Teacher establishes a signal for attention, such raising a hand, clapping in a pattern, "If you can hear my voice, clap once," blinking lights, or playing a sound.
- Teacher reinforces procedures for transitions by practicing them throughout the year.

DISTINGUISHED

Transitions are *seamless*, with *students assuming responsibility* in ensuring their efficient operation.

At the distinguished level of performance, teaching practices may include the following types of activities:

- Students brainstorm a list of transitions that occur throughout the day.
- Students discuss what procedures would work best for each transition and decide how to apply them to each situation.
- Students model transition procedures and correct each other when procedures are not followed.
- Group members monitor the time it takes to get into groups.
- Students decide which attention signal will work best for their group and remind each other about using it.
- Students indicate that they need a practice session to reinforce the procedures for transitions.

The tools that follow will help you explore how to put the activities of these high levels of performance into practice in your classroom.

Management of Transitions

Element Reflection

✔ **Teacher tool**   __ **Student tool**

1. Describe some indications of poorly handled transitions between, for example, large- and small-group work.

2. To what extent do you teach your students how to transition from one activity to another, have them practice the routines, and then give them feedback?

Domain 2

Developing Classroom Transitions

✔ **Teacher tool**   ✔ **Student tool**

To make sure that you smoothly transition from one activity to another, you should plan routines and teach them to students. You can also solicit input from your students about procedures.

EXAMPLE TRANSITION PROCEDURES

Transition	Possible Procedure
Entering the classroom	Go directly to your assigned seat. Note instructions on board. Begin work.
Leaving the classroom	Wait for the signal from the teacher. Collect materials. Line up when your row or group is called.
Moving from individual to group work	Wait for the signal from the teacher. Gather materials needed for the task. Move quietly to your group.

List other transitions for which you need a procedure.

Transition	Procedure

Domain 2

Element

Management of Materials and Supplies

Description

The procedures for distributing and collecting materials are a clear indication of a teacher's experience. Experienced teachers have all necessary materials at hand and have taught students to perform the routines with minimum disruption to the flow of instruction.

A Closer Look

To help you recognize the subtle differences between the higher levels of performance for this element, note the keywords emphasized in the descriptions and review the activities common to those levels.

PROFICIENT

Routines for handling materials and supplies occur *smoothly*, with *little loss of instructional time*.

At the proficient level of performance, teaching practices may include the following types of activities:

- Teacher purposefully teaches routines to students.
- Teacher color codes the location of supplies so that students know where they belong.
- Teacher takes a picture of the proper placement of supplies and puts it above the area.
- Teacher provides baskets for work labeled with what goes in each basket.
- A basket of supplies is placed in the middle of each group so that students have access to needed materials.
- Homework is placed in an individual folder to be turned in to the teacher. Teacher places homework back in the folder with feedback.
- Teacher creates a student folder that includes activities the students can do when they are finished with their work.

DISTINGUISHED

Routines for handling materials and supplies are *seamless*, with *students assuming some responsibility* for smooth operation.

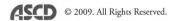

At the distinguished level of performance, teaching practices may include the following types of activities:

- Students have input into how systems are working and suggest revisions.
- Students assume responsibility for making systems work.
- Students take initiative in a range of procedures related to materials and supplies, such as passing out papers, collecting everything needed by their table group, or putting art materials away neatly and efficiently.

The tools that follow will help you explore how to put the activities of these high levels of performance into practice in your classroom.

Management of Materials and Supplies

Element Reflection

✔ **Teacher tool**   __ **Student tool**

1. Describe a classroom in which materials and supplies are not well managed. What does it look like? How can it be dangerous as well as inefficient?

2. What procedures can you teach your students so that they can assume responsibility for materials and supplies?

Domain 2

Teaching Routines Checklist: A Simple Plan

✔ Teacher tool   __ **Student tool**

Use the word *simple* to design your plan for teaching a routine.

☐ **Set Up**
Talk about and set up why the routine is important. Remind students of times when they needed a routine and didn't have one.

☐ **Input**
Describe what the routine will be. Ask for student input on what might work.

☐ **Model**
Show students how the routine looks. Model the steps as if you were the student.

☐ **Practice**
Have the students practice the routine. Give them feedback after the practice and repeat as necessary.

☐ **Learning Experience**
Teaching a routine is the same as any other learning experience: You teach it, model it, and practice it. If students don't get it, you reteach or find a different way of providing the learning needed.

Domain 2

Element

Performance of Noninstructional Duties

Description

Accomplished teachers are masters of multitasking. Where appropriate, students themselves contribute to the design and execution of routines for noninstructional matters. Overall, little instructional time is lost in such activities.

A Closer Look

To help you recognize the subtle differences between the higher levels of performance for this element, note the keywords emphasized in the descriptions and review the activities common to those levels.

PROFICIENT

Efficient systems for performing noninstructional duties are in place, resulting in *minimal loss* of instructional time.

At the proficient level of performance, teaching practices may include the following types of activities:

- Teacher establishes routines for what to do if, for example, a student's pencil breaks, there is a fire drill, a student needs to use the bathroom, a student finishes work early, or a student was absent.
- Teacher uses an attendance board to indicate which students are present, placing their names in the correct area as they enter the room.
- Elementary teacher uses "home folders" for communications from home. Secondary teacher has a basket or bin for communications from home, permissions slips, and so forth.

DISTINGUISHED

Systems for performing noninstructional duties are *well established*, with *students assuming considerable responsibility* for efficient operation.

At the distinguished level of performance, teaching practices may include the following types of activities:

- Students suggest classroom procedures to address the range of situations that arise in a classroom.
- Students use the attendance board as they enter the room. They may also indicate their lunch preference with such a method.

The tools that follow will help you explore how to put the activities of these high levels of performance into practice in your classroom.

Performance of Noninstructional Duties

Element Reflection

✔ **Teacher tool**   __ **Student tool**

1. Audit your own performance of nonclassroom duties. How efficient are they? Could they be streamlined? Which of them have you taught to students?

2. To what extent are students in your class able to assume responsibility for the noninstructional duties? Why is doing so connected to their learning?

Domain 2

☐ 211

Incorporating Pocket Activity Boards

✔ **Teacher tool**   ___ **Student tool**

Pocket activity boards are particularly useful at the elementary level. You can use them for noninstructional duties, for learning activities during filler times, or as an organizer for managing differentiated learning in the classroom.

In planning for pocket activity boards, you may want to consider the following:

1. What function will the board serve?

2. How many pockets will you need?

3. Who will be best served by the chart?

Domain 2

Element

Supervision of Volunteers
and Paraprofessionals

Description

Not every teacher has the benefit of assistance from volunteers and paraprofessionals, but those who do recognize that it takes both organization and management to maximize the benefits of their presence. Volunteers and paraprofessionals must understand their duties and have the skill to carry them out. It is the teacher's responsibility to ensure that these conditions are met.

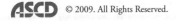

A Closer Look

To help you recognize the subtle differences between the higher levels of performance for this element, note the keywords emphasized in the descriptions and review the activities common to those levels.

PROFICIENT

Volunteers and paraprofessionals are *productively* and *independently* engaged during the *entire* class.

At the proficient level of performance, teaching practices may include the following types of activities:

- Teacher reviews the standards for paraprofessionals in the district or state and discusses them with the paraprofessionals.
- Teacher establishes guidelines for volunteers and reviews them with those involved.
- Teacher gives feedback to paraprofessionals on a regular basis about how their work is progressing.

DISTINGUISHED

Volunteers and paraprofessionals make a *substantive contribution* to the classroom environment.

At the distinguished level of performance, teaching practices may include the following types of activities:

Domain 2

- Teacher meets with volunteers and with them develops guidelines for the work.
- Teacher and paraprofessional review and discuss the standards in the district or state, making revisions to meet their particular situation.
- Teacher and paraprofessional reflect on their work together both formally at scheduled intervals and informally, such as at the end of the day or class period.

The tools that follow will help you explore how to put the activities of these high levels of performance into practice in your classroom.

Domain 2

Supervision of Volunteers and Paraprofessionals

Element Reflection

✔ **Teacher tool** ___ **Student tool**

1. What strategies can you use to make the most of volunteers and paraprofessionals?

2. To what extent do you find that you must train your volunteers and paraprofessionals so that they can contribute to your classroom?

Paraprofessional Professional Development and Reflection Form

✔ **Teacher tool**   __ **Student tool**

In working with paraprofessionals, it's important to review and discuss the guidelines for their work and help them direct their professional development. You can use this form to help paraprofessionals with this process.

Have paraprofessionals review the standards by which they are evaluated in your school or district. Help them identify two or three standards on which to focus this year, and then ask them to outline an action plan, being as specific as possible. Throughout the year, they should note specific actions, courses, or artifacts of success in this area.

Standard	What I Plan To Do	Evidence of Success in This Standard

Domain 2

Component 2c

Action Planning and Reflection

✔ **Teacher tool**   __ **Student tool**

Look over the tools for this component and choose a strategy or strategies that you are committed to trying in your classroom. Then return to this page and record what happened. If there was a change, what evidence indicates the extent to which this strategy was successful? Finally, think about what you might do differently to continue to bring about further growth in this component.

What will I try?	How did it go?	What will I do differently next time?

Domain 2

Component 2d

Managing Student Behavior

OVERVIEW

Managing student behavior can be a challenge to even the most experienced teacher, and this component is perhaps the one that most depends on the others being in place. For example, students will misbehave if they are not engaged in meaningful learning, they will be less likely to be disruptive if the family is involved with the school, and certainly students who feel they are treated with respect are less likely to behave inappropriately.

Elements within this component, such as setting expectations for behavior that have been developed with classroom input and are posted for all to see, are designed to prevent misbehavior. These standards for behavior must be both culturally and developmentally appropriate for individual students and the class.

Student misbehavior is also prevented by teachers continually monitoring the class with the proverbial eyes in the back of their head. This apparent sixth sense is, in reality, a sign of the teachers' expertise in using monitoring strategies that allow them to anticipate areas of possible concern. When teachers must impose intervention strategies, the strategies should allow both the teacher and the students to retain their dignity and return to the task of learning without disturbing the learning of the other students.

SELF-ASSESSMENT

Assess your practice in Component 2d against the levels of performance below, then check the box that best matches the level of your own teaching for each element.

Component 2d: Managing Student Behavior				
	Level of Performance			
ELEMENT	UNSATISFACTORY	BASIC	PROFICIENT	DISTINGUISHED
Expectations	No standards of conduct appear to have been established, or students are confused as to what the standards are.	Standards of conduct appear to have been established, and most students seem to understand them.	Standards of conduct are clear to all students.	Standards of conduct are clear to all students and appear to have been developed with student participation.
	☐	☐	☐	☐

Domain 2

Component 2d

ELEMENT	Level of Performance			
	UNSATISFACTORY	BASIC	PROFICIENT	DISTINGUISHED
Monitoring of student behavior	Student behavior is not monitored, and teacher is unaware of what the students are doing. ☐	Teacher is generally aware of student behavior but may miss the activities of some students. ☐	Teacher is alert to student behavior at all times. ☐	Monitoring by teacher is subtle and preventive. Students monitor their own and their peers' behavior, correcting one another respectfully. ☐
Response to student misbehavior	Teacher does not respond to misbehavior, or the response is inconsistent, is overly repressive, or does not respect the student's dignity. ☐	Teacher attempts to respond to student misbehavior but with uneven results, or there are no major infractions of the rules. ☐	Teacher response to misbehavior is appropriate and successful and respects the student's dignity, or student behavior is generally appropriate. ☐	Teacher response to misbehavior is highly effective and sensitive to students' individual needs, or student behavior is entirely appropriate. ☐

Source: From *Enhancing Professional Practice: A Framework for Teaching, 2nd Edition* (p. 74), by C. Danielson, 2007, Alexandria, VA: ASCD. © 2007 by ASCD. Reprinted with permission.

As a result of this self-assessment, on which element will you focus first? Turn to the pages following to explore the elements of the component in detail. After you've reviewed the tools, you can use the Action Planning and Reflection form to document the results of implementing the strategies in your classroom.

Domain 2

Element

Expectations

Description

Most students are willing to comply with reasonable standards of conduct. However, it's essential that they know what those standards are and, better yet, that they have contributed to their development.

A Closer Look

To help you recognize the subtle differences between the higher levels of performance for this element, note the keywords emphasized in the descriptions and review the activities common to those levels.

PROFICIENT

Standards of conduct are *clear* to *all* students.

At the proficient level of performance, teaching practices may include the following types of activities:

- Teacher posts rules that are visible to all students.
- Teacher shares standards of conduct with families of students.
- Teacher explains and models expectations of classroom behavior for the students.
- Teacher states rules in a positive manner.
- Teacher provides a manageable number of classroom rules.
- Teacher reviews rules with students as necessary as activities in the classroom change, such as before a group learning activity, before individual work while the teacher is working with a small group, or before a special program or speaker.

DISTINGUISHED

Standards of conduct are clear to all students and have been *developed with student participation*.

At the distinguished level of performance, teaching practices may include the following types of activities:

- Students contribute to the classroom code of conduct.

Domain 2

Expectations

- Students are able to explain the standards of conduct to their families and why they are important.
- When rules need revising or are not working, teacher includes students in choosing possible solutions.
- Students propose ideas for how their conduct could change so that the classroom environment is more productive and better supports learning.

The tools that follow will help you explore how to put the activities of these high levels of performance into practice in your classroom.

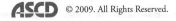
Domain 2

Expectations

Element Reflection

✔ **Teacher tool** ___ **Student tool**

1. What approaches do you use to set clear expectations for student conduct?

2. How can you ensure that students themselves participate in creating such standards?

Domain 2

Creating a Classroom Code of Conduct

__ **Teacher tool**   ✔ **Student tool**

Consider three to five guiding principles for your classroom, and fill them into the worksheet. Then ask students to help outline some rules that might support each principle. Be sure to write principles in a positive way and ask students to do the same. For example, instead of, "No pushing," you could write, "Keep hands and feet to yourself."

Principle 1:

Rule

Rule

Rule

Principle 2:

Rule

Rule

Rule

Principle 3:

Rule

Rule

Rule

 © 2009. All Rights Reserved.

Domain 2

Element

Monitoring of Student Behavior

Description

Experienced teachers are attuned to what is happening in the classroom and can move subtly to help students reengage with the lesson content. When skillfully done, the learning of the other students continues and the intervention goes unnoticed by the rest of the class.

A Closer Look

To help you recognize the subtle differences between the higher levels of performance for this element, note the keywords emphasized in the descriptions and review the activities common to those levels.

PROFICIENT

The teacher is *alert* to student behavior *at all times*.

At the proficient level of performance, teaching practices may include the following types of activities:

- Teacher is alert for potential problems in the classroom.
- Teacher walks around, spending time in each quadrant of the classroom.
- Teacher scans the faces of the students, making eye contact.
- Teacher devises nonverbal signals for individual students to redirect their efforts.
- Teacher makes eye contact with the students potentially misbehaving.

DISTINGUISHED

Monitoring by the teacher is *subtle* and *preventive*. *Students* monitor their own and their peers' behavior, correcting one another respectfully.

At the distinguished level of performance, teaching practices may include the following types of activities:

- Teacher uses proximity to alert a student who has not responded to eye contact. Teacher talks to the student privately if proximity isn't sufficient.
- Students work with the teacher to devise a nonverbal signal to help monitor student behavior.
- Students devise a system for monitoring their own behavior.

- Students apply a system for monitoring their own behavior.
- Students regularly acknowledge the appropriate behavior of each other.

The tools that follow will help you explore how to put the activities of these high levels of performance into practice in your classroom.

Domain 2

Element Reflection

✔ **Teacher tool**   ___ **Student tool**

1. Describe the challenge of monitoring student behavior while attending to all the other tasks of teaching. How do you meet that challenge?

2. What strategies can you use to enlist student participation in ensuring that their classmates' behavior is appropriate?

Domain 2

Monitoring Student Behavior Checklist

✔ Teacher tool   __ **Student tool**

☐ Scan the classroom.

☐ Walk around the classroom.

☐ Provide feedback to students on appropriate behavior.

☐ Look for signs of frustration or confusion.

☐ Move to the students needing redirection.

Domain 2

Element

Response to Student Misbehavior

> **Description**
>
> How teachers respond to student infractions to standards of conduct is an important mark of the teachers' skill. Accomplished teachers try to understand why students are conducting themselves in such a manner, and their response respects the dignity of the student. The best responses are those that are subtle and preventive, although this is not always possible.

A Closer Look

To help you recognize the subtle differences between the higher levels of performance for this element, note the keywords emphasized in the descriptions and review the activities common to those levels.

PROFICIENT

The teacher's response to misbehavior is *appropriate* and *successful* and *respects* the student's dignity, or student behavior is *generally* appropriate.

At the proficient level of performance, teaching practices may include the following types of activities:

- Teacher talks to the student privately to remove the audience of the other students.
- Teacher makes a conscious effort to improve relationships with the student, for example by discussing topics other than school with the student.
- Teacher involves families in respectful ways that enlist their help with the student.
- Teacher puts a sticky note on the student's desk as a reminder of the desired behavior.
- Teacher enlists the help of other student services staff, such as a school counselor, social worker, or school psychologist, for assistance with the student.
- Teacher explains the student's behavior in objective, observable terms free of generalities or emotions.

DISTINGUISHED

The teacher response to misbehavior is *highly effective* and *sensitive* to students' individual needs, or student behavior is *entirely* appropriate.

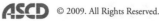

Response to Student Misbehavior

At the distinguished level of performance, teaching practices may include the following types of activities:

- Teacher asks the student for input about what would help prevent undesirable behavior.
- Teacher asks the student to write a letter explaining the misbehavior to the student's family.
- Teacher directs the student to call home in the teacher's presence to explain the misbehavior.
- Teacher reflects on the intervention: Did the misbehavior stop? Did the intervention prevent the reoccurrence of the misbehavior? Did it allow the student to return to learning?
- Teacher asks the student to explain or write about the misbehavior in objective terms.

The tools that follow will help you explore how to put the activities of these high levels of performance into practice in your classroom.

Domain 2

Response to Student Misbehavior

 # Element Reflection

✔ **Teacher tool** ___ **Student tool**

1. Consider several recent student infractions of classroom rules. How do you consistently refer to the classroom expectations in your response?

2. To what extent can you explain some student misbehavior being caused by other factors, such as boredom or insecurity? Would a different instructional design improve the situation?

Domain 2

Response to Student Misbehavior

Reflection on My Behavior

__ **Teacher tool**   ✔ **Student tool**

When students break rules or if their behavior disrupts the class, have the students complete this behavior reflection. Then hold a conference with the students to review the responses and determine how they will make better decisions in the future.

When I (write out specific behavior) _____,

I was violating the principle on our code of conduct that addresses (list principle) _____.

As I reflect on this situation, one of the reasons I might have done this is because…

The next time I am in this situation I will…

Student signature: _____

Domain 2

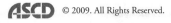

Component 2d

Action Planning and Reflection

✔ Teacher tool   **__ Student tool**

Look over the tools for this component and choose a strategy or strategies that you are committed to trying in your classroom. Then return to this page and record what happened. If there was a change, what evidence indicates the extent to which this strategy was successful? Finally, think about what you might do differently to continue to bring about further growth in this component.

What will I try?	How did it go?	What will I do differently next time?

Domain 2

Component 2e

Organizing Physical Space

OVERVIEW

When space is tight in a school, some teachers are required to float, teaching in different rooms at different times during the day. Such teaching off a cart imposes a genuine hardship on the teachers and illustrates the importance of the physical environment on student learning.

First and foremost, the physical environment must be safe, with no dangling cords or furniture obstructing doors. All students should be able to see and hear, and teachers must accommodate students with special needs. Most teachers have also found benefits in moving the furniture to promote group discussion or project work.

The idea that desks should be organized in rows is a thing of the past. Such an arrangement, which makes talking among classmates difficult, reflects the antiquated view of teaching and learning that held that pupils needed to face forward so that they could listen to the teacher and copy information from the board. Primary classrooms are frequently organized into centers, with a comfortable reading corner, space for scientific inquiry, and an area for art work or blocks. Secondary classrooms use space to promote effective communication and team learning.

SELF-ASSESSMENT

Assess your practice in Component 2e against the levels of performance below, then check the box that best matches the level of your own teaching for each element.

Component 2e: Organizing Physical Space				
	Level of Performance			
ELEMENT	UNSATISFACTORY	BASIC	PROFICIENT	DISTINGUISHED
Safety and accessibility	The classroom is unsafe, or learning is not accessible to some students.	The classroom is safe, and at least essential learning is accessible to most students.	The classroom is safe, and learning is equally accessible to all students.	The classroom is safe, and students themselves ensure that all learning is equally accessible to all students.
	☐	☐	☐	☐

Source: From *Enhancing Professional Practice: A Framework for Teaching, 2nd Edition* (p. 76), by C. Danielson, 2007, Alexandria, VA: ASCD. © 2007 by ASCD. Reprinted with permission.

Domain 2

Component 2e

	Level of Performance			
ELEMENT	UNSATISFACTORY	BASIC	PROFICIENT	DISTINGUISHED
Arrangement of furniture and use of physical resources	The furniture arrangement hinders the learning activities, or the teacher makes poor use of physical resources. ☐	Teacher uses physical resources adequately. The furniture may be adjusted for a lesson, but with limited effectiveness. ☐	Teacher uses physical resources skillfully, and the furniture arrangement is a resource for learning activities. ☐	Both teacher and students use physical resources easily and skillfully, and students adjust the furniture to advance their learning. ☐

Source: From *Enhancing Professional Practice: A Framework for Teaching, 2nd Edition* (p. 76), by C. Danielson, 2007, Alexandria, VA: ASCD. © 2007 by ASCD. Reprinted with permission.

As a result of this self-assessment, on which element will you focus first? Turn to the pages following to explore the elements of the component in detail. After you've reviewed the tools, you can use the Action Planning and Reflection form to document the results of implementing the strategies in your classroom.

Domain 2

Element

Safety and Accessibility

Description

A first requirement of a classroom is that it is a safe physical environment and that all students can see and hear classroom events.

A Closer Look

To help you recognize the subtle differences between the higher levels of performance for this element, note the keywords emphasized in the descriptions and review the activities common to those levels.

PROFICIENT

The classroom is *safe*, and learning is *equally accessible* to all students.

At the proficient level of performance, teaching practices may include the following types of activities:

- Teacher assures that there are established walkways in the classroom and that these walkways are free of clutter. For example, the class has procedures for placing backpacks, books, coats, and so forth in designated areas.
- Teacher provides opportunities for colleagues to observe the classroom and give feedback about the physical arrangement.
- Teacher has electrical and cable cords taped to the floor.
- Teacher ensures that each student has easy access to all resources, materials, and supplies. For example, baskets in the center of groups contain supplies. Bins, books, and folders are easily accessible to all.
- The teacher ensures that potentially dangerous materials, such as chemicals, are stored safely and that students are instructed in how to handle them.
- Teacher ensures that each student is positioned appropriately in the classroom and can see the board, hear the teacher, and access needed materials and supplies.

Domain 2

DISTINGUISHED

The classroom is safe, and *students themselves* ensure that all learning is equally accessible to all students.

At the distinguished level of performance, teaching practices may include the following types of activities:

- Students assist with maintaining a classroom free of clutter. For example, students have input in and follow through with established procedures and respectfully correct each other as necessary.
- Students make suggestions about how traffic flow around the classroom could be more safe and effective.
- Students access resources, materials, and supplies as needed and return these to the designated areas.
- Students ensure that potentially dangerous materials are handled safely.
- Students assume responsibility for ensuring that peers have access to learning. For example, a student would move an overhead to assist a classmate who has impaired vision.

The tools that follow will help you explore how to put the activities of these high levels of performance into practice in your classroom.

Safety and Accessibility

Element Reflection

✔ **Teacher tool**   __ **Student tool**

1. What are some easily recognizable indicators of a classroom that is not safe for students?

2. What approaches could you use to teach your students to be alert to problems of access—for example, not being able to see a whiteboard—both on their own behalf and that of their classmates?

Domain 2

Safety First

✔ **Teacher tool** __ **Student tool**

Determine the safety issues in your classroom caused by technology or other tools that you use for instruction or by the physical setup of the classroom. Then brainstorm how you can modify those factors to make your classroom safer.

CLASSROOM TOOLS

Tool	Safety Issues for the Class	Safety Issues for Individual Students	How to Make the Tool Safe in Your Classroom

Safety and Accessibility

PHYSICAL SPACE

Challenge	Safety Issues	Possible Solutions
Bottlenecks		
Areas for Privacy		
Areas for Group Work		
Areas for Displaying Group Work		
Other		

Domain 2

Element

Arrangement of Furniture and Use of Physical Resources

Description

Accomplished teachers use physical resources, such as electronic and audio/video equipment, skillfully and ensure that the furniture arrangement is conducive to the activities planned for the lesson.

A Closer Look

To help you recognize the subtle differences between the higher levels of performance for this element, note the keywords emphasized in the descriptions and review the activities common to those levels.

PROFICIENT

The teacher uses physical resources *skillfully*, and the furniture arrangement is a *resource* for learning activities.

At the proficient level of performance, teaching practices may include the following types of activities:

- The physical resources, such as flip charts, overhead projection devices, computers, and DVD players, are easily accessible and do not obstruct movement.
- Teacher has color-coded tape on the floor to designate furniture placement based on instruction. For example, yellow tape is the placement for small-group work, red tape for whole-group instruction, and blue tape for class discussion.
- Teacher arranges desks or tables to be free to readily monitor and assist each student.
- Teacher arranges the room so that students can easily form pairs, triads, and small groups.
- Teacher has established clear traffic patterns that connect the learning areas of the room so that students don't have to walk through one area to get to another.
- Vertical space, such as file cabinets, wall dividers, and moveable cabinets, display student work.
- Quiet areas of the room are separate from active areas to minimize distractions.

Arrangement of Furniture and Use of Physical Resources

DISTINGUISHED

Both the teacher and students use physical resources *easily* and *skillfully*, and *students* adjust the furniture to advance their learning.

At the distinguished level of performance, teaching practices may include the following types of activities:

- Students move furniture, as appropriate, to aid instruction and learning.
- Students arrange the classroom according to the type of instruction noted on the board, following color-coded tape on the floor.
- Students move chairs into pairs, triads, and small groups as necessary for learning.
- Students have input into the traffic patterns and point out areas that might disturb their learning.
- Students have their own designated areas where they choose the work that will be displayed.
- Students have input into the location of areas for quiet and activity and contribute to those areas with their own resources.

The tools that follow will help you explore how to put the activities of these high levels of performance into practice in your classroom.

Arrangement of Furniture and Use of Physical Resources

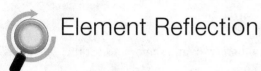

Element Reflection

✔ **Teacher tool**   __ **Student tool**

1. Describe how your different furniture arrangements contribute to the types of learning activities you use.

2. How can you teach your students to contribute to the classroom arrangement?

Domain 2

Arrangement of Furniture and Use of Physical Resources

Designing Your Classroom

✔ **Teacher tool**   __ **Student tool**

ARRANGEMENT 1: DESK CLUSTERS

- For whole-group instruction, students all face forward.
- For pair-sharing, students can easily turn to their neighbors.
- For table sharing, the two students in the front turn to form a group with the two in the back. Note: If students worked at tables, the process would be even easier.

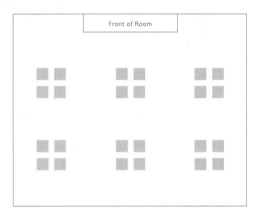

ARRANGEMENT 2: TABLE GROUPS

- For whole-group instruction, modeling, or projection, students simply look over their shoulders to the front of the room.
- For group work, students can easily turn back to the table for eye-to-eye contact.

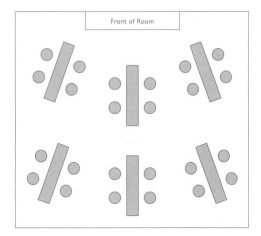

Domain 2

Arrangement of Furniture and Use of Physical Resources

ARRANGEMENT 3: DOUBLE HORSESHOE

- For whole-group discussion, students can face forward.
- For small-group discussion, students can turn to their classmates on the back horseshoe.

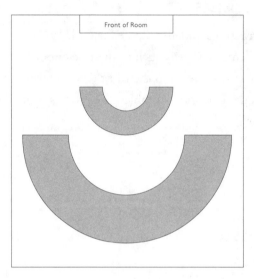

Front of Room

Domain 2

Arrangement of Furniture and Use of Physical Resources

Use the space below to draw your classroom. Consider both the physical resources and furniture arrangement as you set up your room. You will probably want to make several different arrangements for varying learning patterns.

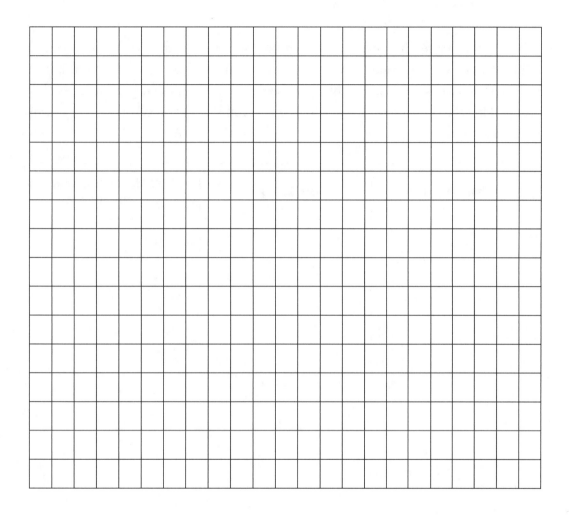

Domain 2

Action Planning and Reflection

✔ **Teacher tool**   __ **Student tool**

Look over the tools for this component and choose a strategy or strategies that you are committed to trying in your classroom. Then return to this page and record what happened. If there was a change, what evidence indicates the extent to which this strategy was successful? Finally, think about what you might do differently to continue to bring about further growth in this component.

What will I try?	How did it go?	What will I do differently next time?

Domain 2

Domain 3

domains

preparation *planning*

instruction *class environment*

professional responsibility

Instruction

Instruction

Domain 3 comprises the components that are at the core of teaching and reflects the primary mission of schools to enhance student learning. Each of the components in this domain represents a distinct aspect of instructional skill. The components are unified through a vision of students developing complex understanding and participating in a community of learners.

In the larger framework for teaching, Domain 3 represents the implementation of the plans that teachers designed in Domain 1. Teachers who successfully execute the components of Domain 1 prepare plans that are suitable to their students, grounded in deep understanding of the content, aligned with state standards, and designed to engage students in important work. In Domain 3, teachers demonstrate through their instructional skills that they can successfully implement those plans.

Accomplished teachers engage their students in meaningful work, which carries significance beyond the next test and which can provide the skills and knowledge necessary for answering important questions or contributing to important projects. Such work is real and significant, and it is important to students and to teachers. Accomplished teachers don't have to motivate their students because the way they organize and present the content, the roles they encourage students to assume, and the student initiative they expect all motivate students to excel.

Based on the results of the self-assessment you took in the introduction (see page 7), turn to the page of the component on which you will focus first. Each of the following sections explores the elements of these components in detail and includes tools that you can use in your professional practice.

Domain 3

Component 3a

Communicating with Students

OVERVIEW

Although nonverbal communication plays an important role in teacher-student interactions, much of a teacher's communication involves language, both oral and written. This language must be clear and expressive so that students understand what they are expected to do and why it's important that they do so. On a basic level, teachers give directions and explain procedural matters, and students shouldn't be left guessing the teacher's intent. More important, teachers explain concepts. They can bring the content to life with clear language and appropriate and imaginative metaphors and analogies. A rich vocabulary and expressive language can enhance students' school experience and, in turn, their lives.

SELF-ASSESSMENT

Assess your practice in Component 3a against the levels of performance below, then check the box that best matches the level of your own teaching for each element.

Component 3a: Communicating with Students				
	Level of Performance			
ELEMENT	UNSATISFACTORY	BASIC	PROFICIENT	DISTINGUISHED
Expectations for learning	Teacher's purpose in a lesson or unit is unclear to students.	Teacher attempts to explain the instructional purpose, with limited success.	Teacher's purpose for the lesson or unit is clear, including where it is situated within broader learning.	Teacher makes the purpose of the lesson or unit clear, including where it is situated within broader learning, linking that purpose to student interests.
	☐	☐	☐	☐
Directions and procedures	Teacher's directions and procedures are confusing to students.	Teacher's directions and procedures are clarified after initial student confusion.	Teacher's directions and procedures are clear to students.	Teacher's directions and procedures are clear to students and anticipate possible student misunderstanding.
	☐	☐	☐	☐

Component 3a

	Level of Performance			
ELEMENT	UNSATISFACTORY	BASIC	PROFICIENT	DISTINGUISHED
Explanations of content	Teacher's explanation of the content is unclear or confusing or uses inappropriate language. ☐	Teacher's explanation of the content is uneven; some is done skillfully, but other portions are difficult to follow. ☐	Teacher's explanation of content is appropriate and connects with students' knowledge and experience. ☐	Teacher's explanation of content is imaginative and connects with students' knowledge and experience. Students contribute to explaining concepts to their peers. ☐
Use of oral and written language	Teacher's spoken language is inaudible, or written language is illegible. Spoken or written language contains errors of grammar or syntax. Vocabulary may be inappropriate, vague, or used incorrectly, leaving students confused. ☐	Teacher's spoken language is audible, and written language is legible. Both are used correctly and conform to standard English. Vocabulary is correct but limited or is not appropriate to the students' ages or backgrounds. ☐	Teacher's spoken and written language is clear and correct and conforms to standard English. Vocabulary is appropriate to the students' ages and interests. ☐	Teacher's spoken and written language is correct and conforms to standard English. It is also expressive, with well-chosen vocabulary that enriches the lesson. Teacher finds opportunities to extend students' vocabularies. ☐

Source: From *Enhancing Professional Practice: A Framework for Teaching, 2nd Edition* (p. 80), by C. Danielson, 2007, Alexandria, VA: ASCD. © 2007 by ASCD. Reprinted with permission.

As a result of this self-assessment, on which element will you focus first? Turn to the pages following to explore the elements of the component in detail. After you've reviewed the tools, you can use the Action Planning and Reflection form to document the results of implementing the strategies in your classroom.

Domain 3

Element

Expectations for Learning

Description

Classrooms are businesslike places where important work takes place. This is not to suggest that they are somber; they may be joyful but businesslike. Teachers communicate the importance of what students are undertaking and clarify what students are learning. Even if the teacher doesn't articulate the desired learning at the outset of a lesson, students are clear about the purpose by the lesson's end.

A Closer Look

To help you recognize the subtle differences between the higher levels of performance for this element, note the keywords emphasized in the descriptions and review the activities common to those levels.

PROFICIENT

The teacher's purpose for the lesson or unit is *clear*, including its position within the *broader learning*.

At the proficient level of performance, teaching practices may include the following types of activities:

- Teacher both writes and verbally explains the purpose of the lesson.
- Teacher invites a few nonvolunteer students to restate the lesson's purpose.
- Teacher revisits the lesson's purpose at various points during the lesson.
- Teacher uses questioning strategies to elicit the lesson's connection to previous learning.
- Teacher invites students to consider the lesson's purpose and react to it at some point during the lesson.
- Teacher creates a graphic organizer to show the position of the current lesson within the larger unit.

DISTINGUISHED

The teacher's purpose for the lesson or unit is clear, situated within the broader learning, and *linked to student interests.*

At the distinguished level of performance, teaching practices may include the following types of activities:

- Teacher weaves student interests, such as those acquired via the student interest or parent surveys on page 61, into communication about the content.
- Teacher articulates to students their various interests, which are accommodated by the lesson.
- Students design a graphic organizer of the purpose of the lesson or unit situated within the broader learning.
- Students write for three minutes about a connection between a personal interest and the lesson's purpose.

The tools that follow will help you explore how to put the activities of these high levels of performance into practice in your classroom.

Domain 3

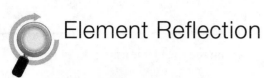

Element Reflection

✔ Teacher tool　　　　　　　__ **Student tool**

1. Why is it important for students to be able to articulate the goals of a lesson or activity?

2. Describe a situation in which it is preferable for students not to be aware of the purposes of a lesson.

Domain 3

Sharing Expectations for Learning

__ **Teacher tool**   ✔ **Student tool**

One strategy for communicating learning expectations to students is companion statement stems "We are learning to...," or WALT, and "What I'm looking for...," or WILF.

For example, the WALT for a lesson on writing paragraphs for 2nd graders might be, "We are learning to write a paragraph describing an object of clothing." And the WILF might be, "What I'm looking for is a clear topic sentence and three supporting statements."

Complete the WALT and WILF chart below and share it with students. Once students are familiar with the format, consider having them help create the WILF after you've shared and discussed the WALT.

We are learning to. . . (WALT)	What I'm looking for. . .(WILF)

Sources:
Primary Resources. (n.d.). *Gareth Pitchford's primary resources.* Retrieved June 8, 2009, from http://www.primaryresources.co.uk
Cohen, M. (2004, January). *A shared policy for positive teaching and learning.* Retrieved June 8, 2009, from http://www.thegrid.org.uk/learning/assessment/generic/documents/shared_policy_positive_teaching.doc

Domain 3

Element

Directions and Procedures

Description

Students must be clear about what they are expected to do during a lesson. Teachers can provide these directions and procedures orally, in writing, or a combination of the two. Some teachers use a board or projection device so that students can refer to it independently.

A Closer Look

To help you recognize the subtle differences between the higher levels of performance for this element, note the keywords emphasized in the descriptions and review the activities common to those levels.

PROFICIENT

The teacher's directions and procedures are *clear* to students.

At the proficient level of performance, teaching practices may include the following types of activities:

- Teacher delivers directions through multiple modalities. For example, the teacher writes the directions, the teacher relays them verbally, or students discuss them in one-minute pair-shares.
- Teacher checks for student understanding of directions or procedures, calling on non-volunteers to explain them in their own words.
- Teacher invites students to ask clarifying questions about directions before beginning a task.
- Teacher models the procedure for the assignment.
- Students follow directions successfully without ongoing, additional clarification.

DISTINGUISHED

The teacher's directions and procedures are clear to students and *anticipate possible student misunderstanding*.

At the distinguished level of performance, teaching practices may include the following types of activities:

- Teacher individualizes directions to accommodate students' learning differences.

Directions and Procedures

- Teacher points out what not to do in addition to what is correct when giving directions.
- Teacher indicates the most challenging aspects of the procedures, such as with an exclamation point or other symbol on written directions.
- Teacher asks students to rank the steps in the directions from easiest to most difficult.
- Teacher invites students to improve the directions or procedures after the activity.

The tools that follow will help you explore how to put the activities of these high levels of performance into practice in your classroom.

Domain 3

Directions and Procedures

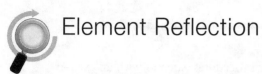

Element Reflection

✔ **Teacher tool**   __ **Student tool**

1. What are indications that students are not clear about what they are expected to do?

2. What strategies do you use to anticipate possible student misunderstandings about the directions for an activity?

Domain 3

Directions and Procedures

Giving Directions to Students Checklist

✔ **Teacher tool**   __ **Student tool**

Ensuring that students understand your directions is essential to moving forward with instruction. When planning your lesson, use this checklist to guide you in giving students directions. Then reflect on what elements of your directions helped or did not help student understanding.

☐ Write directions in student-appropriate language. If some students have reading challenges, provide them with a card that has simpler directions.

☐ Read the directions aloud. You can also have a student do this, if appropriate.

☐ Ask students to think about the directions for one minute and to ask clarifying (wondering) questions about them.

Or

Have students pair-share for one minute about the easiest or hardest part of the directions.

☐ Call on a nonvolunteer student to restate the directions in his own words.

☐ Ask a question about the directions, such as "When should you record your observations in your journal?" or "Which steps are the tricky ones? How do you know? What will you do to not get tricked here?"

☐ Note which students and how many students are able to follow the directions successfully without further clarification.

1. What part of the process you followed for giving directions helped students successfully follow them?

2. What part of the process you followed for giving directions contributed to students not being able to follow them?

3. How can you individualize or adjust the direction procedure for subsequent lessons?

Domain 3

☐ 259

Directions and Procedures

Modifying Directions for Students

✔ **Teacher tool**   __ **Student tool**

Use this template to modify directions for students who may need additional support.

1. Write a set of directions for a forthcoming assignment as you would present them to your class as a whole.

2. Identify the students who might have difficulty understanding and following these directions because they struggle with the language or require greater simplicity.

Students Who Struggle with Directions	Reasons for Struggle

3. Modify the directions to use simpler vocabulary and break them down into steps that are easier to follow.

Domain 3

Element

Explanations of Content

Description

When explaining concepts to students, experienced teachers use vivid language and imaginative analogies and metaphors, connecting explanations to students' interests and lives beyond school.

A Closer Look

To help you recognize the subtle differences between the higher levels of performance for this element, note the keywords emphasized in the descriptions and review the activities common to those levels.

PROFICIENT

The teacher's explanation of content is *appropriate* and *connects* with students' knowledge and experience.

At the proficient level of performance, teaching practices may include the following types of activities:

- Teacher regularly uses graphic organizers to clarify content.
- Teacher regularly clarifies content in multiple ways, using auditory, visual, and kinesthetic approaches. As a result, students listen, view, and do in every lesson.
- Teacher makes use of analogies when explaining content, either by eliciting or by telling.
- Teacher regularly uses text previewing strategies to help students understand the content they read about.

DISTINGUISHED

The teacher's explanation of content is *imaginative* and connects with students' knowledge and experiences. *Students contribute* to explaining content to their peers.

At the distinguished level of performance, teaching practices may include the following types of activities:

- Teacher regularly uses local experts, business people, and community-based resources to illustrate how the content students are studying connects to real life.

Domain 3

- Teacher regularly and overtly connects the content to what students have already learned using graphic organizers and artifacts students previously created.
- Teacher regularly uses an interdisciplinary approach, purposefully connecting current lessons to what students are studying in other content areas.
- Teacher uses the gradual release of responsibility model to have students explain content to peers.

The tools that follow will help you explore how to put the activities of these high levels of performance into practice in your classroom.

Domain 3

Explanations of Content

Element Reflection

✔ Teacher tool   **__ Student tool**

1. How does using metaphor and analogy help you explain complex content to students?

2. Under what conditions is it a good idea for students to explain concepts to their classmates?

Domain 3

Teaching Students to Assume Responsibility for Explaining Content

✔ **Teacher tool**   __ **Student tool**

Accomplished teachers provide a learning environment in which all students can gradually take on responsibility for their own learning. Teachers enable this learning environment by:

- Becoming facilitators of learning or the "guides on the side" rather than solely the "sage on the stage."
- Providing real choices that accommodate a range of learning styles.
- Inviting students to choose what they will do to demonstrate their learning and identify the steps they will take to accomplish the task.
- Emphasizing intrinsic motivation rather than external rewards.

Unit of Study: _____

Step 1—Modeling: I Do, You Watch. Over a period of days or weeks, carefully and overtly model learning behaviors such as explaining content, self-assessment, seeking feedback, goal setting, and reflection.

1. Which aspect of content will I explain to students?

2. After I explain the content, what will I do to help students understand what made my explanation excellent?

3. How will we capture and codify the features of "excellent explaining"?

Domain 3

Explanations of Content

Step 2—Sharing: I Do, You Help. Share exemplars of quality work and teach students to identify quality samples of their own work.

1. Which aspect of content will I explain to students?

2. Before I explain, how will I remind students of the features of excellent explaining that we learned in Step 1?

3. How will I invite students to use the features of excellent explaining to give me feedback about my explanation?

4. When and how will I demonstrate to students that I have incorporated their feedback and improved my explanation?

Domain 3

Step 3—Guiding: You Do, I Help, We Do Together. Assume responsibility with students for explaining the content through guided practice.

1. What aspects of content can students help me explain?

2. How many students should help me explain a content portion during each lesson?

3. How will all students use the features of excellent explaining to give feedback to me and the students who help me explain?

4. How will I use the features of excellent explaining to give feedback to students who explain?

5. How can I, and the students who help me explain, demonstrate that we've incorporated the feedback and improved our explanations?

Domain 3

Explanations of Content

Step 4—Independent: You Do, I Watch. Students practice, demonstrate, and apply learning behaviors that help them become self-directed learners. Assign each student a portion of the content to explain in his own words, using any of the techniques that you've previously modeled and discussed. Then give feedback to students and have students give feedback to each other about their explanations of content.

1. What aspects of content can students explain?

2. How will I support students to ensure that they use the features of excellent explaining to develop and deliver their explanations?

3. How will I ensure that all other students use the features of excellent explaining to give feedback to the students who explain?

Source: Pearson, P. D., & Gallagher, M. C. (1983). The instruction of reading comprehension. *Contemporary Educational Psychology, 8,* 317–244.

Domain 3

Using Analogies Self-Assessment

✔ **Teacher tool**   __ **Student tool**

For each criterion, indicate how often you use it in your practice and your plans for using analogies in your instruction.

Criterion	Frequently	Occasionally	Rarely	Next Steps
I create analogies appropriately to help teach content.				
I use analogies that are familiar to students.				
When I use analogies, I connect them to important outcomes.				
When I use analogies, I make sure students remember the target concept, not just the analogy.				
I make sure that discussion accompanies analogies.				
I involve students in the creation of analogies.				
I'm good at identifying the types of content appropriately taught using analogies.				

Domain 3

Explanations of Content

Using Analogies to Teach Concepts Checklist

✔ **Teacher tool**   __ **Student tool**

☐ Introduce the target concept. (For example, hibernation of bears.)

☐ Cue retrieval of analog. (For example, migration of birds studied previously.)

☐ Identify relevant features of target and analog. (Why would we compare these two things? What do they have in common?)

☐ Map similarities, using a T-chart or Venn diagram.

☐ Indicate where the analogy breaks down, using a T-chart or Venn diagram.

☐ Draw conclusions.

Domain 3

☐ 269

Getting the GIST: Previewing Text

___ **Teacher tool**   ✔ **Student tool**

Use this worksheet to guide you in preparing for the text you will be responsible for reading. Can you get the GIST of the text ahead of time?

G = Graphic Organizers (titles, subtitles, charts, graphs)

1. I've looked at the graphics in the text, and here's what I learned from them:

2. What do I already know about this topic?

3. What am I wondering about?

I = Introduction

1. I've read the introduction, and here are some big ideas I learned from it:

2. How does the introduction connect to the graphic organizers I already viewed?

Explanations of Content

S = Summary

1. I've read the summary and compared it to the introduction, and this is what I believe this section of text is about:

2. What did I learn from the summary that I did not learn from the introduction?

3. What ideas in the summary were also in the introduction?

T = Terms

1. I've read the vocabulary and other terms. Here are some I already knew:

2. Here are some other words that were new to me:

Element

Use of Oral and Written Language

Description

For many students, their teachers' language is their best model of both accurate syntax and a rich vocabulary. These models enable students to emulate such language, making their own more precise and expressive.

A Closer Look

To help you recognize the subtle differences between the higher levels of performance for this element, note the keywords emphasized in the descriptions and review the activities common to those levels.

PROFICIENT

The teacher's spoken and written language is *clear* and *correct*, conforming to standard English. Vocabulary is *appropriate* to the students' ages and interests.

At the proficient level of performance, teaching practices may include the following types of activities:

- Teacher has all documents proofread by a colleague before sending them home.
- Teacher identifies own spelling or grammatical weaknesses and works to correct them.
- Teacher compares own written documents to those of other teachers of the same grade level to compare vocabulary, grammar, and spelling.
- Teacher invites a peer to observe her teaching and to collect any errors in language and to note her vocabulary.

DISTINGUISHED

The teacher's spoken and written language is clear and correct, conforming to standard English. It is also *expressive*, with *well-chosen vocabulary* that enriches the lesson. Teacher finds opportunities to *extend students' vocabularies*.

At the distinguished level of performance, teaching practices may include the following types of activities:

- Teacher presents a word for the day every day and uses it in the lesson and throughout the day.

Use of Oral and Written Language

- Teacher regularly uses a thesaurus to offer synonyms for words within the content.
- Students are rewarded for using well-chosen words.
- Teacher's lesson plans deliberately include a focus on vocabulary, regardless of the content area.
- Teacher adjusts vocabulary for diverse students' needs.
- Teacher works with a peer to develop vocabulary to enrich a particular lesson.

   The tools that follow will help you explore how to put the activities of these high levels of performance into practice in your classroom.

Domain 3

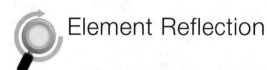

Element Reflection

✔ Teacher tool   __ **Student tool**

1. When is it desirable and when is it not desirable to correct a student's use of nonstandard English?

2. What are some techniques to help students use language in more expressive ways?

Domain 3

Use of Oral and Written Language

Teaching Mainstream ELL Students: Self-Evaluation and Planning

✔ **Teacher tool**   __ **Student tool**

Best Practice	How successful was I in using this strategy?			Notes	How will I adjust my approach for next time?
	Not Very	Marginally	Very		
1. Enunciate clearly but do not raise your voice. Add gestures, point directly to objects, or draw pictures when appropriate.					
2. Write clearly, legibly, and in print.					
3. Develop and maintain routines. Use clear and consistent signals for classroom instructions.					
4. Repeat information and review frequently. If a student does not understand, rephrase or paraphrase in shorter sentences and simpler syntax.					
5. Check often for understanding, and have students demonstrate their learning to show comprehension, instead of asking whether they understand.					
6. Avoid idioms and slang.					
7. Present new information in the context of known information.					

Domain 3

Use of Oral and Written Language

Best Practice	How successful was I in using this strategy?			Notes	How will I adjust my approach for next time?
	Not Very	Marginally	Very		
8. Announce the lesson's objectives and activities, and list instructions step-by-step.					
9. Present information in a variety of ways.					
10. Frequently summarize the salient points of a lesson, and always emphasize key vocabulary words.					
11. Recognize student success overtly and frequently. However, be aware that in some cultures overt, individual praise is considered inappropriate and can therefore be embarrassing or confusing to the student.					

Sources:

Eastern Stream Center on Resources and Training, Region IV Comprehensive Center at AEL, Region XIV Comprehensive Center/Center for Applied Linguistics. (1998). *Help! They don't speak English starter kit for primary teachers.* Oneonta, NY: Eastern Stream Center on Resources and Training.

Reed, B., & Railsback, J. (2003). *Strategies and resources for mainstream teachers of English language learners.* Retrieved July 1, 2009, from http://www.nwrel.org/request/2003may/ell.pdf

Short, D. J. (1991). *Integrating language and content instruction: Strategies and techniques.* Washington, DC: National Clearinghouse for Bilingual Education.

Domain 3

Component 3a

Action Planning and Reflection

✔ **Teacher tool** ___ **Student tool**

Look over the tools for this component and choose a strategy or strategies that you are committed to trying in your classroom. Then return to this page and record what happened. If there was a change, what evidence indicates the extent to which this strategy was successful? Finally, think about what you might do differently to continue to bring about further growth in this component.

What will I try?	How did it go?	What will I do differently next time?

Domain 3

Component 3b

Using Questioning and Discussion Techniques

OVERVIEW

Questioning and discussion techniques are part of the instructional repertoire of every accomplished teacher. Carefully framed questions at a challenging cognitive level encourage students to engage deeply with content, questioning assumptions and exploring the implications of different lines of thought. Questioning can serve many purposes, but this component refers to using questioning and discussion to advance student learning (as opposed to using it to check for understanding, such as in Component 3d: Using Assessment in Instruction, or to return a student to attention, such as Component 2d: Managing Student Behavior).

At the higher levels of teaching performance, all students—not just volunteers—are engaged in true discussion with each other, not just with the teacher. Questioning and discussion at the higher levels could be compared to a game of basketball: the ball is passed among multiple players, or students, of the same team. In contrast, at the lower levels, questioning and discussion could be compared to ping-pong: the ball goes back and forth between the student, usually a volunteer, and the teacher.

SELF-ASSESSMENT

Assess your practice in Component 3b against the levels of performance below, then check the box that best matches the level of your own teaching for each element.

Domain 3

Component 3b

Component 3b: Using Questioning and Discussion Techniques				
	Level of Performance			
ELEMENT	UNSATISFACTORY	BASIC	PROFICIENT	DISTINGUISHED
Quality of questions	Teacher's questions are virtually all of poor quality, with low cognitive challenge and single correct responses, and they are asked in rapid succession. ☐	Teacher's questions are a combination of low and high quality, posed in rapid succession. Only some invite a thoughtful response. ☐	Most of the teacher's questions are of high quality. Adequate time is provided for students to respond. ☐	Teacher's questions are of uniformly high quality, with adequate time for students to respond. Students formulate many questions. ☐
Discussion techniques	Interaction between teacher and students is predominantly recitation style, with the teacher mediating all questions and answers. ☐	Teacher makes some attempt to engage students in genuine discussion rather than recitation, with uneven results. ☐	Teacher creates a genuine discussion among students, stepping aside when appropriate. ☐	Students assume considerable responsibility for the success of the discussion, initiating topics and making unsolicited contributions. ☐
Student participation	A few students dominate the discussion. ☐	Teacher attempts to engage all students in the discussion, but with only limited success. ☐	Teacher successfully engages all students in the discussion. ☐	Students themselves ensure that all voices are heard in the discussion. ☐

Source: From *Enhancing Professional Practice: A Framework for Teaching, 2nd Edition* (p. 82), by C. Danielson, 2007, Alexandria, VA: ASCD. © 2007 by ASCD. Reprinted with permission.

As a result of this self-assessment, on which element will you focus first? Turn to the pages following to explore the elements of the component in detail. After you've reviewed the tools, you can use the Action Planning and Reflection form to document the results of implementing the strategies in your classroom.

Domain 3

Element

Quality of Questions

Description

Questions of high quality cause students to think and reflect, to deepen their understanding, and to test their ideas against those of their classmates. When teachers ask high-quality questions, they ask only a few of them and provide students with sufficient time to think about their response, reflect on the comments of their classmates, and deepen their understanding.

A Closer Look

To help you recognize the subtle differences between the higher levels of performance for this element, note the keywords emphasized in the descriptions and review the activities common to those levels.

PROFICIENT

Most of the teacher's questions are of *high quality*, and the teacher gives *adequate wait time* for students to respond and between the student and teacher response.

At the proficient level of performance, teaching practices may include the following types of activities:

- Teacher structures questions at the higher levels of Bloom's Taxonomy.
- Teacher waits three to five seconds between asking the question and calling on a respondent.
- Teacher pauses three to five seconds *after* a student responds before either answering or calling on another student.

DISTINGUISHED

The teacher's questions are of *uniformly* high quality with adequate wait time, and *students* formulate many questions.

At the distinguished level of performance, teaching practices may include the following types of activities:

- Teacher teaches students about the nature of good questions.
- Teacher shares an age-appropriate version of Bloom's Taxonomy with students.
- Teacher regularly invites students to categorize the questions asked.

Domain 3

- Teacher invites students to identify excellent questions in their, or the teacher's, reading.
- Teacher invites students to create questions prior to the start of a unit.
- Teacher regularly invites students to create higher-order questions related to their other learning.
- Teacher provides feedback to students about the questions they ask.

The tools that follow will help you explore how to put the activities of these high levels of performance into practice in your classroom.

Domain 3

Quality of Questions

Element Reflection

✔ **Teacher tool**   __ **Student tool**

1. What are the challenges in using wait time in your questioning techniques?

2. What are some strategies for teaching students how to formulate higher-level questions for their classmates?

Domain 3

Questioning Strategies Self-Assessment and Planning

✔ **Teacher tool**   __ **Student tool**

Best Practice	I Do Well With This	I Need to Work on This	Notes/Plans for Improvement
1. Allow at least three seconds after posing a question before selecting a respondent.			
2. Wait two to three seconds before responding to a student's answer to a question so that the student has time to supply more information or give an expanded answer.			
3. Students repeat your question in their own words before answering.			
4. Questions are complex, with few questions involving only simple recall of information.			
5. Support student thinking by telling them what you're going to ask when you are giving the assignment.			
6. Students create questions about the content to ask each other.			
7. Most of the questions are higher order.			
8. When a student answers a question, another student supplies details or poses another question related to it, then another student may add to that response.			
9. Provide questioning stems, such as "What might happen if. . .?" or "Your answer seems to suggest...," to students to assist them in responding to each other.			
10. Give students standards for their responses, such as "Be prepared to explain," or "Have opposing points of view to discuss."			
11. Students create devil's advocate questions.			

Domain 3

Monitoring Classroom Questioning

✔ **Teacher tool**   __ **Student tool**

Use this template to monitor your questioning and students' responses. This type of monitoring can help you make instructional decisions about how to move forward with specific students.

Class/Period: _____

Key: + = Student answered question correctly.
        − = Student answered question incorrectly.
        V = Student volunteered to answer.
        A = Student was absent.

Note: Unless otherwise indicated, all respondents are *nonvolunteers*.

Student	Date				

Notes:

Domain 3

Quality of Questions

Monitoring Classroom Questioning Example

Class/Period: <u>Social studies</u>

Key: + = Student answered question correctly.
         − = Student answered question incorrectly.
         V = Student volunteered to answer.
         A = Student was absent.

Note: Unless otherwise indicated, all respondents are *nonvolunteers*.

Student	Date				
	4/27	4/28	5/1	5/3	5/4
Adams	+	+			
Aielo	−	+	−	+	+
Banks	+	A	A	A	+
Bridges	−	−	−	+	+
Case	+	+	+	+	V+
Carrabas	−	−	−	−	+
Davies	+	−	+	+	+
Franks					
Georgio	+	+	+	+	+
Jones	−	−	+	+	−
Kurtz	V−	−	−	+	+
Maru	+	+	+	V+	−
Reyes					+

Notes:
- Three students, Adams, Franks, and Reyes, have not been called on consistently by the teacher.
- Bridges, Carrabas, and Kurtz have answered incorrectly a majority of the time they were called on.

Domain 3

Element

Discussion Techniques

Description

Some teachers confuse discussion with recitation, in which students provide answers to a teacher's questions, which are usually low level, in a type of verbal quiz. In a true discussion, all students share their views on a topic, the teacher guides discussion from one topic to another, and the discussion deepens the understanding of all students.

A Closer Look

To help you recognize the subtle differences between the higher levels of performance for this element, note the keywords emphasized in the descriptions and review the activities common to those levels.

PROFICIENT

The teacher creates a *genuine* discussion among students, *stepping aside* when appropriate.

At the proficient level of performance, teaching practices may include the following types of activities:

- Teacher regularly invites students to respond to other students' comments.
- Teacher regularly invites students to ask questions in response to other students' comments.
- Teacher aims for questioning and discussion among students, rather than strictly between the teacher and students.
- Teacher regularly uses a focused-questioning protocol to keep questions deep and on-topic.
- Teacher often uses Socratic questioning techniques.
- Teacher posts discussion topics on a classroom blog or wiki, where students respond. Teacher tracks quantity and quality of student contributions using a rubric.[1]

DISTINGUISHED

Students assume *considerable* responsibility for the success of the discussion, *initiating* topics and making *unsolicited contributions*.

Domain 3

Discussion Techniques

At the distinguished level of performance, teaching practices may include the following types of activities:

- Teacher involves students in deciding which of an array of appropriate topics the class should explore in meeting specific standards.
- Teacher regularly invites students to reflect on the lesson or content and share their thoughts.
- Teacher shares elements of the focused-questioning protocol with students to structure their schema about the qualities of good discussion.
- Teacher often asks students to prepare a 5–10 minute discussion about a lesson or content using the focused-questioning protocol.
- Teacher shares the qualities of Socratic questioning.
- Teacher often requires students to prepare short discussions of the content using Socratic techniques.
- Teacher regularly provides students with feedback on the quality of both their questions specifically and their participation in the discussion generally.
- Students post and respond to discussion topics on a classroom blog or wiki. They self-assess the quality of their contributions using a teacher-supplied rubric.[1]

The tools that follow will help you explore how to put the activities of these high levels of performance into practice in your classroom.

[1] Calvert, J. (2009). *Blogs in the classroom*. Retrieved June 11, 2009, from http://calvert.wiki.ccsd.edu/page/diff/Blogs+in+the+Classroom/69204799

Domain 3

ASCD 287

Discussion Techniques

Element Reflection

✔ **Teacher tool**   __ **Student tool**

1. What are some practical techniques you can use to ensure that all students have an opportunity to participate in the discussion?

2. How can you teach students to notice when they are dominating a discussion or when some students have not had their voices heard?

Domain 3

Discussion Techniques

Changing the Nature of Discussion

✔ Teacher tool   **__ Student tool**

Discussions are more authentic when students build on each other's responses, instead of relying on the teacher to interject after each response. In this format, the teacher poses a thoughtful question, one student forms a response, another student questions or builds on that response, another student questions or builds further, and so on. Students have to be taught how to approach and develop this type of discussion.

Envision the following characteristics in your classroom and consider how you can teach students to behave in these ways.

1. During a discussion, students use the skills of active listening with their peers:
- Paraphrasing—Students repeat what their peer answered, using their own words.
- Clarifying—Students ask a peer for more information about their response.
- Mediating—Students ask questions of a peer, inviting them to consider new information.

What I will teach my students to empower them to behave in these ways:

2. Students use their body language congruently: they turn to look at the student to whom they are responding instead of facing the teacher.

What I will teach my students to empower them to behave in this way:

3. Students disagree with points of view in ways that are respectful, content-focused, and appropriate to the discussion.

What I will teach my students to empower them to behave in this way:

4. Students monitor the discussion, noting who has and has not participated, and use appropriate questions to involve quieter students in the conversation.

What I will teach my students to empower them to behave in this way:

Domain 3

Integrating Writing into Discussion

✔ **Teacher tool** ___ **Student tool**

A discussion should not rely solely on oral interaction. Writing can be an effective tool for engaging everyone, offering quiet or shy students the opportunity to actively participate and helping focus excessive talkers on another form of expression. Writing also allows for deeper, more elaborate reflection.

Try integrating the following writing activities into class discussions, then reflect on whether they improved engagement and plan how you might adjust the strategy for future lessons.

Discussion Writing Strategy	Date Implemented	Notes/Plans for Improvement
Class Secretaries A class secretary records the discussion and provides a summary to the rest of the class, instead of every student taking individual notes. All students review and correct this record. Rotate so that every student can be class secretary.		
Free Writing Students write for a few minutes to gather their thoughts or come up with new ideas. They might examine a passage in a text, reflect on a given question, or articulate an opinion. Best used before starting discussion on a new topic.		
The One-Minute Paper Students write down their comments, reorganize their ideas, or respond to a specific question. Best used if the discussion is declining or is too intense or students look confused.		
Reflection Papers Students write brief summaries and commentaries of the discussion, evaluating their own role or writing one thing they learned from it. Comments are then shared with the class.		
Student Questions Students write down one or two questions.		

Source: Young, X., & Taylor, M. (1997). Lecture at Cornell University, Ithaca, NY.

Domain 3

Socratic Teaching Guidelines

✔ **Teacher tool**   ___ **Student tool**

Critical thinking is fostered not by answers but by questions. The better the questions, the more powerful the student thinking. Socrates, whose principles endure to this day, created a model for questioning. When Socratic questioning is used as a teaching tool, students pose questions to each other to stimulate thinking and advance conceptual knowledge. Answers to questions lead to further questions, all of which spiral thinking and learning upward. Some types of Socratic questioning are as follows:

Probing Thinking. These types of questions dig into the thinking of the respondent.

- What causes you to say that?
- Could you explain what you mean?
- How does this relate to what we have been talking about?

Probing Assumptions. Students examine hidden assumptions on which their thinking might be based.

- What must be true for your thinking to be correct?
- What other assumptions are possible?

Probing Reasoning. Breaking reasoning down into its component parts, or challenging rationale, can cause deeper and more specific thinking.

- Why do you think so?
- How do you know this?
- What facts are there to support what you are saying?

Probing Alternate Perspectives. These questions help students look at issues from more than one point of view.

- What's another way to look at this?
- Why is this viewpoint stronger than the other one? How do you know?
- What are the strengths and weaknesses of each viewpoint?

Domain 3

Probing Implications and Consequences. Extending an argument to its implications and consequences strengthens thought.

- What might happen next?
- How does this change what we've already learned?

Metaquestioning. Students question the question, identifying the usefulness or value of various questions.

- What was the point of asking that question?
- How does that question help your thinking?
- Which questions were most helpful in advancing your thinking? Least helpful?

Instruct students on this type of discussion and what types of questions they should be asking of each other. Keep track of which students pose which types of questions, and then use that data to determine how you can engage all students in thoughtful discussion.

Class or Period:

Time Frame/Dates:

Student	Probing Thinking	Probing Assumptions	Probing Reasoning	Probing Alternative Perspectives	Probing Implications and Consequences	Metaquestioning

Notes:

Domain 3

Discussion Techniques

Activities for Involving Students in Discussions

✔ **Teacher tool**   __ **Student tool**

Try these activities in your units and lessons to promote discussions that will include all students. Some activities will work better than others depending on the class and type of lesson. Record when you used the strategies and whether they successfully involved students in discussion. Then reflect on whether you'll use that activity again or how you will modify it for this or another lesson.

Activity	Date	Level of Success Not ◄———► Highly 1 2 3 4	Reflection and Modifications
Table Hop/Pass Pose a question and, after giving students a few seconds of think time, hop from table group to table group, calling randomly on one student. The student can respond or pass. After the activity, call on a few students to summarize the various responses.			
Response Cards Orally ask a question or display it on an overhead and have students simultaneously hold up index cards, signs, dry-erase boards, magnetic boards, small chalkboards, or the like to indicate their responses. Response cards can be pre-printed with responses, such as yes/no or A-B-C-D, or write-on cards.			
Hand Signals Students indicate with thumbs-up or thumbs-down whether a given question is true or false or if they understand the content.			

Domain 3

Activity	Date	Level of Success Not ←——→ Highly 1　2　3　4	Reflection and Modifications
Randomly Selecting Students To ensure that all students are called on during discussions, create a random response system using items such as popsicle sticks or numbers to give all students an equal chance of being invited to respond. For example, write each student's name on a popsicle stick and place them in a jar. Then randomly draw out a popsicle stick and ask that student to respond. After the student responds, return the popsicle stick to the jar so that all students will remain actively involved.			

Discussion Rubrics for Online Learning

✔ **Teacher tool**   ✔ **Student tool**

When you use blogs as a discussion technique or otherwise post questions or prompts for students to respond in an interactive online environment, you can evaluate students' participation based on the following rubric. You can also have students evaluate their own contributions with the same rubric.

Discussion board posts are evaluated on the following scale.

Criteria	1	2	3	4
Development of Discussion Topic	• Posts are not developed or may be very short. • No attempt made to connect post to readings or assignments.	• Somewhat substantial posts. • Connection to readings or assignments is not clear or not consistent throughout post.	• Thoughtful, substantial posts. • General connection to readings or assignments.	• Highly thoughtful, substantial posts. • Clear connections to readings or assignments.
Collaboration with Peers	Does not collaborate with peers.	Collaborates with peers without relating discussion to relevant readings or assignments.	Collaborates with peers, relating discussion to relevant readings or assignments.	Collaborates with peers to extend dialogue (e.g., by raising alternate point of view or offering additional resource or connection).
Application of Learning	Irrelevant connections or does not attempt to make connections.	Attempts to connect to personal experience but connection unclear.	Connects discussion topic to relevant personal experiences.	Connects discussion topic to relevant personal experiences in an insightful way.
Timeliness	Does not adhere to time lines.	Mostly on time.	Consistently on time.	Models timeliness for peers.
Use of Language	Language and writing conventions contain multiple and significant errors.	Language and writing conventions contain some errors.	Language and writing conventions are correct.	Language and writing conventions enrich the post.

Domain 3

Element

Student Participation

A Closer Look

To help you recognize the subtle differences between the higher levels of performance for this element, note the keywords emphasized in the descriptions and review the activities common to those levels.

PROFICIENT

The teacher successfully engages *all* students in the discussion.

At the proficient level of performance, teaching practices may include the following types of activities:

- Teacher regularly and consistently uses a variety of techniques for randomly calling on *nonvolunteers* during questioning and discussion.
- Teacher regularly and consistently tracks patterns of calling on nonvolunteer students during discussion.
- Teacher elicits participation through a variety of sensory modes (kinesthetic, verbal, and spatial).
- Teacher announces at the outset of the discussion that students may write a contribution in their journals or on an index card if they were unable to contribute verbally during the discussion time.
- Teacher regularly uses a variety of strategies to ask all students each question during the lesson.

DISTINGUISHED

Students themselves ensure that *all* voices are heard in the discussion.

At the distinguished level of performance, teaching practices may include the following types of activities:

Student Participation

- Teacher instructs students on a variety of techniques, such as using popsicle sticks or cards with students' names on them, for randomly calling on nonvolunteers so that they can use these methods.
- Teacher instructs students on an age-appropriate system for tracking students who have contributed to the discussion and students who have not so that they are aware of who has participated.
- Teacher regularly invites students to use their checklists to frame a question for someone who has not contributed to the discussion.
- Teacher encourages students to build on each other's responses to questions by responding either with a comment or a new question.

The tools that follow will help you explore how to put the activities of these high levels of performance into practice in your classroom.

Domain 3

Student Participation

 # Element Reflection

✔ **Teacher tool**　　　　　　　___ **Student tool**

1. To what extent do students take responsibility for being involved in or taking the lead in the discussion?

2. In a class discussion, most students direct their comments to the teacher rather than to their classmates. How can you teach students to respond to one another while showing respect for each others' views?

Domain 3

Student Participation

Getting Students to Ask the Questions: Self-Assessment

✔ Teacher tool   **__ Student tool**

To help you determine how well you employ discussion techniques, rate yourself on how often you use each point of the following strategies.

Key: R = I do this regularly.
         S = I do this sometimes.
         N = I need to develop this strategy.

Beginning a New Unit

The class thinks of questions that could be asked about the topic.

_____ I use true brainstorming techniques, accepting all contributions without judgment, encouraging students to build on each other's ideas, and encouraging far-out or unusual ideas. The goal is a large number of ideas or questions.

_____ I capture all student questions in writing and use student assistants to help me.

_____ I categorize the students' questions, combining items that overlap or are overly similar, and use symbols to indicate which are most or least interesting and whether they are easy or hard to answer.

_____ I teach a developmentally appropriate form of Bloom's Taxonomy to help students categorize questions from lower- to higher-order.

Questioning Homework

Students form questions about an assignment for the next day's discussion.

_____ I ask students to write three comparison questions about the story they are reading.

_____ I ask students to find the most interesting question left unanswered by the reading.

_____ I ask students to identify the question the author was trying to answer.

_____ I ask students to write a question that will demand at least 10 minutes of thought to answer.

_____ I ask students to find a question that has no answer, or two thousand answers, or an infinite number of answers.

_____ I ask students to ask a question that is the result of a bigger question. Students then ask the rest of the class to identify the bigger question.

_____ I ask students to identify the most important and the least important questions.

Domain 3

The Interview

Before they read a story or see a film about an event, students recreate the familiar scene of a television reporter asking pointed, focused questions to an interviewee.

_____ I tell students in advance that I will ask one of them to be one of the main figures in the story or film once it is over. The rest of the class will take turns asking that student interview questions.

_____ I ask all students to write down at least three questions to ask.

Bigger Questions

Deep questions require thought, and students shouldn't have an answer quickly. Thinking questions can be 1-minute, 5-minute, or 10-minute questions.

_____ I refuse to call on students while they are supposed to be thinking. I encourage students to jot down ideas while they are thinking about questions.

_____ I encourage students to list other questions that may help them answer the original question.

_____ I demonstrate how one question may spawn other questions.

_____ When the time period is over, I have students draw pictures of how their minds jumped and moved and considered.

_____ I show students the structure of thought that should underlie an informed conclusion to a demanding question.

_____ I work through the supporting arguments on the board so that students can see that the main idea is supported by a framework of other thoughts.

_____ I use metaphors, such as tree trunks and roots, to help students visualize a complex process.

Divergent Thinking

Scamper is a set of questioning strategies in which students are taught to ask how to change an existing product, item, or idea by asking how to substitute; combine; add; modify, magnify, or minimize; put to other uses; eliminate; and reverse.

_____ I have students both ask the questions and answer them.

_____ I explain to students how their questions, even though often very divergent, relate to the required content and show a thorough knowledge of the content.

Sources:

Davis, H. B. (1982). _Super think: Strategies for asking thought-provoking questions._ San Luis Obispo, CA: Dandy Lion Publications.

Eberle, R. F. (1972). Developing imagination through scamper. _Journal of Creative Behavior, 6_(3), 199–203.

McKenzie, J., & Davis, H. B. (1986). _Filling the tool box: Classroom strategies to engender student questioning._ Retrieved July 1, 2009, from http://www.fno.org/toolbox.html

Domain 3

Monitoring Participation in Classroom Discussion

✔ **Teacher tool**   __ **Student tool**

Use this template to monitor individual student participation in discussions. The data can help you make instructional decisions about student understanding and next steps for teaching the content.

Class or Period: _____

Date: _____

Key: + = Observed
       A = Student was absent

Student	Initiates Topic	Offers Unsolicited Substantial Contribution	Respectfully Challenges Another Student's Response	Invites Another Student into the Discussion	Probes the Response of Another Student for Clarity	Paraphrases Another Student's Response

Notes:

Domain 3

Monitoring Participation in Classroom Discussion Example

Class or Period: <u>Social studies</u>

Date: <u>6/23</u>

Key: + = Observed

A = Student was absent

Student	Initiates Topic	Offers Unsolicited Substantial Contribution	Respectfully Challenges Another Student's Response	Invites Another Student into the Discussion	Probes the Response of Another Student for Clarity	Paraphrases Another Student's Response
Aielo	+ +	+		+		+ +
Banks		+		+	+	
Bridges	+	+	+ +	+		+
Case	A	A	A	A	A	A
Carrabas	+			+ + +		
Davies		+				
Franks	A	A	A	A	A	+ (entered late)
Georgio	+	+	+		+	+

Notes:
- All students who were present participated in at least one aspect (met one criteria) of the discussion.
- Davies and the absent students need more support or follow-up instruction in how to actively engage in class discussions.
- Carrabas should be invited to participate more often.

Domain 3

Component 3b

Action Planning and Reflection

✔ **Teacher tool**   __ **Student tool**

Look over the tools for this component and choose a strategy or strategies that you are committed to trying in your classroom. Then return to this page and record what happened. If there was a change, what evidence indicates the extent to which this strategy was successful? Finally, think about what you might do differently to continue to bring about further growth in this component.

What will I try?	How did it go?	What will I do differently next time?

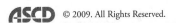   ☐ 303

Component 3c

Engaging Students in Learning

OVERVIEW

Engaging students in learning is the centerpiece of the framework for teaching, and all the other components support it by promoting high levels of student understanding. In contrast to time on task, which refers to whether students are doing what the teacher asked them to do, engagement refers to whether what the teacher asked students to do is sufficiently rigorous to promote deep learning. Engagement requires that teachers hold high expectations for each student.

Student engagement may be hands-on, involving physical activity, but more important it should be minds-on, involving intellectual activity. School, in other words, is not a spectator sport. Mental engagement is

- Mental *work*.
- Real thinking, not just simple recall of facts.
- Often described by students as "difficult, but in a good way."

SELF-ASSESSMENT

Assess your practice in Component 3c against the levels of performance below, then check the box that best matches the level of your own teaching for each element.

Component 3c: Engaging Students in Learning				
	Level of Performance			
ELEMENT	UNSATISFACTORY	BASIC	PROFICIENT	DISTINGUISHED
Activities and assignments	Activities and assignments are inappropriate for students' age or background. Students are not mentally engaged in them. ☐	Activities and assignments are appropriate to some students and engage them mentally, but others are not engaged. ☐	Most activities and assignments are appropriate to students, and almost all students are cognitively engaged in exploring content. ☐	All students are cognitively engaged in the activities and assignments in their exploration of content. Students initiate or adapt activities and projects to enhance their understanding. ☐

Domain 3

Component 3c

ELEMENT	Level of Performance			
	UNSATISFACTORY	BASIC	PROFICIENT	DISTINGUISHED
Grouping of students	Instructional groups are inappropriate to the students or to the instructional outcomes. ☐	Instructional groups are only partially appropriate to the students or only moderately successful in advancing the instructional outcomes of the lesson. ☐	Instructional groups are productive and fully appropriate to the students or to the instructional purposes of the lesson. ☐	Instructional groups are productive and fully appropriate to the students or to the instructional purposes of the lesson. Students take the initiative to influence the formation or adjustment of instructional groups. ☐
Instructional materials and resources	Instructional materials and resources are unsuitable to the instructional purposes or do not engage students mentally. ☐	Instructional materials and resources are only partially suitable to the instructional purposes, or students are only partially mentally engaged with them. ☐	Instructional materials and resources are suitable to the instructional purposes and engage students mentally. ☐	Instructional materials and resources are suitable to the instructional purposes and engage students mentally. Students initiate the choice, adaptation, or creation of materials to enhance their learning. ☐
Structure and pacing	The lesson has no clearly defined structure, or the pace of the lesson is too slow or rushed, or both. ☐	The lesson has a recognizable structure, although it is not uniformly maintained throughout the lesson. Pacing of the lesson is inconsistent. ☐	The lesson has a clearly defined structure around which the activities are organized. Pacing of the lesson is generally appropriate. ☐	The lesson's structure is highly coherent, allowing for reflection and closure. Pacing of the lesson is appropriate for all students. ☐

Source: From *Enhancing Professional Practice: A Framework for Teaching, 2nd Edition* (p. 85), by C. Danielson, 2007, Alexandria, VA: ASCD. © 2007 by ASCD. Reprinted with permission.

Domain 3

As a result of this self-assessment, on which element will you focus first? Turn to the pages following to explore the elements of the component in detail. After you've reviewed the tools, you can use the Action Planning and Reflection form to document the results of implementing the strategies in your classroom.

Element

Activities and Assignments

Description

The core of student engagement, activities and assignments that promote learning are those that require student thinking, emphasize depth over breadth, and may enable students to exercise some choice.

A Closer Look

To help you recognize the subtle differences between the higher levels of performance for this element, note the keywords emphasized in the descriptions and review the activities common to those levels.

PROFICIENT

Most activities and assignment are *appropriate* to students, and *almost all* students are *cognitively engaged* in exploring content.

At the proficient level of performance, teaching practices may include the following types of activities:

- Teacher identifies the types of thinking required by a classroom activity or homework assignment.
- Teacher instructs students in how to draw inferences.
- Teacher differentiates activities and assignments for most students most of the time.
- Teacher incorporates strategies for engaging students, such as making content relevant to student lives, providing students with choice and a sense of control, and capitalizing on peer interactions and the social nature of learning.
- Teacher employs specific strategies to increase engagement when lecturing.

DISTINGUISHED

All students are cognitively engaged in the activities and assignments in their exploration of content. *Students initiate or adapt* activities and projects to enhance their understanding.

At the distinguished level of performance, teaching practices may include the following types of activities:

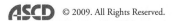

Domain 3

- Teacher routinely invites students to identify the types of thinking required by a classroom activity or homework assignment.
- Teacher invites students' input in designing product or project requirements.
- As appropriate, students negotiate individual learning contracts with the teacher.
- Students initiate, analyze, and evaluate scenarios for role-plays that are authentic to their lives.
- Students initiate changes to an assignment or activity to make it more authentic and meaningful to their lives.
- Teacher encourages students to develop proposals for alternative projects and assignments.
- Students design, experience, and evaluate a service learning educational experience.

The tools that follow will help you explore how to put the activities of these high levels of performance into practice in your classroom.

Domain 3

Activities and Assignments

Element Reflection

✔ **Teacher tool**   __ **Student tool**

1. Should students always be doing activities that engage them intellectually? Is there ever a place for mindless activities?

2. How can you determine whether an activity is engaging for students by examining their work? What would you look for?

Domain 3

Creating Engaging Activities for Students

✔ **Teacher tool**   __ **Student tool**

Students are more likely to be engaged in learning when lessons contain multiple correct answers and pathways to find them, student choice, relevance to students' lives, collaboration, and rigor.

To practice creating engaging activities, revise the less engaging activities for each characteristic to make them more engaging. The first characteristic is done for you. When you're done, turn to page 312 for recommendations on engaging activities.

Characteristics of Engaging Activities	Less Engaging Activity	More Engaging Activity
Multiple Correct Answers and Pathways When the work involves only one correct answer or one correct way to get to the correct answer, it tends to be less engaging than work that has more than one answer or way to get there.	List the five significant events in the Battle of Gettysburg.	Assume the role of a Confederate or Union soldier. Write a letter home, describing the five significant events of the Battle of Gettysburg from your perspective.
Student Choice When students have some degree of choice about what they learn, how they learn it, or how they show what they know, they tend to invest more and learn more.	Learn about the hibernation of bears by reading Chapter 4 and answering the questions at the end of the chapter.	
Relevance When the learning activities have personal meaning for students, they are more likely to be invested in the learning.	Study the features of a persuasive letter, then pretend you are the owner of a candy store who petitions city council for free parking in front of your store.	

Domain 3

Activities and Assignments

Characteristics of Engaging Activities	Less Engaging Activity	More Engaging Activity
Collaboration Learning is a social event. Students can learn from each other and find doing so more engaging. However, you should carefully structure the collaborative activity to produce engagement.	Students work together to answer questions on a worksheet.	
Rigor Learning activities need to be sufficiently challenging, making students really have to think.	Students read some text and answer recall questions.	

Domain 3

MORE ENGAGING ACTIVITIES

Student Choice

Learn about the hibernation of bears by
- Reading Chapter 4.
- Watching a DVD.
- Locating four Internet sources from the provided list.
- Interviewing Mr. Clark, a local expert.

Relevance

Read local newspapers for the arguments about whether skateboarding should be permitted in the city park. List the arguments both for and against skateboarding in the park. Then study the features of persuasive letter writing. Write a personal letter to the town council persuading them of your point of view about skateboarding in the city park. Send your letter and share replies with the class.

Collaboration

Use a jigsaw structure for reading text in which each student has a portion of the reading to digest and summarize. Students share their summaries with their group members, who then create a chart presenting the key ideas from their reading portions to the class.

Rigor

Students read some text, evaluate which three events have the greatest significance, and write a rationale for their thinking. They then compare their rationale with that of other students whose thinking is different, and the students arrive at a consensus.

Domain 3

Activities and Assignments

Checklist for Engaging Students in Lectures

✔ Teacher tool   **__ Student tool**

Many teachers feel that the lecture method of instruction cannot result in student engagement at a high level. Although teachers shouldn't use any method of teaching exclusively, you can make a lecture or minilecture more engaging for students.

As you plan a lesson in which you will deliver a portion in a lecture-based format, incorporate the following characteristics into your lecture. Check off each item as you embed it in your planning.

☐ Present the lecture topic and the learning goals before beginning the lecture.

☐ Invite students to self-assess what they already know about the topic, and elicit a few of these responses.

☐ During the lecture, require everyone to take notes. For younger students, supply a partial outline that they complete during the lecture.

☐ Use visual aids, such as pictures, media, and graphic organizers, to complement the lecture.

☐ At various points in the lecture, ask a question that requires students to refer back to their notes to respond.

☐ When asking questions during the lecture, call on nonvolunteers.

☐ Midway through the lecture, ask a reflection question. Have students either write a response to it or share their thinking with an elbow partner.

☐ At the conclusion of the lecture, ask students to reflect in silence for a few moments to think, formulate a question, make a suggestion, or record their thoughts on the topic.

Reflect on the success of the lecture. What made it successful? What might you change in the future when delivering a lecture-based lesson?

Domain 3

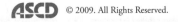

Learning Contract

__ **Teacher tool**   ✔ **Student tool**

A learning contract is a working agreement between a student and the teacher that outlines how that student will meet specific learning objectives. Such a contract permits students to have control over their learning, with teacher approval. It also allows students to design a series of learning experiences that will result in certain types of learning. The teacher must approve the learning contract.

My Name: _____ Teacher Signature: _____

Class/Course: _____ Grade Level: _____

Topic: _____

Learning Objectives	Related Lesson/ Assignment/ Activities (How I will learn?)	Materials or Text Support (Things I'll need in order to learn.)	Evidence of Learning (How will I show that I learned?)	Due Date
I will learn...				
I will learn...				
I will learn...				
I will learn...				
I will learn...				

Domain 3

Activities and Assignments

Self-evaluation: For each learning objective, describe whether you met that objective and the evidence that supports your conclusion.

Teacher evaluation: For each objective, assesses the student's achievement and comment on the evidence.

Domain 3

Activities and Assignments

Alternative Project Proposal

__ **Teacher tool**   ✔ **Student tool**

Students can learn more and become more engaged when they can choose certain aspects of their learning, in appropriate ways, at appropriate times. You can create a menu for students with ways to learn a portion of the content or demonstrate goal achievement. You can also give students the option of creating their own alternatives for learning a portion of the content or demonstrating goal achievement.

Students generally benefit from choosing from a list of teacher-created alternatives initially. As students become more familiar with the process, they can generate their own ideas. Students' success in creating alternatives for their learning depends, in large part, on the quality of the learning goals that you have created and shared.

Distribute the worksheet to students so that they can design their own projects for designated units of study.

Carefully review the description, goals, and criteria for the class assignment. If you decide that you would like to propose an alternative project, follow the steps below:

1. Complete all parts of this form.
2. Submit the completed form to me by _____.
3. Meet with me to review the proposal on a date that we have agreed on.
4. Clarify any questions and complete a project time line.
5. Follow the time line and submit the final project by _____.

Name: _____ Class/Period: _____

1. This project proposal is submitted to take the place of class assignment: _____
2. Briefly describe the project you are proposing as an alternative to the class assignment.

3. Write the learning goals provided for this assignment, and describe the activities you will accomplish to meet those goals. In the last column, describe how you will show me that you have met the learning goal once you have accomplished the proposed activities.

Domain 3

Activities and Assignments

Learning Goals	Proposed Activities	Materials Needed	Completion Date	Evidence of Goal Achievement

4. Based on teacher feedback, my revised proposal is as follows:

5. Time line for project:

Student signature: _____

Teacher signature: _____

Domain 3

Element

Grouping of Students

Description

The nature of the instructional outcomes and the learning needs of the students help determine the way students should be grouped. In some cases, teachers may cluster students with similar backgrounds and skills in the same group. Other times, teachers may spread more advanced students across the different groups. Alternatively, teachers might permit students to select their own groups or could group students randomly.

A Closer Look

To help you recognize the subtle differences between the higher levels of performance for this element, note the keywords emphasized in the descriptions and review the activities common to those levels.

PROFICIENT

Instructional groups are *productive* and *fully appropriate* to the students or to the instructional purposes of the lesson.

At the proficient level of performance, teaching practices may include the following types of activities:

- Teacher uses flexible grouping including whole-class learning; pairs, triads, and quads; student-selected groups; teacher-selected groups; and random groups.
- Teacher decides on the grouping according to the instructional purpose.
- Teacher establishes roles and responsibilities for pairs of students for peer editing of writing assignments.
- Teacher readily adjusts groups when students are absent.
- Teacher assigns students to groups in various ways, such as by interest, readiness, or learning style preference.
- Teacher uses a variety of methods to form groups, such as random, clock partners, by drawing a card or number, or student choice.
- Teacher directly instructs on the roles and responsibilities of group members.

DISTINGUISHED

Instructional groups are productive and fully appropriate to the students or to the instructional purposes of the lesson. *Students* take the *initiative* to influence the formation or adjustment of instructional groups.

At the distinguished level of performance, teaching practices may include the following types of activities:

- Students suggest appropriate opportunities for working in cooperative groups.
- Students evaluate their own effectiveness in the group and the effectiveness of the group as a whole.
- Students keep a record of their involvement in different types of groups.
- Students provide feedback to each other about group participation.

The tools that follow will help you explore how to put the activities of these high levels of performance into practice in your classroom.

Domain 3

Grouping of Students

Element Reflection

✔ **Teacher tool**   __ **Student tool**

1. If student groups are heterogeneous in terms of skill, how do you prevent the more advanced students from feeling bored or from doing all the work themselves?

2. How do student personalities affect group work? How do you control for this?

Domain 3

Evaluating Cooperative Behavior in Small Groups

___ **Teacher tool**   ✔ **Student tool**

Ask students to self-assess and assess each other using the rubric for cooperative behavior in small groups.

Name: _____   Date: _____

1: Needs Improvement	2: Satisfactory	3: Good	4: Excellent
• Works toward group goals only when prompted. • Contributes to the group only when prompted. • Needs occasional reminders to be sensitive to the feelings and learning needs of others. • Participates in needed changes when prompted and encouraged.	• Works toward group goals with occasional prompting. • Contributes to the group with occasional prompting. • Sometimes shows sensitivity to the feelings and learning needs of others. • Participates in needed changes, with occasional prompting.	• Works toward group goals without prompting. • Accepts and fulfills individual role within the group. • Contributes knowledge, opinions, and skills without prompting. • Often shows sensitivity to the feelings and learning needs of others. • Willingly participates in needed changes.	• Consistently and actively works toward group goals. • Is sensitive to the feelings and learning needs of all group members. • Willingly accepts and fulfills individual role within the group. • Consistently and actively contributes knowledge, opinions, and skills. • Values the knowledge, opinion, and skills of all group members and encourages their contributions. • Helps group identify necessary changes and encourages group action for change.

Domain 3

1. How well did you cooperate with your group? Explain why you gave yourself that score.

2. How well did each member of your group work together? Explain your reasoning for each rating.

Element

Instructional Materials and Resources

Description

The instructional materials a teacher selects can have an enormous influence on students' experience. Some teachers are obliged to use a school's or district's officially sanctioned materials. But many teachers use these selectively or supplement them with others of their choosing that are better suited to engaging students in deep learning.

A Closer Look

To help you recognize the subtle differences between the higher levels of performance for this element, note the keywords emphasized in the descriptions and review the activities common to those levels.

PROFICIENT

Instructional materials and resources are *suitable* to the instructional purposes and *engage students* mentally.

At the proficient level of performance, teaching practices may include the following types of activities:

- Teacher has the suitable instructional materials necessary for the lesson available for all students. These may include textbooks, readings, maps, charts, videos, workbooks, or access to the Internet.
- Teacher augments school-issued materials with instructional materials from other suitable sources as permitted or as appropriate.
- Teacher uses artifacts and other found objects to enhance the representation of content.
- Teacher makes explicit the rationale for selecting specific material or resources to support the lesson.
- Teacher enlists online and electronic learning resources to engage students.

Domain 3

DISTINGUISHED

Instructional materials and resources are suitable to the instructional purposes and engage students mentally. *Students* initiate the choice, adaptation, or creation of materials to enhance their learning.

At the distinguished level of performance, teaching practices may include the following types of activities:

- Teacher invites students to create or identify their own learning materials.
- Students suggest additional resources, such as guest speakers, field trips, or performances, for a topic or unit of study.
- Students decide which adaptation of a novel is appropriate for study.

The tools that follow will help you explore how to put the activities of these high levels of performance into practice in your classroom.

Instructional Materials and Resources

Element Reflection

✔ **Teacher tool**   __ **Student tool**

1. Are there advantages to materials made by teachers to purchased materials?

2. How do you know whether the materials and resources you chose helped advance learning? What factors do you use in determining this?

Domain 3

□ 325

Instructional Materials and Resources

Materials to Help Me Learn Checklist

__ **Teacher tool**   ✔ **Student tool**

You can distribute this checklist to students to give them the opportunity to choose how they would like to achieve the instructional outcomes you outline. Be sure to fill in the title and goals first.

Lesson or Unit Title: _____

Lesson or Unit Learning Goals:

1.

2.

3.

Study the learning goals above for the lesson or unit, and then read the list of learning materials below. Select two or three that you would like to use or create to help you achieve those goals.

☐ Reading a book.

☐ Reading an article from a magazine.

☐ Locating information from the Internet.

☐ Interviewing a knowledgeable adult.

☐ Interviewing a knowledgeable student.

☐ Working with a community mentor.

☐ Creating a chart, graphic organizer, or diagram.

☐ Drawing a picture or illustration.

☐ Making a model.

☐ Writing a song, poem, or rap.

☐ Providing a community service.

☐ Developing a dance.

☐ Other materials:

Domain 3

Element

Structure and Pacing

Description

A well-paced lesson, one that doesn't rush students in completing a task or leave students bored, with a well-defined structure is one of the marks of an experienced teacher. In addition, a well-designed lesson includes time for reflection and closure.

A Closer Look

To help you recognize the subtle differences between the higher levels of performance for this element, note the keywords emphasized in the descriptions and review the activities common to those levels.

PROFICIENT

The lesson has a *clearly defined* structure around which the activities are organized, and pacing is *generally appropriate*.

At the proficient level of performance, teaching practices may include the following types of activities:

- Teacher keeps to an organized structure or agenda, but with flexible time frames, to ensure appropriate time for all facets of the lesson.
- Teacher communicates that time is a valuable resource and models efficient use of time in performing noninstructional duties.
- Teacher communicates the agenda or structure both orally and visually, such as by using clocks or tables.
- Students do not have downtime waiting for others to finish.
- Teacher consistently coordinates use of time and space with the learning activity.
- Teacher invites students to contribute ways to use time effectively.
- Teacher invites students to self-evaluate on their productive use of time in the class.

DISTINGUISHED

The lesson's structure is *highly coherent*, allowing *time for reflection and closure*. Pacing is appropriate for *all students*.

At the distinguished level of performance, teaching practices may include the following types of activities:

- Teacher compacts curriculum for students for whom it is appropriate.
- Teacher regularly employs a variety of techniques suitable for lesson closure.
- Teacher invites student self-reflection on the learning experience in daily journals or learning logs.
- Lessons have momentum, and teacher keeps students active from one part of the lesson to another.

The tools that follow will help you explore how to put the activities of these high levels of performance into practice in your classroom.

Structure and Pacing

Element Reflection

✔ **Teacher tool**   __ **Student tool**

1. Describe some signals that students give that indicate a lesson's pace is too slow or too rushed.

2. Why is it important to be sure to incorporate time in a lesson for student reflection and closure?

Domain 3

Action Planning and Reflection

✔ **Teacher tool**   __ **Student tool**

Look over the tools for this component and choose a strategy or strategies that you are committed to trying in your classroom. Then return to this page and record what happened. If there was a change, what evidence indicates the extent to which this strategy was successful? Finally, think about what you might do differently to continue to bring about further growth in this component.

What will I try?	How did it go?	What will I do differently next time?

Domain 3

Component 3d

Using Assessment in Instruction

OVERVIEW

In recent years, the thinking about assessment has changed. In addition to its traditional role at the end of instruction as a way to determine whether students have mastered the content, it is now being used during instruction as well. Assessment is now considered an integral part of instruction.

As a lesson progresses, teachers monitor student learning continuously so that they can adjust instruction midcourse if necessary. Teachers also work toward helping students monitor and adjust their own learning. This, of course, is only possible when students are clear about learning outcomes from the start of instruction.

Another essential part of the assessment loop is feedback, which individualizes instruction and enables students to correct errors and advance understanding. Provided by peers or the teacher, effective feedback is accurate, constructive, substantive, specific, and timely.

SELF-ASSESSMENT

Assess your practice in Component 3d against the levels of performance below, then check the box that best matches the level of your own teaching for each element.

Component 3d: Using Assessment in Instruction				
	Level of Performance			
ELEMENT	UNSATISFACTORY	BASIC	PROFICIENT	DISTINGUISHED
Assessment criteria	Students are not aware of the criteria and performance standards by which their work will be evaluated.	Students know some of the criteria and performance standards by which their work will be evaluated.	Students are fully aware of the criteria and performance standards by which their work will be evaluated.	Students are fully aware of the criteria and performance standards by which their work will be evaluated and have contributed to the development of the criteria.
	☐	☐	☐	☐

Source: From *Enhancing Professional Practice: A Framework for Teaching, 2nd Edition* (p. 89), by C. Danielson, 2007, Alexandria, VA: ASCD. © 2007 by ASCD. Reprinted with permission.

Domain 3

Component 3d

ELEMENT	Level of Performance			
	UNSATISFACTORY	BASIC	PROFICIENT	DISTINGUISHED
Monitoring of student learning	Teacher does not monitor student learning in the curriculum.	Teacher monitors the progress of the class as a whole but elicits no diagnostic information.	Teacher monitors the progress of groups of students in the curriculum, making limited use of diagnostic prompts to elicit information.	Teacher actively and systematically elicits diagnostic information from individual students regarding their understanding and monitors the progress of individual students.
	☐	☐	☐	☐
Feedback to students	Teacher's feedback to students is of poor quality and not provided in a timely manner.	Teacher's feedback to students is uneven, and its timeliness is inconsistent.	Teacher's feedback to students is timely and of consistently high quality.	Teacher's feedback to students is timely and of consistently high quality, and students make use of the feedback in their learning.
	☐	☐	☐	☐
Student self-assessment and monitoring of progress	Students do not engage in self-assessment or monitoring of progress.	Students occasionally assess the quality of their own work against the assessment criteria and performance standards.	Students frequently assess and monitor the quality of their own work against the assessment criteria and performance standards.	Students not only frequently assess and monitor the quality of their own work against the assessment criteria and performance standards but also make active use of that information in their learning.
	☐	☐	☐	☐

Source: From *Enhancing Professional Practice: A Framework for Teaching, 2nd Edition* (p. 89), by C. Danielson, 2007, Alexandria, VA: ASCD. © 2007 by ASCD. Reprinted with permission.

Domain 3

Component 3d

As a result of this self-assessment, on which element will you focus first? Turn to the pages following to explore the elements of the component in detail. After you've reviewed the tools, you can use the Action Planning and Reflection form to document the results of implementing the strategies in your classroom.

Domain 3

Element

Assessment Criteria

Description

For teachers to incorporate assessment strategies into their teaching and for students to monitor their own learning, students must know the criteria for assessment. At the highest level of performance, students themselves have a hand in articulating criteria.

A Closer Look

To help you recognize the subtle differences between the higher levels of performance for this element, note the keywords emphasized in the descriptions and review the activities common to those levels.

PROFICIENT

Students are *fully aware* of the criteria and performance standards by which their work will be evaluated.

At the proficient level of performance, teaching practices may include the following types of activities:

- Teacher writes and speaks the learning criteria, then asks nonvolunteer students to explain the criteria in their own words before students begin the learning and frequently throughout the learning.
- Teacher provides examples and models that embody the criteria and performance standards required of the students (exemplars) as well as poor examples (non-exemplars) so that students can see the difference.
- Any student in the class, when randomly questioned, can articulate the evaluative criteria and performance standards.
- During instruction, the teacher points out aspects of the instruction that connect to the performance standards and criteria.
- Teacher avoids competitive grading and enlists alternatives to letter grades, such as feedback only, or adaptations of letter grades, such as A/B/I (incomplete).
- Teacher makes explicit the relationship between assessment and grading (i.e., report card grades) as appropriate to the age-group, and students are able to explain to others when prompted.

DISTINGUISHED

Students are fully aware of the criteria and performance standards by which their work will be evaluated and have *contributed to the development* of the criteria.

At the distinguished level of performance, teaching practices may include the following types of activities:

- Teacher instructs students about the nature of assessment criteria in developmentally appropriate language.
- Teacher shares performance and content standards with students in student-friendly language, then thinks aloud about the criteria that would be related to these standards. The teacher writes the related criteria beneath the appropriate standard and repeats this process until students are ready to begin contributing ideas for the criteria that might be related to a given content standard.
- Students use the criteria they helped create to score a sample piece of student work.
- Students develop tests or test questions to deepen their understanding of content or topic.
- Teacher regularly indicates the portions of assessment criteria that students helped create.

The tools that follow will help you explore how to put the activities of these high levels of performance into practice in your classroom.

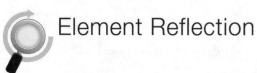

Element Reflection

✔ **Teacher tool**   __ **Student tool**

1. Why is it important for students to understand the assessment criteria you will use to evaluate their work?

2. What are the advantages of students helping design assessment rubrics? What are the challenges?

Domain 3

Rubrics for Providing Feedback on Oral Presentations

✔ **Teacher tool**   ✔ **Student tool**

After devoting energy to their presentations, students typically expect thorough feedback. By using a rubric, you use the same, clear standards for evaluating all students, and students can be familiar with the evaluation criteria if you review it in class before they begin preparing their presentations. Better yet, have students help you design the rubric.

During the presentation, collect actual evidence of what you see and hear on the rubric document. You can then circle or underline the statements on the rubric that match the evidence you collected. After the presentation, have the presenter use the rubric as a self-assessment and turn it in to you before you complete yours. This will give you insight into the speaker's thinking.

Use the following rubrics or create your own. In designing the rubric, make sure to leave space to write comments and specific examples during the presentation itself.

ELEMENTARY RUBRIC

Criteria	Not OK	Could Be Better	Good	Best
Subject	No good ideas.	One or two good ideas.	Some good ideas.	Many good ideas.
Structure	No clear structure.	Beginning, middle, and end are clear sometimes.	Beginning, middle, and end can be recognized.	• Clear beginning, middle, and end. • Easy to understand.
Delivery	Delivery is poor in every way.	• Sometimes not easy to hear. • Too fast or too slow. • Several words pronounced incorrectly. • No expression.	• Mostly easy to hear. • Most words pronounced correctly. • Generally not too fast or too slow. • Some expression.	• Easy to hear. • Not too fast or slow. • Words pronounced correctly. • Lots of expression.

Domain 3

Criteria	Not OK	Could Be Better	Good	Best
Visual Effects	Uses no extras.	Uses few pictures, objects, or demonstrations.	Uses some pictures, objects, or demonstrations.	Uses multiple pictures, objects, or demonstrations appropriately.
Length of Presentation	Time off by 4 or more minutes.	3 minutes too short or too long.	2 minutes too short or too long.	Right on time.

SECONDARY RUBRIC

Criteria	Inadequate	Minimal	Adequate	Superior
Content	• Main focus on irrelevant content. • Knowledge of audience isn't considered.	• Some irrelevant content. • Deviates from topic. • Some vocabulary and concepts beyond the audience's scope of knowledge.	• Main focus on relevant content. • On topic. • Content generally adapted for the audience.	• All content relevant. • Multiple forms of evidence, such as details, generalizations, and examples. • Content personalized for the specific audience.
Organization	• Presentation disorganized. • Audience cannot follow the message.	• Presentation mixed up or random. • Audience must make some assumptions about how ideas are connected.	• Presentation organized. • Audience can follow the logic and sequence of ideas.	• Presentation very organized. • Clearly conveys logic and sequence of ideas.
Delivery	• Volume inappropriate. • Words unclear or pronounced incorrectly. • Presenter doesn't seem interested in the topic. • Body language distracts or sends message contradictory to delivery.	• Sometimes speaks too quietly or too loudly. • Speaks too quickly or too slowly. • Some words unclear or pronounced incorrectly. • Audience has trouble following the message. • Body language does not distract from delivery.	• Volume appropriate. • Speaks at appropriate pace. • Words pronounced clearly and correctly. • Uses body language as appropriate.	• Delivery is clear, calm, and energetic. • Intonation varies depending on the emphasis. • Words pronounced very clearly and correctly. • Uses body language to enhance delivery.

Domain 3

Assessment Criteria

Criteria	Inadequate	Minimal	Adequate	Superior
Visual Effects	• Repetitive with little or no variety. • Inadequate use of visual aids or media.	• Little or no variation. • Little originality or interpretation. • Minimal or no use of visual aids or media.	• Some originality. • Uses some visual aids or media.	• Very original. • Uses appropriate visual aids or media. • Secures the audience's attention.
Length of Presentation	Well outside the specified guidelines.	Too long or too short by a significant amount.	Just under or just over the specified guidelines.	Within the specified guidelines.

Source: Utah Education Network. *Oral presentation rubric.* Retrieved June 9, 2009, from http://www.uen.org/Rubric/rubric.cgi?rubric_id=19

Domain 3

Element

Monitoring of Student Learning

Description

A teacher's skill in eliciting evidence of student understanding is one of the true marks of expertise. Teachers must plan student assessment carefully in advance and then weave it into the lesson. Expert teachers do so seamlessly.

A Closer Look

To help you recognize the subtle differences between the higher levels of performance for this element, note the keywords emphasized in the descriptions and review the activities common to those levels.

PROFICIENT

The teacher monitors the progress of *groups of students* in the curriculum, making *limited* use of diagnostic prompts to elicit information.

At the proficient level of performance, teaching practices may include the following types of activities:

- Teacher asks diagnostic questions of the class and calls on volunteers to respond.
- Teacher occasionally uses strategies such as exit ticket summary statements to elicit information about student learning at the end of a lesson.
- Teacher sometimes uses reflective journal writing during a lesson to elicit information about student learning.
- Teacher identifies students making errors in homework and provides them with extra assistance based on their errors.
- Teacher notes students who, during instruction, seem to have the clearest grasp of the content and sometimes pairs them with those having difficulty.

DISTINGUISHED

The teacher *actively* and *systematically* elicits diagnostic information from *individual students* about their understanding and monitors the progress of individual students.

At the distinguished level of performance, teaching practices may include the following types of activities:

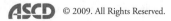

- Teacher regularly uses activities and questions specifically designed to reveal students' understanding of the lesson goals. The teacher analyzes these for patterns of understanding, both by groups and for individuals.
- Teacher can state accurately which students are struggling with which aspects of a lesson's goals, the evidence that confirms this understanding, and how to adjust instruction for them.
- Teacher asks *every student* diagnostic questions using various whole-class response methods to see at a glance which students do and do not understand.
- Teacher communicates information from formative assessment with the students, other teachers, or parents to help coordinate the next instructional steps.

The tools that follow will help you explore how to put the activities of these high levels of performance into practice in your classroom.

Domain 3

Element Reflection

✔ Teacher tool   **__ Student tool**

1. During a lesson, what sources of evidence do you have of the extent of students' understanding of content?

2. For a lesson you will be teaching soon, what are some questions you could pose to all students simultaneously during the lesson that would provide you with information about students' level of understanding?

Domain 3

Strategies for Monitoring Student Learning During Instruction

✔ **Teacher tool**   __ **Student tool**

To elicit specific information about student learning from whole-class responses, try incorporating the following strategies into your lesson. Then look for patterns of understanding within the class and adjust instruction accordingly based on individual responses. If you map out possible instructional adjustments ahead of time, you can easily shift gears during the lesson to increase understanding.

For each strategy, plan how you can modify your instruction if students indicate a lack of understanding. Then reflect on how well the strategy worked in your class and what adjustments, if any, you will make in using that strategy in the future.

Lesson:

Diagnostic Prompt	Lesson Adjustments if Responses Show Lack of Understanding	Notes for the Future
Two-Sided Answer Cards Each student has a card with the word "True" or "Yes" printed on one side and "False" or "No" printed on the other. (The card can have green on one side and red on the other for nonreaders.) The teacher poses a series of carefully constructed questions, and each student holds up the card to show the answer.		
A-B-C-D Cards Each student receives four cards, labeled A, B, C, and D. The teacher displays a multiple-choice question, and every student holds up the letter card that corresponds with their answer. Questions should have two incorrect responses, one correct response, and one nearly correct answer that represents a typical misconception about the content.		

Domain 3

Diagnostic Prompt	Lesson Adjustments if Responses Show Lack of Understanding	Notes for the Future
Sticky Response Midway through the lesson, the teacher asks each student to respond to one or two pivotal questions with a phrase or short sentence on a sticky note. The teacher can scan the answers during the next portion of the lesson.		
Thumbs Up, Down, or Sideways The teacher asks yes-or-no questions, and students answer yes with a thumbs-up, no with a thumbs-down, and unsure with their thumbs sideways.		

Domain 3

Structured Questioning Record

✔ **Teacher tool**   __ **Student tool**

During a discussion, you can elicit diagnostic information about student learning with questions that are carefully constructed to reveal specific understandings. Pose the questions to the class, and select *nonvolunteers* to respond. Maintain a checklist of students who responded and whether their responses were correct or incorrect. For the incorrect responses, note on the checklist how you can adjust instruction accordingly.

Lesson: _____

Key: + = Student answered question correctly.

          − = Student answered question incorrectly.

Student	Question:	Revision for Incorrect Responses:	Question:	Revision for Incorrect Responses:

Domain 3

Using 2+2 Feedback and Exit Tickets

✔ **Teacher tool**   __ **Student tool**

After a lesson, student feedback on your approach to the content will help you gauge how well your teaching strategies worked and how you can modify your lesson plans for future instruction with this class. You can use this strategy with students in upper elementary through high school.

Have students write two compliments, or things that went well for them in the lesson and helped their understanding, and two suggestions, or things that could have improved the lesson or did not go well for them, on an exit ticket. A variation on the activity is having students write their comments on sticky notes and post them on a chart divided into a "compliments" column and a "suggestions" column.

Record the 2+2 responses and then brainstorm how you can modify your instruction to address the suggestions and continue to incorporate successful aspects of the compliments.

Student Compliment	How can I incorporate this in future lessons?

Source: Adapted from Allen, D., & LeBlanc, A. (2005). *Collaborative peer coaching that improves instruction: The 2+2 performance appraisal model.* Thousand Oaks, CA: Corwin Press.

Domain 3

Element

Feedback to Students

Description

Feedback on learning is an essential element of a rich instructional environment. Without it, students have to guess at how they are doing and how to improve their work. Valuable feedback should be timely, constructive, substantive, accurate, and specific.

A Closer Look

To help you recognize the subtle differences between the higher levels of performance for this element, note the keywords emphasized in the descriptions and review the activities common to those levels.

PROFICIENT

The teacher's feedback to students is *timely* and of *consistently high quality*.

At the distinguished level of performance, teaching practices may include the following types of activities:

- Teacher provides feedback in writing, orally, and through modeling.
- Teacher invites students to summarize the feedback in their own words.
- Students can articulate the strengths and weaknesses or errors in their learning based on the feedback.
- Teacher uses developmentally appropriate language when giving feedback.
- Teacher reflects periodically on the quality of feedback to ensure that it is substantive, constructive, accurate, and specific.

DISTINGUISHED

The teacher's feedback to students is timely and of consistently high quality. *Students use feedback* in their learning.

At the distinguished level of performance, teaching practices may include the following types of activities:

- Teacher regularly provides a variety of feedback, including written, verbal, and modeling, to all students and individualizes the type of feedback according to the needs of the student.

- All feedback specifies the strengths and weaknesses or errors and how to improve.
- Teacher keeps track of the feedback and follows up to ensure that students are using the feedback to advance their learning. If students are not using the feedback, the teacher investigates how to improve feedback to make it more useful.
- Teacher notes when and where students use feedback in their learning and reinforces their doing so.
- Students are able to articulate how they used feedback in their learning or their work.

The tools that follow will help you explore how to put the activities of these high levels of performance into practice in your classroom.

Domain 3

Element Reflection

✔ **Teacher tool**   __ **Student tool**

1. Feedback to students should be timely. What would you consider "timely"? How does it change depending on the grade level or the subject?

2. How can you encourage students to use feedback from you or from other students in their learning?

Domain 3

Am I Giving Good Feedback?

✔ **Teacher tool**   __ **Student tool**

Use the following guidelines to periodically assess the feedback you give students.

Qualities of Feedback	Recommendations	How effective is my feedback? How can I improve it?
Timely Points to Consider: • When to give feedback. • How often to give feedback.	• Give feedback as often as possible. • Immediate feedback is usually best. • Feedback should drive learning and be useful to the student.	
Accurate Points to Consider: • Teachers must know content to give accurate feedback. • A climate of safety is important so that students understand that making mistakes is part of learning.	• Find and point out errors in students' responses, both written and oral. • For written work, don't point out every error of the same type. Once you have pointed out an error and explained why it's wrong, have the student locate other instances of the same problem.	
Mode Point to Consider: • Feedback can be written, oral, or by demonstration.	• Don't write paragraphs if a quick comment will do. • Give written feedback on written work.	
Substantive Points to Consider: • Feedback should fully inform the student about the strengths and weaknesses of the work or the thinking. • Feedback should be focused and strategic.	• Be sure to explain when students ask why. • Don't give too much or too little feedback. Too much feedback can overwhelm, while not enough prevents learning. • Don't try to give feedback about everything. Decide in advance what aspects of the work you will focus on and then limit yourself to commenting on those items. Let students know which aspects you will focus on.	

Domain 3

Feedback to Students

Qualities of Feedback	Recommendations	How effective is my feedback? How can I improve it?
Constructive Point to Consider: • Good feedback improves learning.	• Be sure feedback tells students what they did well and what they need to do next to improve. • Follow up to see whether students are using your feedback. Is their learning improving? • See if students can articulate in their own words exactly how to improve their learning, based on the feedback.	
Specific Points to Consider: • Encouragement is not feedback. • Feedback tells a student exactly what was right and wrong. • Focus feedback on the topic.	• Question individuals to see if they understand your feedback in the way you intended. • Choose words that position the student as the doer in the next steps that should result from feedback.	

Domain 3

Element

Student Self-Assessment
and Monitoring of Progress

Description

The mark of when students have assumed responsibility for their learning is when they monitor their own learning and take appropriate action. They can only do this if the criteria for learning are clear and if they have been taught how to self-monitor progress.

A Closer Look

To help you recognize the subtle differences between the higher levels of performance for this element, note the keywords emphasized in the descriptions and review the activities common to those levels.

PROFICIENT

Students *frequently* assess and monitor the *quality of their own work* against the assessment criteria and performance standards.

At the proficient level of performance, teaching practices may include the following types of activities:

- Teacher gives students rubrics at the start of a learning sequence. Together they discuss the rubric and generate a few examples.
- Students work in groups to translate the rubrics into their own language, or the teacher initially presents the rubric in "kid language."
- Teacher refers to the rubric frequently during instruction, showing students how the rubric reflects the important learning.
- Teacher provides examples of the rubric product at various levels of performance so that students understand the difference between the lower and higher levels.
- Students formatively assess their own work, and the teacher provides feedback about their accuracy.
- Students discuss their self-assessments and each other's assessments, comparing them for greater accuracy.

DISTINGUISHED

Students frequently assess and monitor the quality of their own work against the assessment criteria and performance standards, and they also *actively use* that information in their learning.

At the distinguished level of performance, teaching practices may include the following types of activities:

- Students make corrections to their own work following their self-assessments.
- Students can articulate the specific learning they acquired through self-assessment.
- Students can express to parents or teachers how later versions of their work have improved from first versions.
- Students keep records of their own performance on assessments and reflect on these, noting growth and patterns within the learning.
- Students analyze their performance on a test, noting errors and suggesting ways to improve their learning.

The tools that follow will help you explore how to put the activities of these high levels of performance into practice in your classroom.

Domain 3

Student Self-Assessment and Monitoring of Progress

Element Reflection

✔ **Teacher tool** ___ **Student tool**

1. How do you involve students in assessing their own work against specific criteria? How could you increase this practice?

2. What do students need to learn to accurately assess their own work against provided criteria?

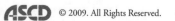

Student Self-Reflection on Learning

✔ Teacher tool   __ **Student tool**

To help students build awareness of their own learning and become comfortable monitoring their own progress, you can scaffold their learning with prompts and questions.

After a lesson, post the following questions or prompts on an overhead, a PowerPoint slide, whiteboard, or blackboard. Have students respond on index cards or in journals. You can then collect and analyze their comments and provide group or individual feedback.

REFLECTION QUESTIONS FOR STUDENTS

- What two new things have I learned about _____ today?

- What do I still want to know about _____ ?

- What do I still want to find out more about _____?

- I struggled with _____ in today's lesson.

- I found _____ to be easy in today's lesson.

- I already knew _____ about the subject of today's lesson.

PROMPTS FOR STUDENTS

- As I consider this lesson today…

- I think today's lesson was challenging because…

- I feel successful with today's learning because…

- I will use this learning in the future to…

- Today's lesson is important because…

Action Planning and Reflection

✔ **Teacher tool**   __ **Student tool**

Look over the tools for this component and choose a strategy or strategies that you are committed to trying in your classroom. Then return to this page and record what happened. If there was a change, what evidence indicates the extent to which this strategy was successful? Finally, think about what you might do differently to continue to bring about further growth in this component.

What will I try?	How did it go?	What will I do differently next time?

Domain 3

Component 3e

Demonstrating Flexibility and Responsiveness

OVERVIEW

Even the most carefully designed lesson occasionally requires midcourse correction, and it takes considerable skill to be able to move to plan B on short notice. Teachers must be attuned to their students and their learning, which closely relates to Component 3d: Using Assessment in Instruction. There are three types of situations that call for flexibility of teaching:

1. An activity is not working procedurally.
2. A spontaneous event presents an opportunity for valuable learning.
3. One or more students have difficulty learning the desired content.

In each of these situations, the teacher must make decisions during instruction to make the experience more valuable for students by drawing on a repertoire of alternative activities or strategies and rapidly implementing one or more. To pull it off, teachers need courage and confidence, both of which come from experience. This kind of instructional flexibility is more difficult for novices, who by definition have fewer tools in their teaching toolbox.

SELF-ASSESSMENT

Assess your practice in Component 3e against the levels of performance below, then check the box that best matches the level of your own teaching for each element.

Component 3e: Demonstrating Flexibility and Responsiveness				
	Level of Performance			
ELEMENT	UNSATISFACTORY	BASIC	PROFICIENT	DISTINGUISHED
Lesson adjustment	Teacher adheres rigidly to an instructional plan, even when a change is clearly needed. ☐	Teacher attempts to adjust a lesson when needed, with only partially successful results. ☐	Teacher makes a minor adjustment to a lesson, and the adjustment occurs smoothly. ☐	Teacher successfully makes a major adjustment to a lesson when needed. ☐

Source: From *Enhancing Professional Practice: A Framework for Teaching, 2nd Edition* (p. 91), by C. Danielson, 2007, Alexandria, VA: ASCD. © 2007 by ASCD. Reprinted with permission.

Domain 3

	Level of Performance			
ELEMENT	UNSATISFACTORY	BASIC	PROFICIENT	DISTINGUISHED
Response to students	Teacher ignores or brushes aside students' questions or interests. ☐	Teacher attempts to accommodate students' questions or interests, although the pacing of the lesson is disrupted. ☐	Teacher successfully accommodates students' questions or interests. ☐	Teacher seizes a major opportunity to enhance learning, building on student interests or a spontaneous event. ☐
Persistence	When a student has difficulty learning, the teacher either gives up or blames the student or the student's home environment. ☐	Teacher accepts responsibility for the success of all students but has only a limited repertoire of instructional strategies to draw on. ☐	Teacher persists in seeking approaches for students who have difficulty learning, drawing on a broad repertoire of strategies. ☐	Teacher persists in seeking effective approaches for students who need help, using an extensive repertoire of strategies and soliciting additional resources from the school. ☐

Source: From *Enhancing Professional Practice: A Framework for Teaching, 2nd Edition* (p. 91), by C. Danielson, 2007, Alexandria, VA: ASCD. © 2007 by ASCD. Reprinted with permission.

As a result of this self-assessment, on which element will you focus first? Turn to the pages following to explore the elements of the component in detail. After you've reviewed the tools, you can use the Action Planning and Reflection form to document the results of implementing the strategies in your classroom.

Element

Lesson Adjustment

Description

Experienced teachers are able to make both minor and major adjustments to a lesson during instruction, if necessary. Such adjustments depend on a teacher's store of alternate instructional strategies and the confidence to make a shift when needed.

A Closer Look

To help you recognize the subtle differences between the higher levels of performance for this element, note the keywords emphasized in the descriptions and review the activities common to those levels.

PROFICIENT

The teacher makes a *minor* adjustment to the lesson, and the adjustment occurs *smoothly*.

At the proficient level of performance, teaching practices may include the following types of activities:

- Teacher continuously uses whole-class assessment techniques (see Component 3d on page 331) to understand who is and is not learning and why.
- Teacher identifies the aspects of a lesson that are likely to cause confusion and plans for alternative approaches in advance.
- When making a minor lesson adjustment, the teacher lets students know about it and solicits their feedback about how it's working.
- Teachable moments are always connected to content standards and learning objectives.
- During instruction, teacher regularly prompts for student interests that relate to the content.

DISTINGUISHED

The teacher successfully makes a *major adjustment* to a lesson when needed.

At the distinguished level of performance, teaching practices may include the following types of activities:

- Teacher accurately diagnoses difficulties with the lesson based on regular, whole-class assessment.

Domain 3

- Teacher identifies likely content and activity challenges in the original lesson and designs a second lesson that avoids those challenges. If an informal assessment reveals student difficulties, the teacher implements the backup lesson.
- Teacher accurately weighs the value of implementing a major adjustment against the loss of the planned instruction.
- Teacher reveals to students the reasons for making a major lesson change and gets their feedback about its success.
- The teacher invites students to connect a teachable moment to the appropriate content standard or learning objective.
- When students have difficulties with the lesson, the teacher probes them for additional information so that the lesson adjustment accurately addresses the problem.

The tools that follow will help you explore how to put the activities of these high levels of performance into practice in your classroom.

Lesson Adjustment

Element Reflection

✔ **Teacher tool**   __ **Student tool**

1. During a lesson, what indicates that you need to make an adjustment?

2. How effective are your lesson adjustments? How do you know?

Domain 3

Action Flow Lesson Plan ✔ **Teacher tool**   __ **Student tool**

By anticipating areas where students may have problems understanding, you can increase your flexibility and responsiveness by planning adjustments such as reteaching or increasing or decreasing the pace.

Study the lesson plan flow chart below and note how it plans for the possible difficulties of confusion or low understanding. Then plan an action flow lesson of your own.

SAMPLE ACTION FLOW LESSON

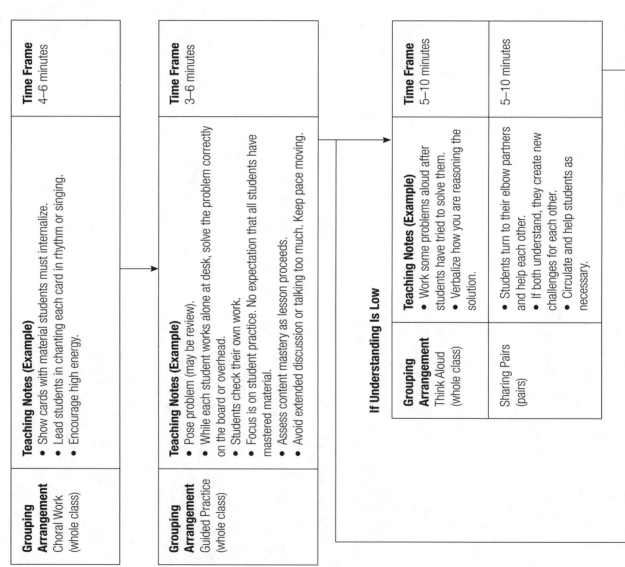

Grouping Arrangement	Teaching Notes (Example)	Time Frame
Choral Work (whole class)	• Show cards with material students must internalize. • Lead students in chanting each card in rhythm or singing. • Encourage high energy.	4–6 minutes

Grouping Arrangement	Teaching Notes (Example)	Time Frame
Guided Practice (whole class)	• Pose problem (may be review). • While each student works alone at desk, solve the problem correctly on the board or overhead. • Students check their own work. • Focus is on student practice. No expectation that all students have mastered material. • Assess content mastery as lesson proceeds. • Avoid extended discussion or talking too much. Keep pace moving.	3–6 minutes

If Understanding Is Low

Grouping Arrangement	Teaching Notes (Example)	Time Frame
Think Aloud (whole class)	• Work some problems aloud after students have tried to solve them. • Verbalize how you are reasoning the solution.	5–10 minutes
Sharing Pairs (pairs)	• Students turn to their elbow partners and help each other. • If both understand, they create new challenges for each other. • Circulate and help students as necessary.	5–10 minutes

Lesson Adjustment

If Understanding Is High

Grouping Arrangement	Teaching Notes (Example)	Time Frame
Think Aloud (whole class)	• Introduce easy example of new problem, thinking aloud when working on the board or overhead. • Pose similar problem for students to try by themselves. • Work the problem on board, again thinking aloud. • Pose a slightly harder problem, let them try it, then invite a student to show the solution on board. • Continue at comfortable pace, and move on before interest lags.	6–12 minutes

Grouping Arrangement	Teaching Notes (Example)	Time Frame
Review, Test (whole class)	• Write problem on board. • Pause to let students begin working and check that they are. • Work the problem correctly on the board, and students correct their own work. • Proceed through set of problems. • Avoid giving instruction on how to solve problems. • Focus is on review, self-correction, and personal challenge. • Pace is sufficiently brisk to maximize student involvement.	4–8 minutes

Grouping Arrangement	Teaching Notes (Example)	Time Frame
Voting Strategy (whole class)	• Give students a few moments to assess their learning process or learning outcomes and to express themselves. • Ask how many took risks on today's review, how many strengthened old understandings, how many like the way they handled today's test. • Students respond by raising their hands or thumbs-up, thumbs-down. • Use information to plan for following lesson.	1–2 minutes

Source: Harmin, M. (1994). *Inspiring active learning: A handbook for teachers.* Alexandria, VA: ASCD.

Domain 3

Element

Response to Students

Description

Occasionally during a lesson an unexpected event will present a true teachable moment. A skilled teacher can capitalize on such opportunities.

A Closer Look

To help you recognize the subtle differences between the higher levels of performance for this element, note the keywords emphasized in the descriptions and review the activities common to those levels.

PROFICIENT

The teacher *successfully accommodates* students' questions or interests.

At the proficient level of performance, teaching practices may include the following types of activities:

- Teacher regularly uses strategies that elicit student questions about the lesson topic.

- Teacher decides whether to answer student questions during the lesson or at a later time, depending on the appropriateness of the question and the teacher's knowledge of the content.

- Teacher identifies related student interests, through such strategies as KWL, and incorporates them into the lesson plan.

DISTINGUISHED

The teacher seizes a *major opportunity* to enhance learning, building on *student interest* or a *spontaneous event*.

At the distinguished level of performance, teaching practices may include the following types of activities:

- Teacher regularly surveys students about their interests (see Component 1b on page 41) to get to know students well and builds on interests if the opportunity arises.

Response to Students

- Teacher realizes that every spontaneous event is not a major opportunity, which is defined as an event or student interest that can be incorporated to make the content standard or learning objective more effective and relevant.
- Teacher uses questioning strategies designed to elicit student interests as they relate to the content standard.
- Teacher is aware of the content standards of the past, present, and future and can seize interests and events to relate them to the standard or objective being explored currently as well as to those that have already been explored or will be explored in the future.

The tools that follow will help you explore how to put the activities of these high levels of performance into practice in your classroom.

Domain 3

 Element Reflection

✔ **Teacher tool** ___ **Student tool**

1. How do you determine whether to follow up on a student's interest during a lesson?

2. What is the best response when a student asks a question during a lesson, particularly when it is irrelevant to the topic at hand?

Domain 3

KWL Teaching Strategy

__ **Teacher tool**   ✔ **Student tool**

KWL is a teaching strategy that helps students develop tactical ways to learn new material through questioning and finding information from reliable sources. This strategy can be effective in promoting independence in learning.

The role the teacher plays in the KWL process depends on the students' ages and stages of development. If you are using the model for the first time, you should direct the process and model the steps.

K = What Is Known According to Prior Knowledge

Using the KWL worksheet with your students, ask them what they already know about a given topic. Generate as many ideas about the topic as possible, relying on pupils' prior knowledge. As a class, categorize the information.

W = What Pupils Want to Learn

Have students formulate questions that they want to investigate that bring more meaning and clarity to the topic. Students may generate more questions as the lesson proceeds, and students look for answers through reading, researching, or collecting information from sources provided by the teacher or from sources students found independently.

L = What Pupils Learn After Instructional Events

Students categorize the new information they have learned and create statements about the topic, which they record on the chart. They can then present this information in a summary or outline (writing exercise) or with a graphic organizer (mapping or charts).

Domain 3

STUDENT KWL CHART

What do you already know about this topic?	What do you want to know about this topic?	What have you learned about this topic?

Domain 3

Element

Persistence

Description

When students have difficulty learning, committed teachers don't give up. They seek alternate approaches to help their students be successful, displaying a keen sense of efficacy.

A Closer Look

To help you recognize the subtle differences between the higher levels of performance for this element, note the keywords emphasized in the descriptions and review the activities common to those levels.

PROFICIENT

The teacher *persists* in seeking approaches for students who have difficulty learning, drawing on a *broad repertoire* of strategies.

At the proficient level of performance, teaching practices may include the following types of activities:

- Teacher identifies the students most at risk for learning difficulties in each lesson.
- Teacher surveys other teachers for ways to accommodate student learning difficulties.
- When students have difficulty learning, the teacher analyzes the reasons by asking the student and considering the nature of the lesson tasks, drawing accurate, insightful conclusions about the source of the problem.
- Teacher uses multiple sources, including Web-based resources, classroom-based resources, and other teachers, to design alternative approaches for students having difficulty.

DISTINGUISHED

The teacher persists in seeking effective approaches for students who need help, using an *extensive repertoire* of strategies and *soliciting additional resources* from the school.

At the distinguished level of performance, teaching practices may include the following types of activities:

Persistence

- Teacher seeks assistance from guidance counselors, school psychologists, and other non-classroom specialists for students who may benefit from these services.
- Teacher frequently seeks approaches and strategies for students from other teachers.
- Teacher analyzes strategies for struggling learners that were unsuccessful, accurately determining the reasons they did not work.
- When the teacher is uncertain about the reasons for students' lack of success, the teacher elicits family input or colleague observations and analysis.
- The teacher takes personal responsibility for the learning of every student, regardless of the challenges involved in teaching them.

The tools that follow will help you explore how to put the activities of these high levels of performance into practice in your classroom.

Domain 3

Persistence

Element Reflection

✔ **Teacher tool**   __ **Student tool**

1. When students are having difficulty, how do you find other approaches to assist you?

2. How do you support and guide students so that they want to stick with tasks and want to improve their performance?

Domain 3

□ 371

Teacher Peer Observation Record Form

✔ **Teacher tool**   __ **Student tool**

Teachers can learn much from observing other teachers—and from hearing feedback from colleagues who observe them. Schedule a monthly cross-observation with another teacher in the school to identify each other's effective persistence with struggling learners. The two of you should agree on an objective for the observation beforehand and follow it up with a conversation in which you document your learning on the peer observation sheet. During team meetings, share what you have learned from cross-observations with the group.

Date: _____

Teacher Observing: _____

Teacher Being Observed: _____

1. Objective of Observation (What do I hope to learn about engaging the struggling learner by observing?)

2. What did I see/hear from the observed teacher that I can apply in my practice to more effectively engage struggling learners?

3. What will I change about my practice as a result of what I saw and heard today?

Domain 3

Component 3e

Action Planning and Reflection

✔ **Teacher tool** ___ **Student tool**

Look over the tools for this component and choose a strategy or strategies that you are committed to trying in your classroom. Then return to this page and record what happened. If there was a change, what evidence indicates the extent to which this strategy was successful? Finally, think about what you might do differently to continue to bring about further growth in this component.

What will I try?	How did it go?	What will I do differently next time?

Domain 3

Domain 4

Professional Responsibilities

Professional Responsibilities

The components of Domain 4 are associated with being a true professional educator, encompassing the roles that teachers assume in addition to the ones they have in the classroom with students. Although students rarely notice these activities, and parents and the larger community see them only intermittently, they are vital to preserving and enhancing the profession. Educators begin some of these activities, such as maintaining records and communicating with families, as soon as they enter the profession because they are integral to their work with students. Teachers develop other activities, such as participating in a professional community, after their first few years of teaching once they've mastered, to some degree, the details of classroom management and instruction.

The work of professional educators manifestly extends beyond their work in the classroom, and participation in these activities is what separates highly professional educators from their less proficient colleagues. When teachers present evidence of their work in this area—through logs, summaries of their work on school and district committees, or descriptions of workshops for parents—they are frequently surprised and impressed by the extent of their professional engagement.

Based on the results of the self-assessment you took in the introduction (see page 7), turn to the page of the component on which you will focus first. Each of the following sections explores the elements of these components in detail and includes tools that you can use in your professional practice.

Component 4a

Reflecting on Teaching

OVERVIEW

Reflecting on teaching encompasses the teacher's thinking after any instructional event, including planning, implementation, assessment, and follow-up to instruction. By considering how these elements affected learning, teachers can determine where to make revisions and what aspects of the process they will continue in future lessons.

Teachers may reflect on their practice independently or through collegial conversations, journal writing, examining student work, informal observations, and conversations with students. Furthermore, teachers must learn how to reflect with accuracy and specificity and how to apply that learning to future teaching. Through supportive and deep questioning, mentors, coaches, and supervisors can help teachers acquire and develop the skill of reflecting on teaching. Over time, this way of thinking and analyzing instruction through the lens of student learning becomes a habit of mind, which in turn leads to improved teaching and learning.

SELF-ASSESSMENT

Assess your practice in Component 4a against the levels of performance below, then check the box that best matches the level of your own teaching for each element.

Component 4a

	Component 4a: Reflecting on Teaching			
	Level of Performance			
ELEMENT	UNSATISFACTORY	BASIC	PROFICIENT	DISTINGUISHED
Accuracy	Teacher does not know whether a lesson was effective or achieved its instructional outcomes, or teacher profoundly misjudges the success of a lesson. ☐	Teacher has a generally accurate impression of a lesson's effectiveness and the extent to which instructional outcomes were met. ☐	Teacher makes an accurate assessment of a lesson's effectiveness and the extent to which it achieved its instructional outcomes and can cite general references to support the judgment. ☐	Teacher makes a thoughtful and accurate assessment of a lesson's effectiveness and the extent to which it achieved its instructional outcomes, citing many specific examples from the lesson and weighing the relative strengths of each. ☐
Use in future teaching	Teacher has no suggestions for how a lesson could be improved another time the lesson is taught. ☐	Teacher makes general suggestions about how a lesson could be improved another time the lesson is taught. ☐	Teacher makes a few specific suggestions of what could be tried another time the lesson is taught. ☐	Drawing on an extensive repertoire of skills, teacher offers specific alternative actions, complete with the probable success of different courses of action. ☐

Source: From *Enhancing Professional Practice: A Framework for Teaching, 2nd Edition* (p. 94), by C. Danielson, 2007, Alexandria, VA: ASCD. © 2007 by ASCD. Reprinted with permission.

As a result of this self-assessment, on which element will you focus first? Turn to the pages following to explore the elements of the component in detail. After you've reviewed the tools, you can use the Action Planning and Reflection form to document the results of implementing the strategies in your classroom.

Element

Accuracy

Description

As teachers gain experience, their reflections on practice become more accurate. Teachers can also provide specific examples from the lesson to support their judgments.

A Closer Look

To help you recognize the subtle differences between the higher levels of performance for this element, note the keywords emphasized in the descriptions and review the activities common to those levels.

PROFICIENT

The teacher makes an *accurate assessment* of a lesson's effectiveness and the extent to which it achieved its instructional outcomes and can cite *general* references to support the judgment.

At the proficient level of performance, teaching practices may include the following types of activities:

- Teacher assesses the results of instructional activities and determines whether, in general, they were effective in achieving the desired outcomes.
- Teacher assesses the quality of the questions asked during the lesson by citing several examples of responses that indicate student understanding.
- Teacher uses a journal to reflect on student behavior during instruction, identifying students' actions toward one another during various points of the lesson.
- Teacher reflects on the effectiveness of instructional groups by noting students' participation, conversations, and behavior.
- Teacher completes a reflection form with accurate responses about the lesson.

DISTINGUISHED

The teacher makes a *thoughtful* and *accurate* assessment of a lesson's effectiveness and the extent to which it achieved its instructional outcomes, citing *many specific* examples from the lesson and *weighing the relative strengths* of each.

At the distinguished level of performance, teaching practices may include the following types of activities:

Domain 4

380

Accuracy

- Teacher prompts students to reflect on what they've learned during the lesson and uses these reflections to assess the lesson's effectiveness.
- Teacher identifies specific learning standards that students mastered and those that will need to be reinforced with additional instruction and practice.
- Teacher reflects on the effectiveness of instructional groups by assigning student monitors in each group to collect data about the participation of each group member. In addition, all students participate in a reflection activity in which they make connections between group participation and learning.
- Teacher reflects on a component of the lesson by reviewing evidence collected by a peer or supervisor and then using the rubric for that component to self-assess based on the evidence. The teacher cites specific examples to support the rubric language.
- At the end of the lesson, students complete an entry in their learning log, which the teacher uses to assess the overall effectiveness of the lesson.

The tools that follow will help you explore how to put the activities of these high levels of performance into practice in your classroom.

Element Reflection

 ✔ **Teacher tool** ____ **Student tool**

1. Under what conditions might you make an inaccurate assessment of the success of a lesson?

2. What resources can you draw on to locate specific strategies to improve a lesson?

Accuracy

Lesson Reflection Questionnaire

✔ **Teacher tool** ___ **Student tool**

1. Compare your expectations for the lesson with how it actually went.

2. To what extent did you meet the instructional goals? What is the evidence of this?

3. What were the similarities and differences between what you had planned and what actually happened?

4. Did you make any modifications to your plan during the lesson?

☐ 383

Domain 4

5. Describe any changes you would make if you were to teach this lesson again to the same group of students.

6. The next time you teach this lesson, what are some of the outcomes you would want to happen again?

7. Think about the results you got. How did the way you designed the lesson help yield those results?

8. Did this lesson reveal any aspects of your practice that would benefit from focused professional development?

Accuracy

Analyzing the Effectiveness of an Activity or Assignment

✔ **Teacher tool**   __ **Student tool**

Collect several samples of student work in response to an activity or assignment—home-work, a worksheet, project guidelines, or a problem to solve—that reflect the full range of student ability. Also gather any feedback you offered to students on their work. Answer the following questions to help you analyze the effectiveness of the assignment or activity.

1. What is the concept you intended your students to learn or explore?

2. How does this assignment fit with the prior and future learning of the class?

3. Why did you decide to organize the assignment in this manner? That is, how does this approach advance student understanding?

4. Consider the student work, both of the class as a whole and of those for whom you have samples. What does it tell you about their level of understanding? What does it say about their perseverance?

5. If you had the opportunity to make this same assignment again, would you do it in the same way? If you would alter it, explain why.

6. Given the student work, what do you plan to do next with these students?

Domain 4

Learning Logs

__ **Teacher tool**   ✔ **Student tool**

Student responses in learning logs reveal important information about their learning and the effectiveness of the lesson presented. Students can volunteer to share an idea from their learning logs. On some days, teachers should read all student learning log entries to determine if students understand a new concept. Occasionally, students can use their learning logs to do a think-pair-share activity.

BEFORE INSTRUCTION

Ask students to write about the previous day's lesson, a concept that they are having difficulty with, or an idea or question that comes to mind about their learning. Consider using the following prompts.

- Choose a word from the board and explain this term or concept in your learning log.

- Think about the essential question on the board. Respond to the question in your learning log. Example: Based on our understanding of _____, what connections can we make to our own lives?

- Develop and write two questions that can be answered based on last night's homework.

AFTER A LESSON

Ask students to list facts that they learned or explain the day's activities. They could also write questions, problems, concerns, feelings, observations, or personal connections about the day's lesson. Consider using the following prompts.

- Summarize what you learned about _____.

- What questions do you still have?

- What would you like to know more about?

- Give two examples of _____.

- How did you contribute to the group activity today?

- How did the group's participation contribute to your learning today?

- Do you learn best on your own or with others? How do you know?

- What aspects of today's lesson supported your learning?

- What aspects of today's lesson interfered with your learning?

- Develop a question about today's lesson, and trade your question with a partner. Write down answers or comments about your partner's question.

Element

Use in Future Teaching

Description

For reflections to be useful, teachers must use them to make adjustments to their practice. As their experience and expertise increases, teachers draw on an ever-increasing repertoire of strategies to inform these plans.

A Closer Look

To help you recognize the subtle differences between the higher levels of performance for this element, note the keywords emphasized in the descriptions and review the activities common to those levels.

PROFICIENT

The teacher makes a *few specific* suggestions about what to try another time when teaching the lesson.

At the proficient level of performance, teaching practices may include the following types of activities:

- Based on a reflection of the rubric language and supporting evidence for a chosen component of the framework for teaching, the teacher identifies specific ways to improve instruction.
- The teacher plans to modify a worksheet, which students found confusing.
- During a post-observation conference, the teacher decides to redesign the lesson so that students are in smaller groups to allow for greater participation and engagement by all students.

DISTINGUISHED

Drawing on an *extensive repertoire* of skills, the teacher offers *specific alternative* actions, complete with the *probable success* of different courses of action.

At the distinguished level of performance, teaching practices may include the following types of activities:

- The teacher provides several alternative resources for students, including options for students of varying levels of readiness and learning style.

Domain 4

Use in Future Teaching

- Based on entries students have made in their learning logs, the teacher regroups students for the next lesson according to their areas of interest in the topic.
- After examining samples of student writing, the teacher develops a series of minilessons, sequenced and differentiated according to the needs indicated by the students' work.

The tools that follow will help you explore how to put the activities of these high levels of performance into practice in your classroom.

Element Reflection

✔ **Teacher tool**   __ **Student tool**

1. What obstacles do you encounter in using the results of your reflections to plan future lessons?

2. How can your colleagues help you analyze your lessons and plan future instruction?

Assessing Specific Aspects of a Lesson

✔ **Teacher tool**   __ **Student tool**

After a lesson, use this template to analyze the individual parts of the lesson to determine what was successful, what you may need to adjust, and whether students would benefit from any adjustments.

Item	How successful was it? Not ← → Highly 1 2 3 4 5 6 7 8 9 10	How do you know? (What evidence do you have?)	What could I have done differently?	Why might this be better for at least some students?
Instructional Goals				
Activities				
Materials Used				
Grouping of Students				
Pace of the Lesson				

Use in Future Teaching

Reflecting on Professional Reading

✔ **Teacher tool**   __ **Student tool**

As part of a study group, assigned professional reading, or individual professional reading, use the six sentence stems below to reflect on what you learned from your professional reading and how your learning is connected to your own thinking.

Name: _____

Professional Reading:

Author(s): _____

Date(s) Read: _____

1. The quotes that really struck me are…

2. What I learned has implications for me because…

3. I wonder…

4. This information connects with what I already knew because…

5. To summarize, I learned…

6. I could use this new learning to…

Source: Gianakouros, K. (n.d.). *Reflecting on my professional reading.* (Available from Clarkstown Central School District, 62 Middletown Road, New City, New York 10956) Adapted with permission.

Action Planning and Reflection

✔ Teacher tool   **__ Student tool**

Look over the tools for this component and choose a strategy or strategies that you are committed to trying in your classroom. Then return to this page and record what happened. If there was a change, what evidence indicates the extent to which this strategy was successful? Finally, think about what you might do differently to continue to bring about further growth in this component.

What will I try?	How did it go?	What will I do differently next time?

Component 4b

Maintaining Accurate Records

OVERVIEW

One of the indispensable responsibilities of professional educators is keeping accurate records of both instructional and noninstructional events. This includes student completion of assignments, student progress in learning, and records of noninstructional activities that are part of the day-to-day functions in a school. These records inform teachers' interactions with students and parents and allow teachers to monitor learning and adjust instruction accordingly, so it's important for teachers to be proficient in their record keeping.

The methods of keeping records vary as much as the type of information being recorded. For example, records of formal assessments may be electronic spreadsheets or databases, which allow teachers to analyze items and individualize instruction. Less formal means of keeping track of student progress may include anecdotal notes that are kept in student folders. Whatever the strategy, experienced teachers have established routines that allow record keeping to be smooth and efficient.

SELF-ASSESSMENT

Assess your practice in Component 4b against the levels of performance below, then check the box that best matches the level of your own teaching for each element.

Component 4b: Maintaining Accurate Records				
	Level of Performance			
ELEMENT	UNSATISFACTORY	BASIC	PROFICIENT	DISTINGUISHED
Student completion of assignments	Teacher's system for maintaining information on student completion of assignments is in disarray.	Teacher's system for maintaining information on student completion of assignments is rudimentary and only partially effective.	Teacher's system for maintaining information on student completion of assignments is fully effective.	Teacher's system for maintaining information on student completion of assignments is fully effective. Students participate in maintaining the records.
	☐	☐	☐	☐

Source: From *Enhancing Professional Practice: A Framework for Teaching, 2nd Edition* (p. 97), by C. Danielson, 2007, Alexandria, VA: ASCD. © 2007 by ASCD. Reprinted with permission.

Domain 4

Component 4b

ELEMENT	Level of Performance			
	UNSATISFACTORY	BASIC	PROFICIENT	DISTINGUISHED
Student progress in learning	Teacher has no system for maintaining information on student progress in learning, or the system is in disarray. ☐	Teacher's system for maintaining information on student progress in learning is rudimentary and only partially effective. ☐	Teacher's system for maintaining information on student progress in learning is fully effective. ☐	Teacher's system for maintaining information on student progress in learning is fully effective. Students contribute information and participate in interpreting the records. ☐
Noninstructional records	Teacher's records for noninstructional activities are in disarray, resulting in errors and confusion. ☐	Teacher's records for noninstructional activities are adequate, but they require frequent monitoring to avoid errors. ☐	Teacher's system for maintaining information on noninstructional activities is fully effective. ☐	Teacher's system for maintaining information on noninstructional activities is highly effective, and students contribute to its maintenance. ☐

Source: From *Enhancing Professional Practice: A Framework for Teaching, 2nd Edition* (p. 97), by C. Danielson, 2007, Alexandria, VA: ASCD. © 2007 by ASCD. Reprinted with permission.

As a result of this self-assessment, on which element will you focus first? Turn to the pages following to explore the elements of the component in detail. After you've reviewed the tools, you can use the Action Planning and Reflection form to document the results of implementing the strategies in your classroom.

Element

Student Completion of Assignments

Description

Most teachers, particularly at the secondary level, need to keep track of student assignments, including both whether the assignments were completed and students' success in completing them.

A Closer Look

To help you recognize the subtle differences between the higher levels of performance for this element, note the keywords emphasized in the descriptions and review the activities common to those levels.

PROFICIENT

The teacher's system for maintaining information on student completion of assignments is *fully effective*.

At the proficient level of performance, teaching practices may include the following types of activities:

- Teacher maintains an up-to-date list of assignments that students haven't turned in, which is posted in the classroom for students to access.
- Teacher has created a page on the class Web site where students can check on any missing assignments.
- Teacher keeps track of student completion of assignments in a grade book.
- Teacher uses an online grade book to record attendance, student grades, and comments daily.
- For assignments that the teacher does not routinely collect for a grade, the teacher periodically checks and records student completion. For instance, the teacher can collect homework from a random sample of students or conduct a walk-through during independent seatwork when students must display homework.

DISTINGUISHED

The teacher's system for maintaining information on student completion of assignments is fully effective. *Students participate* in maintaining the records.

At the distinguished level of performance, teaching practices may include the following types of activities:

- Teacher and students maintain an up-to-date list of assignments that students haven't turned in that is posted in the classroom for students to access and update daily.
- Each month, the teacher provides students with a calendar that lists assignments that will be due throughout the month. The calendar includes spaces for students to record when they turned in the assignment and when the teacher returned it.
- Teacher provides a date stamp for students to mark their assignments with the actual date of completion when they turn them in.
- A student is responsible for entering assignments on a board located on a side wall in the classroom so that students can refer to it for long-term assignments and coming tests.

The tools that follow will help you explore how to put the activities of these high levels of performance into practice in your classroom.

Student Completion of Assignments

Element Reflection

✔ **Teacher tool**   __ **Student tool**

1. What Internet resources are available to help you keep track of student assignments?

2. What procedures could you use to enlist students' own energies in keeping track of their outstanding assignments?

Element

Student Progress in Learning

Description

To plan instruction, teachers need to know where individual students are in their learning. Teachers can collect this information formally or informally, but they must update it frequently.

A Closer Look

To help you recognize the subtle differences between the higher levels of performance for this element, note the keywords emphasized in the descriptions and review the activities common to those levels.

PROFICIENT

The teacher's system for maintaining information on student progress in learning is *fully effective*.

At the proficient level of performance, teaching practices may include the following types of activities:

- Teacher maintains a spreadsheet that lists instructional outcomes and competencies for each unit of study, recording students' progress according to the outcomes they have mastered.
- Teacher uses sticky notes to capture anecdotal comments about student learning during class. The teacher may take notes during small-group discussions, writing conferences, and independent work. The teacher transfers the notes to student folders at the end of each day.

DISTINGUISHED

The teacher's system for maintaining information on student progress in learning is fully effective. *Students contribute* information and participate in interpreting the records.

At the distinguished level of performance, teaching practices may include the following types of activities:

- At the midpoint and end of each quarter, both the teacher and students participate in a process to determine student progress. Using tools provided by the teacher, students calculate numerical grade averages and complete a self-assessment that includes criteria for nonachievement factors that contribute to learning, such as effort and class participation. Students have the opportunity to provide evidence to support their self-assessments.

- As part of an end-of-year evaluation, students select samples of writing from their portfolios that reflect their growth throughout the year. The evaluation includes a written reflection from the students documenting their strengths and areas for growth.
- Students use an online portfolio to create and manage products that infuse audio, image, text, and video. These portfolios allow students to create views to periodically share their collections with the class or with the world at large, if the teacher permits it.[1]

The tools that follow will help you explore how to put the activities of these high levels of performance into practice in your classroom.

---

[1] Calvert, J. (2009). *Blogs in the classroom.* Retrieved June 11, 2009, from http://calvert.wiki.ccsd.edu/page/diff/Blogs+in+the+Classroom/69204799

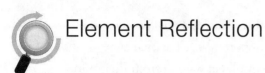

Element Reflection

☑ **Teacher tool**   ___ **Student tool**

1. What techniques, both formal and informal, can you use to monitor student progress in learning?

2. How can you involve students in recording their own progress in learning?

Element

Noninstructional Records

Description

Noninstructional records are those that need to be kept for all the details of school life outside of the classroom. Examples are such things as knowing which students have returned their permission slips for a field trip or which students have paid for their school pictures.

A Closer Look

To help you recognize the subtle differences between the higher levels of performance for this element, note the keywords emphasized in the descriptions and review the activities common to those levels.

PROFICIENT

The teacher's system for maintaining information on noninstructional activities is *fully effective*.

At the proficient level of performance, teaching practices may include the following types of activities:

- The teacher uses a class list to keep track of permission slips that have been turned in.
- The teacher uses a school-based program to enter contact information about each student.
- The teacher uses a school-based program to take attendance at the start of each class.

DISTINGUISHED

The teacher's system for maintaining information on noninstructional activities is *highly effective*, and *students contribute* to its maintenance.

At the distinguished level of performance, teaching practices may include the following types of activities:

- Students in an elementary setting have a system, developed by the teacher, for taking attendance and counting lunch choices.

- In a secondary classroom, teachers have assigned a student in each class period to take attendance. This may be done electronically or with a class list provided by the teacher.

The tools that follow will help you explore how to put the activities of these high levels of performance into practice in your classroom.

Noninstructional Records

Element Reflection

✔ **Teacher tool** ___ **Student tool**

1. How can you avoid the paper blizzard that is the consequence of a poor system—or no system at all—for keeping track of noninstructional items, such as permission slips for a field trip?

2. What system could you institute to engage students in maintaining the system for noninstructional records?

Domain 4

Strategies for Keeping Track of Noninstructional Records

✔ **Teacher tool**   __ **Student tool**

Review the ideas below for ways to keep track of noninstructional records, and then plan how you can adapt the strategies for your own classroom.

Tool Ideas and Suggested Materials	Items Included in My Tool	Location of My Tool
Opening of School Year File Materials: • class rules and procedures • a list of school supplies students need • a seating chart • a welcome letter to the students and parents • icebreaker activities and journal ideas for the first day of school		
Student Files Materials: • copies of notes sent home to parents • copies of notes received from parents • conference notes • behavior contracts • any special health requirements		(Should be a confidential location.)
Faculty File Materials: • school memos • faculty handbook • staff addresses and phone numbers • a school calendar		
Field Trip File Materials: • field trip brochures • contact names and phone numbers • bus information • maps • prices for various past and possible visits *Post a class list on a large envelope in this file.*		
Volunteer File Materials: • student list • seating chart list of tasks to complete • general guidelines for volunteers *Post a large thank-you note to all volunteers here.*		

Noninstructional Records

Tool Ideas and Suggested Materials	Items Included in My Tool	Location of My Tool
Substitute File Materials: • seating chart • student list • class rules • name and location of colleague nearby • specials and break times • lesson plans for the day • emergency procedures • extra worksheets • the location of supplies • allergies of students		

Component 4b

Action Planning and Reflection

✔ **Teacher tool**   __ **Student tool**

Look over the tools for this component and choose a strategy or strategies that you are committed to trying in your classroom. Then return to this page and record what happened. If there was a change, what evidence indicates the extent to which this strategy was successful? Finally, think about what you might do differently to continue to bring about further growth in this component.

What will I try?	How did it go?	What will I do differently next time?

Component 4c

Communicating with Families

OVERVIEW

It is well known that family participation in the education of their children enhances students' learning. Although families' ability to participate in their children's learning varies widely, it is the teachers' responsibility to provide opportunities for them to participate in a meaningful way.

Teachers establish relationships with families by communicating with them about the instructional program and individual students and by inviting families to be part of the education process itself. Although the level of family involvement tends to be higher at the elementary level, regular communication with families of older students is just as important, if not more important. A teacher's effort to communicate with families demonstrates that the teacher cares, which families of students of all ages value.

SELF-ASSESSMENT

Assess your practice in Component 4c against the levels of performance below, then check the box that best matches the level of your own teaching for each element.

Component 4c: Communicating with Families				
	Level of Performance			
ELEMENT	UNSATISFACTORY	BASIC	PROFICIENT	DISTINGUISHED
Information about the instructional program	Teacher provides little or no information about the instructional program to families.	Teacher participates in the school's activities for family communication but offers little additional information.	Teacher provides frequent information to families, as appropriate, about the instructional program.	Teacher provides frequent information to families, as appropriate, about the instructional program. Students participate in preparing materials for their families.
	☐	☐	☐	☐

Source: From *Enhancing Professional Practice: A Framework for Teaching, 2nd Edition* (p. 100), by C. Danielson, 2007, Alexandria, VA: ASCD. © 2007 by ASCD. Reprinted with permission.

Component 4c

ELEMENT	Level of Performance			
	UNSATISFACTORY	BASIC	PROFICIENT	DISTINGUISHED
Information about individual students	Teacher provides minimal information to families about individual students, or the communication is inappropriate to the cultures of the families. Teacher does not respond, or responds insensitively, to family concerns about students. ☐	Teacher adheres to the school's required procedures for communicating with families. Responses to family concerns are minimal or may reflect occasional insensitivity to cultural norms. ☐	Teacher communicates with families about students' progress on a regular basis, respecting cultural norms, and is available as needed to respond to family concerns. ☐	Teacher provides information to families frequently on student progress, with students contributing to the design of the system. Response to family concerns is handled with great professional and cultural sensitivity. ☐
Engagement of families in the instructional program	Teacher makes no attempt to engage families in the instructional program, or such efforts are inappropriate. ☐	Teacher makes modest and partially successful attempts to engage families in the instructional program. ☐	Teacher's efforts to engage families in the instructional program are frequent and successful. ☐	Teacher's efforts to engage families in the instructional program are frequent and successful. Students contribute ideas for projects that could be enhanced by family participation. ☐

Source: From *Enhancing Professional Practice: A Framework for Teaching, 2nd Edition* (p. 100), by C. Danielson, 2007, Alexandria, VA: ASCD. © 2007 by ASCD. Reprinted with permission.

As a result of this self-assessment, on which element will you focus first? Turn to the pages following to explore the elements of the component in detail. After you've reviewed the tools, you can use the Action Planning and Reflection form to document the results of implementing the strategies in your classroom.

Domain 4

Element

Information About the Instructional Program

A Closer Look

To help you recognize the subtle differences between the higher levels of performance for this element, note the keywords emphasized in the descriptions and review the activities common to those levels.

PROFICIENT

The teacher provides *frequent* information to families, as appropriate, about the instructional program.

At the proficient level of performance, teaching practices may include the following types of activities:

- Teacher provides a handout at open house or back-to-school night with a syllabus of the course, including units of study, homework and grading procedures, contact information for the teacher, and so forth.
- Teacher provides a weekly or monthly newsletter to parents. This might include information about the learning that precedes the homework or current class activities, such as community and school service projects, field trips, or concerts.
- Teacher maintains a Web page for the class that includes a calendar and updates on classroom activities.
- Teacher sends home an introductory letter to families during the summer that describes expectations for the school year; lists the teacher's contact information if the parents have any questions; and includes refresher activities, such as summer reading strategies, writing tips, or math strategies.

DISTINGUISHED

The teacher provides frequent information to families, as appropriate, about the instructional program. *Students participate* in preparing materials for their families.

At the distinguished level of performance, teaching practices may include the following types of activities:

- Students and teacher prepare materials for open house or back-to-school night. These materials include information about the units of study, homework and grading policies, expectations for student work and behavior, and comments from the students about what they want to learn in this class.
- Students write a monthly or weekly newsletter. Groups of students write the newsletter, with each student focusing on a different aspect of the class. One student, on a rotating basis, is the editor of the newsletter.
- Students run a blog that talks about different aspects of the class. The teacher invites parents to leave comments on the blog.[1]

The tools that follow will help you explore how to put the activities of these high levels of performance into practice in your classroom.

[1] Calvert, J. (2009). *Blogs in the classroom*. Retrieved June 11, 2009, from http://calvert.wiki.ccsd.edu/page/diff/Blogs+in+the+Classroom/69204799

Information About the Instructional Program

Element Reflection

✔ **Teacher tool** ___ **Student tool**

1. What strategies do you currently use to inform families about your instructional program? What additional strategies could you use?

2. How could you enlist your students' help in ensuring that their families understand your instructional program?

☐ 411

Communicating with Parents Using a Newsletter

✔ **Teacher tool**   __ **Student tool**

Newsletters can help you communicate to those at home what is happening in the instructional program during the school day. You can create the newsletter yourself or you can have students contribute the content. Use the following examples to help you develop your own classroom newsletter.

EXAMPLE NEWSLETTER BY A TEACHER

3rd Grade Community News

Ms. Chalfin's Class   Friday, May 8, 2009

Overview of the Week

Reader's Workshop

This week we began developing "theories" about characters, in preparation for our upcoming writing unit on literary essays. We focused on the character of Ramona, in *Ramona Quimby, Age 8*.

We also read our Community Read, *Mrs. Spitzer's Garden*. This is a great book about a teacher who cultivates a garden, just like she helps foster growth in children. It is a beautiful story about the appreciation of teachers. It helped me reflect, having pride in my profession!

Read Aloud

We finished *Ramona Quimby, Age 8*. Many students have decided to continue the series and have checked out books from our Media Center.

Writer's Workshop

This week we took our last District Writing Prompt. The kids seemed to enjoy the prompt (Imagine you are flying a kite and a sudden gust of wind lifts you off the ground. Write a story about what happens.) Ask your child what happened to them in their story!

Endangered Animal Quilt Update

Quilts are still due next Friday, May 15. Please make sure that your child refers to the diagram in the packet to assemble their work. Also, make sure they complete the "student" section of the rubric. They have the opportunity to honestly grade themselves and then I will grade them.

Other Important News

• The *Literary Lion* is hot off the press. This magazine features many writing pieces from students in our class! If you are interested in a copy, please send in $3 in an envelope requesting a magazine.
The office has asked classroom teachers to inform parents that if any phone numbers change in your family (home, cell, or work), to please let the office know. Thanks!

Math Workshop

This week we studied probability. We learned that probability is the likelihood of an event. Talk to your child about how probability is a common concept (e.g., the weather forecast, whether they will be able to have a sleepover or not, a coin toss, or baseball statistics—what's the chance of the player hitting a grand slam?)

Grammar

This week we continued learning about simple and compound sentences.

Spelling

This week we had our Unit 14 Word Preview.

Social Studies

This week was our last week of Junior Achievement. We experienced being bankers. We learned how to write a check, fill out a deposit slip, and balance a checkbook.

Mr. Valenti presented us with Certificate of Achievement awards.

Soon, we will move into our Connecticut study.

Science

This week we took a break from science because of the district assessments. Soon we will start plant and animal adaptations.

- We are in need of more dry-erase markers. If you have a chance to pick some up, that would be greatly appreciated. Thanks!
- If you don't have plans on Mother's Day at 1:30 p.m., the Bethel Land Trust is having their annual meeting, and you can enjoy a free presentation with a live arctic wolf! What a great connection to our endangered species project! The event will be held at Bennett Park (14 Shelter Rock Road) in Bethel.
- The ABC Countdown sheet is coming home today. It starts on Monday. Please keep this in a safe place!

Specials for the Week of May 11

Mon	Tues	Wed.	Thurs	Fri
Art	Media	Music	Gym	Art

Wear sneakers on Thursday.

Upcoming Events

- Monday, May 11: Start of ABC Countdown
- Tuesday, May 12: District DRP
- Thursday, May 14: Recorder Concert/Art Show
- Friday, May 15: Animal Quilts Due

Source: From J. Chalfin, 2007, Bethel, CT: Frank A. Berry School. Adapted with permission.

EXAMPLE NEWSLETTER BY STUDENTS

Augusto wrote our 8th newsletter!

COMMUNITY NEWS
Published by Ms. Chalfin's 3rd Grade Class

Week of: 10/8/07   Featured Writer: Augusto

Monday	Tuesday
We did not have school because it was Columbus Day.	Students had vacation and the teachers had school.

Wednesday	Thursday
In science, we measured ourselves and our teddy bears using a measuring tape.	During Writer's Workshop, we published our stories.

Friday	Upcoming Events
We had computers with Mrs. Bassett.	• Happy Halloween • oct. 31st • Trick or Treat

Highlight of the Week

Bring Your Bear To school Day.

Source: From the work of the 3rd grade class of J. Chalfin, 2007, Bethel, CT: Frank A. Berry School. Reprinted with permission.

Element

Information About Individual Students

A Closer Look

To help you recognize the subtle differences between the higher levels of performance for this element, note the keywords emphasized in the descriptions and review the activities common to those levels.

PROFICIENT

The teacher communicates with families about students' progress on a *regular basis*, respecting cultural norms, and is *available as needed* to respond to family concerns.

At the proficient level of performance, teaching practices may include the following types of activities:

- Teacher creates a monthly schedule to contact parents with updates about students or the instructional program. The schedule may include dates for newsletters to be sent home, e-mail announcements to individuals or the whole class, phone calls, or personal notes.

- Teacher creates a form letter, which then only takes a minute to fill out, to communicate with parents about individual students. This recognizes the child as an individual and respects the parents enough to tell them so. The letter has a checklist of levels of behavior, work and attitude, and suggested actions for the parent ranging from a hug for a job well done to a conference. Parents may be required to sign and return the form to ensure that they have seen it. The teacher sends home letters as needed.

- Teacher sends a monthly progress report, generated by the school-based software program, to all parents. The report provides parents with updated information on their students' progress.

DISTINGUISHED

The teacher provides information to families *frequently* on student progress, with *students contributing* to the design of the system. Response to family concerns is handled with *great* professional and cultural sensitivity.

At the distinguished level of performance, teaching practices may include the following types of activities:

- Each Friday, students complete a "Homework Success" report that lists any missing assignments for the week. Parents sign and students return the report on Monday.

- Teacher uses an online grade book so that families can access these records privately at any time to monitor the progress of their children.

- At the end of each class or day, students write their reflections in a learning log. Reflections relate to what they have learned that class or day and may be driven by a teacher prompt or question or may be driven by students. The teacher uses this time to jot a note to parents of several students each day to communicate with them about their students, and students take the learning logs home each night for a parent or guardian to sign. Parents may also respond in the log with a question or comment. The teacher checks learning log signatures each morning. The process and frequency for using this strategy varies according to the age and level of the students. For younger students, the learning log is teacher-driven at first, with the whole class brainstorming and then deciding on one idea that is written on the board for everyone to copy into their logs. As the year progresses, the process becomes more student-driven and individualized. At the secondary level, after the process has been modeled for students, they write independently. The frequency may vary from daily to weekly to several times each month.

- Teacher arranges parent-teacher-student conferences twice a year. In preparation, students self-assess their strengths and areas for growth and write two goals they want to work toward. During the conferences with their parents, students present their reflection and goals for the rest of the school year.

The tools that follow will help you explore how to put the activities of these high levels of performance into practice in your classroom.

Information About Individual Students

Element Reflection

✔ Teacher tool　　　　　　　**__ Student tool**

1. To what extent are you able to use technology to keep families up-to-date about the progress their children are making in school?

2. What modifications do you find that you have make to the school's "official" reporting systems for parents to accommodate parents' varied education and cultural backgrounds?

Parent Conference Record

✔ **Teacher tool**   __ **Student tool**

Student: _____ Date: _____

Teacher: _____ Grade: _____

SUBJECT: MATH

Unit Assessment	Date	Grade

Notes to Parent/Guardian:

SUBJECT: READING

Unit Assessment	Date	Matching	Multiple Choice	Free Response

Information About Individual Students

Common Assessment	Date	Score

Notes to Parent/Guardian:

SUBJECT: WRITING

Common Assessment	Date	Score	Goal

Notes to Parent/Guardians:

OTHER SUBJECT AREA INFORMATION

WORK HABITS/CLASSROOM BEHAVIORS

If you have any questions of concerns about your child's progress, please feel free to contact me anytime.

_____
Teacher signature

_____
Parent/Guardian signature   Date

Family Contact Log

✔ **Teacher tool**   __ **Student tool**

Scheduling and documenting regular contact with student's families can ensure that you are monitoring how regularly you are communicating and what you are sharing. Be sure to share something positive about each student whenever you contact the family. Use this log to support your outreach to student's families.

Name: _____

School: _____ School Year: _____

Date	Person Contacted	Type of Contact (person, phone, virtual)	Purpose	Outcome

Information About Individual Students

Communicating with Families Self-Assessment

✔ Teacher tool   **__ Student tool**

Use this self-assessment to determine your strengths and challenges in communicating with families of students in your classes. Check all statements that apply, and list evidence that supports each statement.

✔	Statement	Evidence
	I contact parents when their child has accomplished or done something positive.	
	I follow up with parents who do not attend meetings or conferences.	
	I provide parents with strategies to help their children learn.	
	I use various modes to communicate with families about the instructional program.	
	I work toward establishing a relationship of mutual respect between the home and school.	
	I give parents opportunities to volunteer both in and out of the classroom.	
	Parents frequently volunteer to help.	
	I frequently survey parents about their concerns or questions about their child's education.	

Information About Individual Students

✔	Statement	Evidence
	I use feedback from families to inform my instructional program.	
	I frequently update parents about their child's progress in learning.	
	I provide ongoing opportunities for parents to participate in their child's education.	
	I provide a means for parents to access a monthly calendar that includes assignments, updates, and events.	

1. What are your areas of strength?

2. What areas will you now focus on?

Element

Engagement of Families in the Instructional Program

Description

Accomplished teachers make a concerted effort to incorporate students' out-of-school lives in the classroom learning environment.

A Closer Look

To help you recognize the subtle differences between the higher levels of performance for this element, note the keywords emphasized in the descriptions and review the activities common to those levels.

PROFICIENT

The teacher's efforts to engage families in the instructional program are *frequent* and *successful*.

At the proficient level of performance, teaching practices may include the following types of activities:

- Teacher attends parent-teacher association meetings, luncheons, picnics, evening coffees, and home visits whenever possible.
- Teacher creates a survey that includes questions about both the student and family, such as interests, hobbies, and areas of expertise, for parents to complete during the first few weeks of school.
- Teacher creates a parent resource directory that lists parents' occupations, skills, hobbies, and interests along with their availability and willingness to share these resources with the class.
- Teacher invites parents to student presentations such as science fairs, author's teas, class plays, media demonstrations, or poetry jamborees.
- Teacher creates assignments, such as interviewing, polling, or collecting information about the household, that require students to engage with members of their immediate and extended family.

DISTINGUISHED

The teacher's efforts to engage families in the instructional program are frequent and successful. *Students contribute* ideas for projects that could be enhanced by family participation.

At the distinguished level of performance, teaching practices may include the following types of activities:

- Parent volunteers work with students to write the weekly or monthly class newsletter, working with the newsletter group in class on selected days during the month.
- Students host and invite parents to classroom or school events, such as science fairs, author's teas, poetry jamborees, or geography bees.
- Students suggest activities they might undertake at home to extend their learning.

The tools that follow will help you explore how to put the activities of these high levels of performance into practice in your classroom.

Engagement of Families in the Instructional Program

 Element Reflection

✔ **Teacher tool** ___ **Student tool**

1. How can you incorporate students' family lives into assignments?

2. How do you elicit students' suggestions for family involvement? How do you vet their suggestions?

Summer Assignment Letters

✔ **Teacher tool**   __ **Student tool**

Summer assignments prepare students for the instructional program in the coming school year while providing families the opportunity to get involved with student learning. Adapt the following letters to parents of 3rd graders to suit your needs.

SUMMER READING LETTER: 3RD GRADE

Dear parents,

Your child should be reading daily this summer! Have him carry a book to the park, to camp, in the car, to the beach—wherever. Think about starting a reading partnership or book club with your child in which you take turns reading and talking about what you have read. You can also show your child that reading can be both engaging and relaxing.

It's important for children to have a balanced reading diet, so encourage your child to read from a variety of genres, like fiction and nonfiction, poetry, mysteries, biographies, and fantasy.

Looking ahead to the coming school year, 3rd graders build up their reading stamina to about 35–40 minutes. Have your child take the Summer Reading Challenge and build up to that amount of sustained reading. You can start the summer by having your child read independently for 20 minutes, then increase time every few weeks.

Your child will learn a lot in 3rd grade about applying comprehension strategies to different types of books, and you can help him get a jumpstart on these strategies. When your child is reading, prompt him to think about what is happening:

- Can you tell me what's happened so far? (Retell the important events.)
- What are you thinking? (Developing ideas about what they've read.)
- What do you think is going to happen? (Predict.)
- Can you say why you think that? Let's keep reading and see…
- Wait. There are so many details here. Let's reread this part. (Rereading.)
- Let's stop and try to picture it. (Envisioning.)
- I'm confused here…that last part didn't make sense to me. Can we go back and reread a bit? (Monitoring for sense.)
- This reminds me of… (Connecting to an experience, another text, or something in the world.)

If your child is having trouble figuring out a difficult word, you can ask:

- What would make sense here? Could it be…? Try it… (Have them use the sentence to figure out the word.)
- Are there chunks of the word that look familiar to you?
- What's the first part? Have you read all the way across the word?

Domain 4

- Rewind. Now try it again to make it smooth. Does it make sense?
- Does the word look right and sound right? (Please, do not say "sound it out.")

The more practice your child has reading, the more fluent he will become. Invite your child to read to you and give him independent time as well.

Good luck!

Source: From J. Chalfin, 2007, Bethel, CT: Frank A. Berry School. Adapted with permission.

SUMMER WRITING LETTER: 3RD GRADE

Dear parents,

Encourage your child to keep a writer's notebook this summer. She can carry her notebook around on adventures or typical summer activities and write down her ideas in any form: poems, fictional stories, nonfiction accounts, lists, or random thoughts. Remind your child that the entries don't have to be finished products.

First, have your child make the composition notebook her own by decorating it with photographs, stickers, or artifacts that represent memories. Now the notebook is ready for her to experiment in.

I showed the class my writer's notebook today during the "Moving Up" ceremony, so your child should have a good idea of what I expect.

Have your child bring the notebook to school in the fall. She might use some of these entries throughout the year!

Source: From J. Chalfin, 2007, Bethel, CT: Frank A. Berry School. Adapted with permission.

SUMMER MATH LETTER: 3RD GRADE

Dear parents,

It is important for 3rd graders to be able to automatically recall (within three to five seconds) basic addition and subtraction facts. Over the summer, you can use some simple strategies to help your child hone his skills. Better yet, if you make it a game, it can be fun.

Addition and Subtraction War

(Partner)

Materials: Playing cards, without face cards

How to Play:

- Split the deck in half, and give half to each player.
- Decide whether you are adding or subtracting.
- Each player flips over a card. Mentally add or subtract the numbers. Whoever says the answer first keeps both cards and puts them in a separate pile.
- When you run out of cards, count up how many cards you have in your pile. Whoever has the most wins!

Addition and Subtraction Flashcards

(Partner or alone)

Materials: Flashcards, prepared with addition and subtraction problems

How to Play:

- Flip over a flashcard and say the answer.
- If you say the answer in three to five seconds, put it in the "I Know" pile. If you don't know the answer, put it in the "I Don't Know" pile.
- Once you have made it through the whole pile, go through the "I Don't Know" pile until all the cards are in the "I Know" pile.

Facts on the Go

As you are setting the table for dinner, driving in the car, or taking a walk, quiz your child on a few basic addition and subtraction problems.

Practice Doubles, Doubles +/- 1

Examples of doubles: $5 + 5$ or $7 + 7$

Example of double $+1$: $5 + 6$ (I know $5 + 5 = 10$, so 1 more is 11.)

Example of double -1: $5 + 4$ (I know $5 + 5 = 10$, so 1 less is 9.)

Source: From J. Chalfin, 2007, Bethel, CT: Frank A. Berry School. Adapted with permission.

Action Planning and Reflection

✔ **Teacher tool**   ___ **Student tool**

Look over the tools for this component and choose a strategy or strategies that you are committed to trying in your classroom. Then return to this page and record what happened. If there was a change, what evidence indicates the extent to which this strategy was successful? Finally, think about what you might do differently to continue to bring about further growth in this component.

What will I try?	How did it go?	What will I do differently next time?

Component 4d

Participating in a Professional Community

OVERVIEW

First and foremost, schools are environments that should promote student learning. However, to make this possible, teachers must work with their colleagues to share strategies, collaborate, and plan for the success of individual students. Schools are, in other words, professional organizations for teachers that only realize their full potential when teachers regard themselves as members of a professional community. This community is characterized by mutual support and respect and recognition of all teachers' responsibility to constantly seek ways to improve their practice.

Inevitably, teachers' duties extend beyond the doors of their classrooms to include activities related to the entire school and larger district. Activities include such things as school and district curriculum committees or engagement with the parent-teacher organization. Experienced teachers assume leadership roles in these activities.

SELF-ASSESSMENT

Assess your practice in Component 4d against the levels of performance below, then check the box that best matches the level of your own teaching for each element.

Component 4d: Participating in a Professional Community			
	Level of Performance		
ELEMENT	UNSATISFACTORY	BASIC	PROFICIENT	DISTINGUISHED
Relationships with colleagues	Teacher's relationships with colleagues are negative or self-serving. ☐	Teacher maintains cordial relationships with colleagues to fulfill duties that the school or district requires. ☐	Relationships with colleagues are characterized by mutual support and cooperation. ☐	Relationships with colleagues are characterized by mutual support and cooperation. Teacher takes initiative in assuming leadership among the faculty. ☐

Component 4d

ELEMENT	Level of Performance			
	UNSATISFACTORY	BASIC	PROFICIENT	DISTINGUISHED
Involvement in a culture of professional inquiry	Teacher avoids participation in a culture of inquiry, resisting opportunities to become involved. ☐	Teacher becomes involved in the school's culture of inquiry when invited to do so. ☐	Teacher actively participates in a culture of professional inquiry. ☐	Teacher takes a leadership role in promoting a culture of professional inquiry. ☐
Service to the school	Teacher avoids becoming involved in school events. ☐	Teacher participates in school events when specifically asked. ☐	Teacher volunteers to participate in school events, making a substantial contribution. ☐	Teacher volunteers to participate in school events, making a substantial contribution, and assumes a leadership role in at least one aspect of school life. ☐
Participation in school and district projects	Teacher avoids becoming involved in school and district projects. ☐	Teacher participates in school and district projects when specifically asked. ☐	Teacher volunteers to participate in school and district projects, making a substantial contribution. ☐	Teacher volunteers to participate in school and district projects, making a substantial contribution, and assumes a leadership role in a major school or district project. ☐

Source: From *Enhancing Professional Practice: A Framework for Teaching, 2nd Edition* (p. 103), by C. Danielson, 2007, Alexandria, VA: ASCD. © 2007 by ASCD. Reprinted with permission.

As a result of this self-assessment, on which element will you focus first? Turn to the pages following to explore the elements of the component in detail. After you've reviewed the tools, you can use the Action Planning and Reflection form to document the results of implementing the strategies in your classroom.

Domain 4

Element

Relationships with Colleagues

Description

Members of a professional community don't think of themselves as independent contractors. Rather, they regard their work with students as part of a larger school effort and their close relationships with colleagues as a critical part of that effort.

A Closer Look

To help you recognize the subtle differences between the higher levels of performance for this element, note the keywords emphasized in the descriptions and review the activities common to those levels.

PROFICIENT

Relationships with colleagues are characterized by *mutual support* and *cooperation*.

At the proficient level of performance, teaching practices may include the following types of activities:

- Teacher interacts with grade-level or department colleagues on a regular basis, discussing how to improve instruction for all students.
- Teacher shares newly acquired instructional strategies with colleagues on a regular basis.
- Teacher works with grade-level or department colleagues to identify areas of student need that they can address together.
- Teacher participates as a member of the school-based professional development team, creating opportunities for collaboration and job-embedded learning.
- Teacher regularly demonstrates a willingness to work collaboratively with colleagues to develop and implement new ideas.
- Teacher regularly examines the practices, policies, and procedures of the school to evaluate their effect on student learning.
- Teacher engages in analysis, reflection, discussion, and debate with the intent to improve instructional practice.

DISTINGUISHED

Relationships with colleagues are characterized by mutual support and cooperation. The teacher *takes initiative* in assuming *leadership* among the faculty.

At the distinguished level of performance, teaching practices may include the following types of activities:

- Teacher has created an area on the school Web site where teachers can post effective classroom strategies.
- Teacher hosts an after-school book study on a jointly determined book to assist colleagues in planning to meet an identified student need.
- Teacher encourages colleagues to pursue National Board certification and hosts after-school support groups for those involved.
- Teacher leads a school-based professional development team, convening meetings and organizing job-embedded learning opportunities for faculty members.
- Teacher demonstrates a willingness to challenge practices, policies, and procedures of the school if they are not having the desired effect on student learning.

The tools that follow will help you explore how to put the activities of these high levels of performance into practice in your classroom.

Element Reflection

✔ **Teacher tool** ___ **Student tool**

1. How do you maintain supportive and respectful relationships with your colleagues?

2. What strategies do you use to prevent colleagues from being disrespectful toward each other?

Professional Study Group Announcement

✔ **Teacher tool** ____ **Student tool**

Professional study groups can be used to focus on instructional initiatives in a school, in a district, or among a team of teachers. Use these examples to develop your own study group invitation or registration form.

PROFESSIONAL STUDY GROUP ANNOUNCEMENT EXAMPLE 1

Title: Link Elementary Professional Study Group: *Engaging Readers and Writers with Inquiry* (Wilhem)

Description: This study group will enable professionals to build their knowledge base around inquiry in reading and writing. The participants will, first, become familiar with study groups—why they are so important and what procedures make them successful. Then the participants will be able to decide what portions of the text to read when. During the first few sessions, the group will be facilitated by the instructor, and then each member will have an opportunity to lead or co-lead the team. The group may decide to explore video resources or even extend their work to include inquiry-based lesson studies and walkthroughs, for which they would receive training. The professional study group is connected to both the building and district's vision and strategic plan.

Instructor:	Elementary Learning Facilitator
Dates:	March 27, April 10, April 24, May 8, May 22 (five sessions)
Time:	2:45–4:15 p.m. (1½ hours)
Place:	Link Elementary (room TBA)
Compensation:	7½ hours, equivalent to ½ inservice credit
Participants:	Untenured and tenured teachers
Requirements:	Participants are expected to arrive on time, have readings completed, and fully participate in the discussions.
Limit:	10

Source: Gianakouros, K. *Office of instruction and professional development Link Elementary professional study group.* (Available from Clarkstown Central School District, 62 Middletown Road, New City, New York 10956) Adapted with permission.

PROFESSIONAL STUDY GROUP ANNOUNCEMENT EXAMPLE 2

Join the Club!

Clarkstown Central School District offers professional learning and professional learning credit through PROFESSIONAL BOOK STUDY GROUPS

What is a book study group?

More and more schools are recognizing that some of the most meaningful professional development experiences come directly from teachers. Professional study groups, which often are run like conventional book clubs, are taking place in many school districts. Study groups provide teachers the opportunity to learn not only from the books they read and study together, but also from each other.

The social learning experience that a study group provides can help each teacher grow professionally. Research has shown that the conversations staff members have with one another about their practice can lead to significant improvements in instruction and, therefore, significant improvements in student learning. In addition to individual growth, the school culture is improved.

Tell me more!

There will be a group that will meet at _____. The group members will decide which book(s) to study and when the sessions will take place. _____will facilitate the group. If you are interested, please e-mail the facilitator. Be sure to write which days of the week you are able to meet and whether you would prefer before or after school (1–1½ hours). The group will be open to the entire district and the maximum is 12 people, so first come, first served.

Source: Gianakouros, K. *Join the club!* (Available from Clarkstown Central School District, 62 Middletown Road, New City, New York 10956) Adapted with permission.

Study Group Meeting Record

✔ Teacher tool   **__ Student tool**

You can use this meeting record as an evolving action plan document. Be sure to follow up on the results of your action at the subsequent meeting. By reviewing the meeting records, you can determine whether you are on track for achieving the goal of the study group or whether you need to make changes to the format in future meetings or for future study groups.

Meeting Date:

Topic:

Participants:

Agenda	Notes	Next Steps

Element

Involvement in a Culture of Professional Inquiry

Description

Professional teachers recognize that they have an obligation to continue their learning throughout their careers by participating in a culture of inquiry. This culture recognizes the expertise that resides within the walls of every school and devises techniques to capture and share that expertise.

A Closer Look

To help you recognize the subtle differences between the higher levels of performance for this element, note the keywords emphasized in the descriptions and review the activities common to those levels.

PROFICIENT

The teacher *actively participates* in a culture of professional inquiry.

At the proficient level of performance, teaching practices may include the following types of activities:

- Teacher participates in a discussion group with colleagues about student test data to determine appropriate instructional strategies for struggling students.
- Teacher participates in school-based professional development and shares ideas to promote increased understanding among colleagues.
- Teacher conducts action research in the classroom to determine areas of student need.
- Teacher continually reviews education Web sites and shares pertinent sites with colleagues.
- Teacher regularly collaborates with colleagues, which may include special area teachers, school specialists, content-area specialists, or special educators, to plan instruction that meets the needs of all learners.
- Teacher participates in a "circle of friends" or study group to examine student work.

DISTINGUISHED

The teacher takes a *leadership role* in promoting a culture of professional inquiry.

At the distinguished level of performance, teaching practices may include the following types of activities:

- Teacher initiates and leads a discussion group with colleagues about student test data to determine appropriate instructional strategies for struggling students.
- Teacher develops a needs assessment to address school-based professional development areas to focus on for the year.
- Teacher facilitates school-based professional development for colleagues.
- Teacher attends university classes to learn how to enhance instructional practices and shares new knowledge with colleagues.
- Teacher conducts action research in the classroom to determine areas of student need and discusses findings with colleagues, brainstorming additional strategies to adjust instruction.
- Teacher facilitates a bimonthly meeting of teachers to examine student work.

The tools that follow will help you explore how to put the activities of these high levels of performance into practice in your classroom.

Involvement in a Culture of Professional Inquiry

Element Reflection

✔ **Teacher tool**   __ **Student tool**

1. What specific actions can you take to communicate to colleagues the value of ongoing professional learning?

2. How can you encourage reluctant colleagues to share their expertise with one another?

☐ 441

Domain 4

Element

Service to the School

Description

All schools include projects and responsibilities beyond the actual teaching of students that teachers must be undertake. In some schools, the teachers are compensated for their work outside the classroom. At other schools, the teachers divide the work among themselves.

A Closer Look

To help you recognize the subtle differences between the higher levels of performance for this element, note the keywords emphasized in the descriptions and review the activities common to those levels.

PROFICIENT

The teacher *volunteers* to participate in school events, making a *substantial contribution*.

At the proficient level of performance, teaching practices may include the following types of activities:

- Teacher participates in back-to-school night and prepares a common handout, explaining the curriculum to be taught for the year for all grade-level or department colleagues.
- Teacher attends parent-teacher association meetings and shares ideas for possible areas of focus for the year.
- Teacher assists at school events, such as food drives or school Olympics.
- Teacher participates in the school carnival by having students make creative items for the silent auction.
- Teacher participates in events such as the monthly Family Math Night, teaching families strategies to support students at home.
- Teacher volunteers to chaperone one or more field trips for various student groups throughout the year.

Domain 4

DISTINGUISHED

The teacher volunteers to participate in school events, making a substantial contribution, and assumes a *leadership role* in at least one aspect of school life.

At the distinguished level of performance, teaching practices may include the following types of activities:

- Teacher coordinates such activities as the food drive or school Olympics.
- Teacher coordinates the annual school talent show or other identified yearly event.
- Teacher serves as a club sponsor and coordinates its annual fundraising event.
- Teacher initiates and coordinates the community service program, in which students from across the district participate in volunteer activities.

The tools that follow will help you explore how to put the activities of these high levels of performance into practice in your classroom.

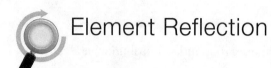

Element Reflection

✔ **Teacher tool**   __ **Student tool**

1. What opportunities are available for you to become involved in schoolwide efforts to improve the school?

2. How can you engage colleagues in schoolwide efforts to strengthen the school's program?

Element

Participation in School and District Projects

Description

Some school and district projects, such as curriculum committees or assessment design efforts, are major undertakings that require a series of meetings over an extended period of time. Professional and experienced educators find ways to incorporate such work into their daily schedules.

A Closer Look

To help you recognize the subtle differences between the higher levels of performance for this element, note the keywords emphasized in the descriptions and review the activities common to those levels.

PROFICIENT

The teacher *volunteers* to participate in school and district projects, making a *substantial* contribution.

At the proficient level of performance, teaching practices may include the following types of activities:

- Teacher participates in school-based discussion groups to determine appropriate instructional strategies for students based on assessment data.
- Teacher mentors teachers new to the school.
- Teacher attends training designed to share appropriate strategies for mentors.
- Teacher participates in a district-level initiative to develop a wellness policy.
- Teacher participates in a committee to develop a revised curriculum for new teacher training.
- Teacher is a member of school-based and districtwide committees.

DISTINGUISHED

The teacher volunteers to participate in school and district projects, making a substantial contribution, and assumes a *leadership role* in a major school or district project.

At the distinguished level of performance, teaching practices may include the following types of activities:

- Teacher initiates a schoolwide discussion group about student test data. The teacher then facilitates biweekly meetings to determine appropriate instructional strategies for teachers to use with struggling students.
- Teacher participates in districtwide committees that shape the direction of curriculum and instructional decisions for all students.
- Teacher leads a school-based conversation to update colleagues about districtwide decisions.
- Teacher facilitates districtwide professional development activities for new and experienced teachers.
- Teacher leads the district committee on health and wellness and is a liaison between the school board and community members.

The tools that follow will help you explore how to put the activities of these high levels of performance into practice in your classroom.

Participation in School and District Projects

Element Reflection

✔ **Teacher tool**   ___ **Student tool**

1. How does your involvement in school or district initiatives benefit student learning?

2. Describe how you convinced colleagues to participate with you in an important school or district project.

Professional Community Log

✔ **Teacher tool**   __ **Student tool**

You can keep track of how you actively participate in your professional community with a professional community log.

Name: _____

School: _____

School Year: _____

Date	Event (e.g., workshop, conference, class)	Benefits

Source: From *The Handbook for Enhancing Professional Practice: Using the Framework for Teaching in Your School* (p. 164), by C. Danielson, 2008, Alexandria, VA: ASCD. © 2008 by ASCD. Adapted with permission.

Participation in School and District Projects

Rating Your Professional Community Participation

✔ **Teacher tool**   __ **Student tool**

At the end of the school year, use the chart to reflect on your role in the professional community and the quality of your participation.

Characteristic The teacher's participation in a professional community demonstrates these, as appropriate.	**Little or None**	**Moderate**	**Extensive**
Participation in school affairs that • Is active and freely given. • Reflects a leadership role with colleagues. • Is supportive of the school's mission for student learning.			
Relationships with colleagues that • Are mutually supportive and respectful. • Demonstrate leadership in instructional affairs.			
Contribution to the school's community of inquiry that • Reflects the needs of the school. • Is built on the assumption of every student's obligation toward ongoing learning.			

Source: From *The Handbook for Enhancing Professional Practice: Using the Framework for Teaching in Your School* (p. 161), by C. Danielson, 2008, Alexandria, VA: ASCD. © 2008 by ASCD. Adapted with permission.

In the areas that you rated "little or none" or "moderate," how can you improve next year?

Action Planning and Reflection

✔ Teacher tool   **__ Student tool**

Look over the tools for this component and choose a strategy or strategies that you are committed to trying in your classroom. Then return to this page and record what happened. If there was a change, what evidence indicates the extent to which this strategy was successful? Finally, think about what you might do differently to continue to bring about further growth in this component.

What will I try?	How did it go?	What will I do differently next time?

Component 4e

Growing and Developing Professionally

OVERVIEW

Teaching is a complex profession, and teachers need to continuously grow and develop to keep their skills current. As the academic disciplines themselves evolve, educators have to constantly refine their understanding of how to engage students in learning. As a result, growth in content, pedagogy, and information technology are essential to good teaching. By staying informed and increasing their skills, teachers become more effective and are able to lead their colleagues.

Job-embedded professional development, such activities as joint planning, study groups, and lesson study, provide opportunities for teachers to learn from each other. In addition, professional educators increase their effectiveness in the classroom by belonging to professional organizations, reading professional journals, attending education conferences, and taking university classes. As they gain experience and expertise, educators find ways to contribute to their colleagues and to the profession.

SELF-ASSESSMENT

Assess your practice in Component 4e against the levels of performance below, then check the box that best matches the level of your own teaching for each element.

Component 4e: Growing and Developing Professionally				
	Level of Performance			
ELEMENT	UNSATISFACTORY	BASIC	PROFICIENT	DISTINGUISHED
Enhancement of content knowledge and pedagogical skill	Teacher engages in no professional development activities to enhance knowledge or skill. ☐	Teacher participates in professional activities to a limited extent when they are convenient. ☐	Teacher seeks out opportunities for professional development to enhance content knowledge and pedagogical skill. ☐	Teacher seeks out opportunities for professional development and makes a systematic effort to conduct action research. ☐

Source: From *Enhancing Professional Practice: A Framework for Teaching, 2nd Edition* (p. 105), by C. Danielson, 2007, Alexandria, VA: ASCD. © 2007 by ASCD. Reprinted with permission.

Component 4e

	Level of Performance			
ELEMENT	UNSATISFACTORY	BASIC	PROFICIENT	DISTINGUISHED
Receptivity to feedback from colleagues	Teacher resists feedback on teaching performance from either supervisors or more experienced colleagues.　☐	Teacher accepts, with some reluctance, feedback on teaching performance from both supervisors and professional colleagues.　☐	Teacher welcomes feedback from colleagues, when made by supervisors, or when opportunities arise through professional collaboration.　☐	Teacher seeks out feedback on teaching from both supervisors and colleagues.　☐
Service to the profession	Teacher makes no effort to share knowledge with others or to assume professional responsibilities.　☐	Teacher finds limited ways to contribute to the profession.　☐	Teacher participates actively in assisting other educators.　☐	Teacher initiates important activities to contribute to the profession.　☐

Source: From *Enhancing Professional Practice: A Framework for Teaching, 2nd Edition* (p. 105), by C. Danielson, 2007, Alexandria, VA: ASCD. © 2007 by ASCD. Reprinted with permission.

As a result of this self-assessment, on which element will you focus first? Turn to the pages following to explore the elements of the component in detail. After you've reviewed the tools, you can use the Action Planning and Reflection form to document the results of implementing the strategies in your classroom.

Element

Enhancement of Content Knowledge and Pedagogical Skill

Description

Teachers have a professional obligation to continually engage in professional learning. Teaching is so complex that it is never perfect, and teachers can always improve. Ongoing learning, therefore, is the mark of a professional, not a sign of deficiency.

A Closer Look

To help you recognize the subtle differences between the higher levels of performance for this element, note the keywords emphasized in the descriptions and review the activities common to those levels.

PROFICIENT

The teacher *seeks out* opportunities for professional development to enhance content knowledge and pedagogical skill.

At the proficient level of performance, teaching practices may include the following types of activities:

- Teacher attends district-sponsored professional development activities related to his subject area or grade level.
- Teacher offers professional development activities for colleagues at the school.
- Teacher attends university classes related to her content area.
- Teacher reads educational periodicals for current information about effective instructional strategies.
- Teacher visits colleagues' classrooms to enhance his own instructional skills.
- Teacher continuously seeks better, more effective ways to help students.
- Teacher works in collaborative teams to examine how lessons align with the state learning standards mapped in the curriculum.
- Teacher works with colleagues to design benchmark assessments to measure how students are demonstrating that they understand the skills and strategies that were taught.
- Teacher checks assessment results and adjusts instruction according to research-based practices.

DISTINGUISHED

The teacher seeks out opportunities for professional development and makes a *systematic effort* to conduct action research.

At the distinguished level of performance, teaching practices may include the following types of activities:

- Teacher attends professional development activities and then shares implementation strategies with colleagues.
- Teacher applies newly acquired knowledge and skills and determines their effect on students' learning.
- Teacher conducts research in her classroom and shares results with colleagues at conferences.
- Teacher leads a study group with colleagues.
- Teacher reads monthly educational periodicals and shares pertinent articles with colleagues.
- Teacher develops a schedule for colleagues in a team or department to visit each other's classrooms.
- Teacher leads grade-level or department meetings that are designed for professional learning.

The tools that follow will help you explore how to put the activities of these high levels of performance into practice in your classroom.

Enhancement of Content Knowledge and Pedagogical Skill

Element Reflection

✔ **Teacher tool**   __ **Student tool**

1. What opportunities do you have to enhance your content knowledge and pedagogical skill? What opportunities should be available but are not?

2. How can you encourage colleagues to continually work on improving their professional knowledge and skill?

Focusing Your Professional Growth

✔ Teacher tool   **__ Student tool**

If you are creating a growth plan for a group, each member should answer these questions independently. Depending on the nature of their work with students, and their prior training and experiences, the goal and teaching standards may vary for each person.

You can use your results from the Four Domains Self-Assessment (see page 7) to help focus your efforts on a particular component of the framework for teaching. Continue your reflection by considering

- Student learning data.
- Strategic goals from your district, building, grade level, or department.
- Feedback from your instructional leader or colleagues.
- Personal motivation and interests.

Once you've chosen a focus for your professional growth, continue generating your plan with additional tools for self-assessment, the Professional Growth Plan Considerations (see page 457) and the Content Knowledge Survey (see page 460). Then fill out the Professional Growth Plan on page 462.

1. Based on your self-assessment, list the components of teaching that you are most likely to target for your professional growth.

2. From the list above, consider the areas that influence student learning and can be supported with available resources. Of those components, what specific elements are most relevant to your self-assessment?

Professional Growth Plan Considerations

✔ Teacher tool   **__ Student tool**

After you've chosen a focus for your professional development (see page 456), you can continue generating your growth plan using this self-assessment tool as well as the Content Knowledge Survey (see page 460) before filling out the Professional Growth Plan on page 462.

You can improve your professional skills through a variety of modes. A few of the in-school options that you can embark on with colleagues in your school are collegial circles, peer coaching or teaching rounds, and action research. When developing your professional development plan, consider if any of these methods might work for your situation.

Collegial Circle

Three to eight colleagues with a common interest or goal meet throughout the school year to investigate a topic related to their professional practice, apply their learning, and review their findings with one another. Collegial circles can involve conversation, workshops, videos, visitations, book studies, Web cases, or outside presenters.

Peer Coaching/Teaching Rounds

Note: It is recommended that teachers who choose this model receive training in peer observation.
Teachers work in one or more pairs within a coaching group to observe each other's classes to provide feedback through conferences before and after the observation to offer ongoing support.

Action Research

One or more teachers or colleagues explore a particular question by collecting data, organizing and analyzing that data, and drawing conclusions. Action research can involve collegial conversation, research, workshops, professional readings, visitations, webcasts, or outside presenters.

For each growth plan element, review the considerations and then make recommendations for your professional development plan.

Domain 4

Enhancement of Content Knowledge and Pedagogical Skill

Growth Plan Element	Considerations	Recommendations
1. What format will you use?	• Collegial circles, portfolio development, action research, peer coaching • Working with peers, independently, with department teams, or a combination	
2. What is the goal of the plan? How is it stated?	• Individual, team, building, or district goals • How does it result in the continuous improvement of student learning? • Aligned to one or more standards of teaching	
3. What is the time line of the plan?	• Single- or multi-year plan	
4. What methods or strategies will you use?	• Action research, videotaping, self-assessment, college courses, workshops, visitation days, classroom observations, mentoring	

Enhancement of Content Knowledge and Pedagogical Skill

Growth Plan Element	Considerations	Recommendations
5. What resources or support do you need?	• Classroom materials, student materials, journals, workshops, books, collegial time, technology, release time, administrative support	
6. What are the indicators of progress?	• Student work, videotapes of classes, peer observation, journals, parent responses, student responses, statistical measures, performance assessment, case studies, professional portfolios, benchmarks, state assessments	

Content Knowledge Survey

✔ Teacher tool   __ **Student tool**

Use this survey to help you assess your knowledge of the subject areas you teach. If you teach more than one subject at the middle or secondary level, you may choose to complete the survey for each subject.

- In the first column, list the content knowledge standards from the national association in your subject area or state and local standards.
- In the second column, list specific evidence of your strengths in meeting each standard.
- In the third column, list how you would like to improve to better meet the content standards.

Content Standards	Strengths	Areas for Growth

Enhancement of Content Knowledge and Pedagogical Skill

Professional Growth Plan Protocol

✔ **Teacher tool**   __ **Student tool**

Customize this example of a district protocol to fit your professional growth plan. If your district or school would like to develop such a protocol, you can use this as a guide.

PROFESSIONAL GROWTH PLAN PROTOCOL EXAMPLE

- For tenured teachers/colleagues as of September _____, and teachers who have been in a continuous annual appointment for more than three years, participation will be in lieu of classroom observations for that teacher for that year, with the exception of teachers in their summative year.

- With building approval, nontenured teachers in their second and third years may participate, but their participation will not replace the contractual requirements for observations.

- An initial conference will be held between participating teachers or groups and their administrator. The purpose will be to answer any questions the teacher or administrator may have about goals, process, or documentation.

- All participants will document their activities with artifacts that illustrate the teachers' learning or activities. The type of documentation necessary will depend on the teacher's goals and specific alternative selected.

- Each participant will have a midyear update meeting with the principal or district administrator. This meeting may be with the group or with each individual in a group.

- Each participant will compose a short reflection about the year's experience and share it with the principal in preparation for the end-of-year conference. This reflection will not be part of the participant's evaluation for the year.

- All participants will have an individual meeting with their principal or a district administrator at the conclusion of the project to discuss the project's outcomes. The principal or designee will use information from the end-of-year conference to complete the teacher's evaluation for that year.

SUGGESTED TIME LINE

By August 15
   Teachers/colleagues should complete and submit a Professional Growth Plan form to the building principal.

By September 10
   The principal will notify each contact person with any questions about the intended project.

By October 15
   Initial learning conference scheduled.

By January 15
   Midyear learning conference scheduled.

Domain 4

Professional Growth Plan

✔ **Teacher tool**   __ **Student tool**

After you've chosen a focus for your professional development (see page 456), and based on the self-assessments Professional Growth Plan Considerations (see page 457) and the Content Knowledge Survey (see page 460), complete your professional growth plan.

Teacher: _____ Date: _____

GOAL

1. What is your learning goal? What are *you* intending to learn?

2. What is your rationale for selecting this goal?

3. What effect do you anticipate this goal will have on student learning?

STANDARDS
Which components of the framework for teaching will this goal address?

EVIDENCE
What evidence will you collect that will help you document and measure the progress toward this goal?

Teacher signature: _____

Administrator signature: _____

Enhancement of Content Knowledge and Pedagogical Skill

Professional Development Log

✔ **Teacher tool**   __ **Student tool**

Use the professional development log to document the types of professional development you participate in, how they aligned with your professional development plan, and the benefits of the activities to your professional growth.

Name: _____

School: _____

School Year: _____

Date	Event (e.g., workshop, conference, class)	Benefits

Source: From *The Handbook for Enhancing Professional Practice: Using the Framework for Teaching in Your School* (p. 164), by C. Danielson, 2008, Alexandria, VA: ASCD. © 2008 by ASCD. Adapted with permission.

Domain 4

Professional Growth Plan Teacher Reflection

✔ **Teacher tool**   __ **Student tool**

Review the content knowledge survey and the professional growth plan that you filled out at the beginning of the year, and then answer the following questions. You can use your responses as a starting point for an end-of-year conversation with your principal or other administrator.

1. In what areas did you grow as a teacher during the year?

2. What is the evidence of this growth?

Element

Receptivity to Feedback
from Colleagues

Description

A mark of a true professional is the willingness to hear suggestions from a colleague with an open mind. Colleagues typically offer suggestions with the aim of enhancing student learning, not criticizing the work of teachers. Professional educators accept suggestions in the spirit in which they were intended.

A Closer Look

To help you recognize the subtle differences between the higher levels of performance for this element, note the keywords emphasized in the descriptions and review the activities common to those levels.

PROFICIENT

The teacher *welcomes feedback* from colleagues, from supervisors, or through professional collaboration.

At the proficient level of performance, teaching practices may include the following types of activities:

- Teacher responds to observation feedback from supervisors or colleagues to improve teaching and learning.
- After receiving feedback from a colleague, teacher invites the colleague to review and comment on the changes she made to an instructional plan or teaching strategy.
- Teacher participates in the collaborative examination of student work to improve instruction and student learning.
- Teacher participates in peer coaching to improve instruction and student learning.

DISTINGUISHED

The teacher *seeks out* feedback on teaching from both supervisors and colleagues.

At the distinguished level of performance, teaching practices may include the following types of activities:

- Teacher invites a supervisor and colleagues into his classroom to observe and provide feedback.
- Teacher videotapes her practice and asks colleagues and supervisors for feedback about a specific goal.
- Teacher facilitates the collaborative examination of student work to improve instruction and student learning.
- Teacher meets with colleagues or supervisors to discuss professional learning plan goals and action steps.

The tools that follow will help you explore how to put the activities of these high levels of performance into practice in your classroom.

Element Reflection

✔ **Teacher tool**   __ **Student tool**

1. Everyone finds it difficult to accept suggestions from colleagues. How do you convey to colleagues that you are open to their suggestions about instruction?

2. How can you help colleagues give feedback in ways that are respectful and promote thinking?

Domain 4

Element

Service to the Profession

A Closer Look

To help you recognize the subtle differences between the higher levels of performance for this element, note the keywords emphasized in the descriptions and review the activities common to those levels.

PROFICIENT

The teacher *participates actively* in assisting *other educators*.

At the proficient level of performance, teaching practices may include the following types of activities:

- Teacher serves as a cooperating teacher for student teachers.
- Teacher hosts grade-level or department planning meetings.
- Teacher is a mentor to new teachers on staff.
- Teacher welcomes colleagues into the classroom to observe instruction.

DISTINGUISHED

The teacher *initiates* important activities to *contribute to the profession*.

At the distinguished level of performance, teaching practices may include the following types of activities:

- Teacher coordinates assignments of student teachers for a department or team.
- Teacher provides training sessions and discussion groups for cooperating teachers.
- Teacher writes articles for a professional publication.
- Teacher is a district-level trainer, delivering professional development related to content and pedagogy.

- Teacher coordinates a visitation schedule for colleagues to observe one another's classrooms.

The tools that follow will help you explore how to put the activities of these high levels of performance into practice in your classroom.

Service to the Profession

Element Reflection

✔ **Teacher tool**　　　　　__ **Student tool**

1. How do you share insights you gain from professional journals with colleagues?

2. How can you persuade your colleagues to overcome a natural hesitation to share their insights about teaching?

Component 4e

Action Planning and Reflection

✔ **Teacher tool**   __ **Student tool**

Look over the tools for this component and choose a strategy or strategies that you are committed to trying in your classroom. Then return to this page and record what happened. If there was a change, what evidence indicates the extent to which this strategy was successful? Finally, think about what you might do differently to continue to bring about further growth in this component.

What will I try?	How did it go?	What will I do differently next time?

Domain 4

Component 4f

Showing Professionalism

OVERVIEW

This component focuses on the ways teachers demonstrate professionalism in both their service to students and to the profession. Teachers at the highest levels of performance in this component put students first, regardless of how this might be contrary to long-held assumptions or past practice or might be more difficult or less convenient. Accomplished teachers have a strong moral compass and are guided by what is in the best interest of students.

Teachers can exhibit professionalism in a number of ways: Interactions with colleagues are conducted with honesty and integrity. Teachers are aware of student needs and access resources to intervene and provide help that may extend beyond the classroom. Teachers advocate for their students by seeking greater flexibility in the ways school rules and policies are applied, even if that means challenging traditional views and the education establishment.

Professionalism is also displayed in the ways teachers approach problem solving and decision making—with student needs in mind. Finally, teachers consistently adhere to school and district policies and procedures but are willing to work to improve those that may be outdated or ineffective.

SELF-ASSESSMENT

Assess your practice in Component 4f against the levels of performance below, then check the box that best matches the level of your own teaching for each element.

Component 4f: Showing Professionalism				
	Level of Performance			
ELEMENT	UNSATISFACTORY	BASIC	PROFICIENT	DISTINGUISHED
Integrity and ethical conduct	Teacher displays dishonesty in interactions with colleagues, students, and the public.	Teacher is honest in interactions with colleagues, students, and the public.	Teacher displays high standards of honesty, integrity, and confidentiality in interactions with colleagues, students, and the public.	Teacher can be counted on to hold the highest standards of honesty, integrity, and confidentiality and takes a leadership role with colleagues.
	☐	☐	☐	☐

Component 4f

ELEMENT	Level of Performance			
	UNSATISFACTORY	BASIC	PROFICIENT	DISTINGUISHED
Service to students	Teacher is not alert to students' needs. ☐	Teacher's attempts to serve students are inconsistent. ☐	Teacher is active in serving students. ☐	Teacher is highly proactive in serving students, seeking out resources when needed. ☐
Advocacy	Teacher contributes to school practices that result in some students being ill served by the school. ☐	Teacher does not knowingly contribute to some students being ill served by the school. ☐	Teacher works to ensure that all students receive a fair opportunity to succeed. ☐	Teacher makes a concerted effort to challenge negative attitudes or practices to ensure that all students, particularly those traditionally underserved, are honored in the school. ☐
Decision making	Teacher makes decisions and recommendations based on self-serving interests. ☐	Teacher's decisions and recommendations are based on limited though genuinely professional considerations. ☐	Teacher maintains an open mind and participates in team or departmental decision making. ☐	Teacher takes a leadership role in team or departmental decision making and helps ensure that such decisions are based on the highest professional standards. ☐
Compliance with school and district regulations	Teacher does not comply with school and district regulations. ☐	Teacher complies minimally with school and district regulations, doing just enough to get by. ☐	Teacher complies fully with school and district regulations. ☐	Teacher complies fully with school and district regulations, taking a leadership role with colleagues. ☐

Source: From *Enhancing Professional Practice: A Framework for Teaching, 2nd Edition* (pp. 107–108), by C. Danielson, 2007, Alexandria, VA: ASCD. © 2007 by ASCD. Reprinted with permission.

Component 4f

As a result of this self-assessment, on which element will you focus first? Turn to the pages following to explore the elements of the component in detail. After you've reviewed the tools, you can use the Action Planning and Reflection form to document the results of implementing the strategies in your classroom.

Domain 4

Element

Integrity and Ethical Conduct

Description

Professional educators have a clear sense of what is right, and their actions are guided by the principles of ethics. They can be trusted to keep their word and to not sacrifice their moral standards for short-term expediency.

A Closer Look

To help you recognize the subtle differences between the higher levels of performance for this element, note the keywords emphasized in the descriptions and review the activities common to those levels.

PROFICIENT

Teacher displays *high standards* of honesty, integrity, and confidentiality in interactions with colleagues, students, and the public.

At the proficient level of performance, teaching practices may include the following types of activities:

- Teacher implements methods that ensure that student records, including test scores, anecdotal comments, and student progress reports, are kept private and confidential.
- Teacher maintains scrupulous records for the collection of money from students, inviting colleagues or students to help improve the system.
- Teacher is careful not to betray confidences about colleagues in the school.

DISTINGUISHED

The teacher can be counted on to hold the *highest standards* of honesty, integrity, and confidentiality and takes a *leadership role* with colleagues.

At the distinguished level of performance, teaching practices may include the following types of activities:

- Teacher takes a leadership role in ensuring that all student records are maintained in a confidential manner.
- Teacher steps in, when necessary, to ensure that colleagues maintain confidentiality of student records, making the point firmly but with tact.

- Teacher takes a leadership role in developing a schoolwide system for collecting funds from students for such things as school pictures.
- Teacher ensures that colleagues do not betray confidences about one another, conveying that to do so is unprofessional.

The tools that follow will help you explore how to put the activities of these high levels of performance into practice in your classroom.

Domain 4

Integrity and Ethical Conduct

 Element Reflection

✔ **Teacher tool** ___ **Student tool**

1. Describe a situation that presented an ethical dilemma for you.

2. How can you contribute to a culture within the school in which high ethical standards of conduct are the norm?

☐ 477

Domain 4

Element

Service to Students

Description

Highly professional educators are guided in their judgments by what is in the best interest of students, including students across the entire school. This frequently involves seeking out help for students beyond the confines of their own classrooms. Experienced teachers try to ensure that students' academic needs as well as their physical and psychological needs are met.

A Closer Look

To help you recognize the subtle differences between the higher levels of performance for this element, note the keywords emphasized in the descriptions and review the activities common to those levels.

PROFICIENT

The teacher is *active* in serving students.

At the proficient level of performance, teaching practices may include the following types of activities:

- Teacher volunteers to participate in a before- or after-school homework support club.
- Teacher refers students in need to a peer mentoring program.
- Teacher quietly donates used clothing to students in need.

DISTINGUISHED

The teacher is *highly proactive* in serving students, seeking out resources when needed.

At the distinguished level of performance, teaching practices may include the following types of activities:

- Teacher develops an after-school homework club, enlisting student volunteers and colleagues to provide support on designated days throughout the week.
- Teacher organizes a faculty clothing drive to which colleagues donate gently used clothing that is then distributed to students in need.
- Teacher arranges for a panel of experts from the community, such as university professors, health care workers, or representatives from local service organizations, to speak at a faculty

Service to Students

meeting or conference day to outline the local resources available for students with special needs.

The tools that follow will help you explore how to put the activities of these high levels of performance into practice in your classroom.

Service to Students

 # Element Reflection

✔ **Teacher tool** ___ **Student tool**

1. Give an example from your professional life of a time when a colleague overlooked the best interest of students in making a decision or recommendation.

2. How can you contribute to a culture of service to students in your school?

Domain 4

Service to Students

Forming a Homework Club Checklist

✔ **Teacher tool** _____ **Student tool**

To help you implement a homework club, complete the checklist.

☐ Select a room or rooms for the club.

☐ Decide how often you should have the club, at what time, and how long the sessions will last. (This can change as the club becomes a more common resource for teachers.)

☐ Recruit student volunteers and make sure they are clear on their responsibilities and the importance of their role. (See the Homework Club Guidelines for Volunteers on page 482.)

☐ Provide teachers with a form to use to refer students to the homework club. It should include space for the teacher to explain the reason for referring the student and a permission slip for parents to sign. (See the Homework Club Referral Form on page 483.)

☐ Create an attendance sheet for students to sign in. Make sure you have a system in place so that there's a fresh sheet for every session.

☐ Create an attendance sheet for volunteers to sign in.

☐ Create feedback forms for volunteers to fill out about each student for teachers.

☐ Design a system for compiling a list of the needs of students who will be attending the homework club so that the volunteers know what help students need. The list will need to be updated and distributed to homework club rooms weekly.

Homework Club Guidelines for Volunteers

✔ **Teacher tool**   __ **Student tool**

Teachers who are proactive in developing resources to support their students may want to try implementing a homework club using volunteers to support student learning. You can distribute these instructions to volunteers to help ensure a high-quality program. Edit them as needed to suit your situation.

EXAMPLE GUIDELINES

Homework Club volunteers provide an important resource for the students referred to the program by their teachers. Volunteers are expected to make this time with students worthwhile and to make a difference in their academic progress.

Please make your assigned times at Homework Club a priority. If you cannot make it to an assignment for any reason, please notify the Homework Club coordinator as soon as possible to report your absence. Remember, a student is counting on you!

- Please arrive at your assignment on time, which is 2:10 p.m. at the middle schools and 3:00 p.m. at the elementary schools.
- Go directly to the assigned Homework Club room.
- Mark your attendance on the Homework Club attendance sheet in the Homework Club room.
- Each week, an updated student information form that includes the student's area of need is sent to each Homework Club. Please refer to it when necessary.
- After each session, Homework Club volunteers will complete a teacher feedback form for each student and will place it in the teacher feedback folder on the desk of the front office secretary.

Homework Club Referral Form

__ **Teacher tool**   ✔ **Student tool**

Customize this form to use when referring students to your homework club. You fill out the top portion and then send the form home with the student as a permission slip for a parent's or guardian's signature.

Student Name: _____ Grade: _____

Referring Teacher: _____ Subject: _____

Homework Club is available for students after school Monday through Thursday.

Student will attend Homework Club on _____.
                                                            Date(s)

Student will attend Homework Club for

_____ Make-up assignment   _____ Homework   _____ Class project   _____ Extra help

IMPORTANT REMINDERS
- Students are invited to join Homework Club on a first-come, first-served basis.
- If students have more than one unexplained absence, they are asked to no longer attend Homework Club.
- Any student with more than one behavioral complaint by a Homework Club volunteer will be asked to no longer attend Homework Club.

....

Parents/Guardians: Please choose the mode of transportation that your child will be using to get home from school:

_____ Parent/guardian pickup (no later than 4:00 p.m.)   _____ Late bus

**Please be advised that if the parent has not arrived before the late bus leaves, the student will be placed on the appropriate late bus.

PARENT/GUARDIAN CONTACT INFORMATION

Name(s): _____   Phone Number: _____
(Include names of any persons authorized to pick up student after school.)   (Where you can be reached while the student
                                                                                is in Homework Club.)

☐ 483

Domain 4

Peer Mentor Program Referral Form

✔ **Teacher tool**　　　　　__ **Student tool**

If you have a peer mentor program at your school, referrals will go more smoothly if the mentors know why students were referred to them and when they are available. You can ask all teachers to use this form when referring students to a peer mentor. Feel free to adapt the form to suit your needs.

Student: _____ Date of Referral: _____

Grade: _____ School: _____

Teacher: _____

Parent/Guardian: _____

Address: _____

_____

Phone: _____

Siblings: _____

This student is being referred because he/she is struggling in the following areas: (check all that apply)

☐ School Performance　　　☐ Classroom Behavior

☐ Self-Esteem/Confidence　　☐ Other: _____

In what specific ways do you think a mentor can help this student?

When is this student available to meet with a mentor?

Additional Comments:

_____　　_____

Referring Teacher Signature　　　　　　　　　　　　Date

Element

Advocacy

Description

Advocacy entails teachers going to bat for students, particularly those who are traditionally underserved by the school. This occasionally leads teachers to challenge long-held beliefs among their colleagues.

A Closer Look

To help you recognize the subtle differences between the higher levels of performance for this element, note the keywords emphasized in the descriptions and review the activities common to those levels.

PROFICIENT

The teacher works to ensure that *all students* receive a fair opportunity to succeed.

At the proficient level of performance, teaching practices may include the following type of activity:

- For students with special needs, teacher arranges a meeting of all involved staff members to explain ways that the staff can successfully work with the students. Parents are invited to attend these meetings, which occur shortly after the start of school, to provide additional insight and suggestions for helping their students succeed in the school environment.

DISTINGUISHED

The teacher makes a *concerted effort* to *challenge negative attitudes or practices* to ensure that all students, particularly those traditionally underserved, are honored in the school.

At the distinguished level of performance, teaching practices may include the following types of activities:

- Teacher provides information to colleagues, which may be in the form of an after-school workshop, about academic and behavioral interventions that support students with disabilities.

- Teacher researches programs to address bullying, including several successful intervention programs currently available to schools, and makes a presentation to faculty.

The tools that follow will help you explore how to put the activities of these high levels of performance into practice in your classroom.

Advocacy

Element Reflection

✔ Teacher tool   __ **Student tool**

1. It's not always easy to advocate for students, particularly those who are traditionally underserved by schools. Describe a situation in which you have done so.

2. How can you contribute to a culture in your school in which all teachers recognize the importance of ensuring that all students have advocates for their well-being?

Element

Decision Making

Description

Professional educators advocate for decisions that are based on data and in the best interest of students, rather than based on teachers' own convenience or tradition alone.

A Closer Look

To help you recognize the subtle differences between the higher levels of performance for this element, note the keywords emphasized in the descriptions and review the activities common to those levels.

PROFICIENT

The teacher maintains an *open mind* and *participates* in team or departmental decision making.

At the proficient level of performance, teaching practices may include the following type of activity:

- Upon request, teacher contributes ideas and data needed to make team-, department-, or building-level decisions that may include determining the master schedule, determining the assignment of students to teachers, determining program and course offerings, or aligning curriculum and resources to needs of students.

DISTINGUISHED

The teacher takes a *leadership role* in team or departmental decision making and helps ensure that such decisions are based on the *highest professional standards*.

At the distinguished level of performance, teaching practices may include the following types of activities:

- Teacher leads team, grade-level, or department discussions for the purpose of making recommendations or decisions that may include determining the assignment of students to teachers, determining program and course offerings, or aligning course offerings and teaching assignments to the needs of students.

Decision Making

- Teacher solicits and organizes specific data and feedback from colleagues necessary to make team or departmental decisions.

The tools that follow will help you explore how to put the activities of these high levels of performance into practice in your classroom.

Domain 4

Decision Making

Element Reflection

✔ **Teacher tool** ___ **Student tool**

1. Describe a situation in which you changed your mind about a course of action after hearing the positions taken by your colleagues.

2. How can you help discourage colleagues from advancing positions based on what seem to you to be self-serving interests?

Domain 4

Element

Compliance with School and District Regulations

Description

Every school and district establishes guidelines for professional conduct. Some of these are incorporated into the district's negotiated agreement, but in all cases they reflect essential professional obligations.

A Closer Look

To help you recognize the subtle differences between the higher levels of performance for this element, note the keywords emphasized in the descriptions and review the activities common to those levels.

PROFICIENT

The teacher *complies fully* with school and district regulations.

At the proficient level of performance, teaching practices may include the following types of activities:

- Teacher is consistent and on time in attendance at team and faculty meetings.
- Teacher is consistent and on time in completing and submitting required reports and paperwork.
- Teacher dresses appropriately for the school setting, reflecting a professional image and serving as a model to students.
- Teacher abides by district regulations about videotaping or photographing students.

DISTINGUISHED

The teacher complies fully with school and district regulations, taking a *leadership role* with colleagues.

At the distinguished level of performance, teaching practices may include the following type of activity:

- Teacher organizes a district team to address violations of school policies relating to cell phone use during class.

The tools that follow will help you explore how to put the activities of these high levels of performance into practice in your classroom.

Compliance with School and District Regulations

Element Reflection

✔ **Teacher tool**   __ **Student tool**

1. Describe a situation in which you have worked with colleagues to change a school or district regulation that you thought undermined the school's primary mission.

2. What should be your approach if you discover that colleagues are cutting corners in their compliance with school and district regulations? Should you speak with them? If so, how?

Domain 4

Component 4f

Action Planning and Reflection

✔ Teacher tool   **__ Student tool**

Look over the tools for this component and choose a strategy or strategies that you are committed to trying in your classroom. Then return to this page and record what happened. If there was a change, what evidence indicates the extent to which this strategy was successful? Finally, think about what you might do differently to continue to bring about further growth in this component.

What will I try?	How did it go?	What will I do differently next time?

Domain 4

About the Authors

Charlotte Danielson is an education consultant based in Princeton, New Jersey, and developed the framework for teaching. She has taught at all levels, from kindergarten through college, and has worked as an administrator, curriculum director, and staff developer in school districts in several regions of the United States. Danielson also served as a consultant to hundreds of school districts, universities, intermediate agencies, and state department of education in virtually every state and in many other countries. In her consulting work, she has specialized in aspects of teacher quality and evaluation, curriculum planning, performance assessment, and professional development. For several years she served on the staff of Educational Testing Service (ETS) and was involved in many significant projects, including designing the assessor training program for Praxis III: Classroom Performance Assessments.

Darlene Axtell is currently an independent consultant and member of the Danielson Group. Since 1997 she has been working with school districts across the United States, Canada, and abroad, helping them implement the framework for teaching into all areas of the school setting. Axtell has been a classroom teacher at the elementary and middle school levels, a school counselor at the middle school and high school levels, and a staff developer. In the administrative arena, she has been a supervisor of school counseling, coordinator of curriculum instruction and assessment, and principal of a middle school.

Paula Bevan is a national consultant with the Danielson Group who specializes in designing and implementing teacher and principal evaluation systems. She also trains evaluators to function in valid and reliable ways and provides external teacher observations and feedback to help schools improve teacher evaluation. An expert in the framework for teaching, Bevan offers a wide variety of training and consultation services related to it.

Bernadette Cleland is a member of the Danielson Group; a national trainer and consultant with ETS; and a consultant assisting numerous districts around the United States in developing evaluation systems, mentoring programs, and professional development based on the framework for teaching. She also delivers graduate-level courses for school districts using the framework as the focus of study. Cleland has taught English/language arts and social studies at the elementary, middle, high school, and post-secondary levels and was a middle school principal and high school associate principal in Vermont.

Candi McKay is an education consultant and member of the Danielson Group, providing professional development to school districts and state service agencies throughout the United States. She facilitates the design and implementation of teacher evaluation systems and professional learning plans that are customized to the needs of teachers at every stage of their careers. McKay works extensively with school leadership teams to enhance their skills in classroom observation, collegial conversation, and professional learning.

Elaine Phillips is an education consultant and charter member of the Danielson Group. She works with districts and schools nationwide in their use of the framework for teaching for teacher evaluation, observation, mentoring, coaching, and professional development. She also teaches online and develops online courses. Phillips began her career as a high school English teacher and has also been the director of a gifted/talented program, the director of curriculum and instruction in Minnesota, and a national trainer for ETS.

Karyn Wright is currently the director of Teacher Induction and Mentoring for the Clark County School District in Las Vegas, Nevada. She has been a teacher, curriculum consultant, assistant principal, staff development coordinator, and human resources director in the Clark County School District. A former trainer for ETS, Wright is now a consultant with the Danielson Group, assisting teachers and administrators across the country in designing appropriate professional development, mentoring and induction programs, and teacher evaluation systems based on the framework for teaching.

The Danielson Group, founded by Charlotte Danielson, offers customized consulting and training for teachers and administrators to assist them in applying the framework for teaching for observation and feedback, reflective conversations, and mentoring. Learn more at www.danielsongroup.org.

RELATED ASCD RESOURCES: FRAMEWORK FOR TEACHING

At the time of publication, the following ASCD resources were available (ASCD stock numbers appear in parentheses). For up-to-date information about ASCD resources, go to www.ascd.org.

Books

Enhancing Professional Practice: A Framework for Teaching, 2nd Edition by Charlotte Danielson (#106034). Also available as PDF e-book.

Enhancing Student Achievement: A Framework for School Improvement by Charlotte Danielson (#102109). Also available as PDF e-book.

The Handbook for Enhancing Professional Practice: Using the Framework for Teaching in Your School by Charlotte Danielson (#106035). Also available as PDF e-book.

An Introduction to Using Portfolios in the Classroom by Charlotte Danielson and Leslye Abrutyn (#197171)

Teacher Evaluation to Enhance Professional Practice by Charlotte Danielson and Thomas L. McGreal (#100219). Also available as PDF e-book.

Teacher Leadership That Strengthens Professional Practice by Charlotte Danielson (#105048). Also available as PDF e-book.

Videos and Mixed Media

Electronic Forms and Rubrics for Enhancing Professional Practice: A Framework for Teaching by Charlotte Danielson (#108123DL)

Enhancing Professional Practice: Elementary DVD with Charlotte Danielson (#609093)

Enhancing Professional Practice: Middle School DVD with Charlotte Danielson (#609094)

Enhancing Professional Practice: High School DVD with Charlotte Danielson (#609095)

Teaching for Understanding Professional Inquiry Kit by Charlotte Danielson (#196212)

Networks

Visit the ASCD Web site (www.ascd.org) and click on Networks under About ASCD for information about professional educators who have formed groups around topics, including "Performance Assessment for Leadership" and "Assessment for Learning." Look in the Network Directory for current facilitators' addresses and phone numbers.

For more information: send e-mail to member@ascd.org; call 1-800-933-2723 or 1-703-578-9600, press 1; send a fax to 1-703-575-5400; or write to Information Services, ASCD, 1703 N. Beauregard St., Alexandria, VA 22311-1714 USA.